Delivering Voice over IP Networks

Delivering Voice over IP Networks

DANIEL MINOLI
EMMA MINOLI

WILEY COMPUTER PUBLISHING

John Wiley & Sons, Inc.
New York • Chichester • Weinheim • Brisbane • Singapore • Toronto

Publisher: Robert Ipsen
Editor: Marjorie Spencer
Managing Editor: Brian Snapp
Text Design & Composition: North Market Street Graphics, Lancaster, PA

Library of Congress Cataloging-in-Publication Data

Minoli, Daniel, 1952–
    Delivering voice over IP networks / Daniel Minoli, Emma Minoli.
      p.   cm.
    Includes bibliographical references (p.   ) and index.
    ISBN 0-471-25482-7 (cloth : alk. paper)
    1. TCP/IP (Computer network protocol) 2. Digital telephone
systems. 3. Computer networks. 4. Data transmission systems.
I. Minoli, Emma. II. Title.
TK5105.585.M6 1998
621.385—DC21   97-48368
                                                         CIP

Printed in the United States of America
10 9 8 7 6 5 4 3 2

Contents

Chapter 3:   Issues in Packet Voice Communication   79

Chapter 4:   Voice Technologies for Packet-Based Voice Applications   121

Chapter 5:   Technology and Standards for Low-Bit-Rate Vocoding Methods   149

Chapter 6:   Voice over IP and the Internet   181

Chapter 7:   Voice over the Internet Case Study: Benefits-Management Outsourcing   235

Appendix: Case Study: Lucent Technologies' Internet Telephony Server—SP (ITS-SP) 255

Preface

First there was the mainframe. Then there was the desktop. Then there was the enterprise network. Then came the intranet. This synthesis has evolved to the point where, as some say, "the computer is the network." But, in fact, we are now entering a quantum-change phase in the corporate landscape, whereby *the corporation is the network.*" A company's economic well-being, its ability to make money and achieve productivity breakthroughs, and its capacity to sustain stock market value, all depend on having in place a multimedia, multipoint, multiservice, high-speed network.

The concept of the efficient use of a common pool of resources (e.g., communication links) being shared by a number of queued customers (e.g., different applications) goes back to the teletraffic studies of the 1920s and the computer network architecture goals of the 1960s (invention of packet services), 1970s (ARPA work leading to the Internet), 1980s (T1-based enterprise networks, ISDN, and B-ISDN), and 1990s (the reduction of communications to IP and the Web).

Because of all the flurries to activities in enterprise networking, the question naturally arises if it makes economic sense to carry voice over data networks. Three variants are possible: (1) voice over frame relay, (2) voice over ATM, and (3) voice over IP (i.e., over routed enterprise networks and the Internet).

Integration has already found reasonable effectiveness in the context of small office/home office (SOHO) locations. The final step in that direction is the support of voice and fax over the same enterprise network or intranet that is supporting the management information systems (MIS) function. However, since voice technology has been around for over a century and digital voice has been depolyed since the early 1960s, the pertinent questions for corporate network planners are as follows: Is voice over packet networks a practical reality? What is the quality of voice, and what are the technical challenges? Is there interworking equipment between PBXs or the key system and the router? And, are there standards for voice over packet networks?

The emergence of Asynchronous Transfer Mode as well as Frame Relay voice solutions is giving impetus to the whole question of voice over enterprise data networks. Quality of service (QoS) plays a crucial role in the support of isochronous traffic, particularly for IP-based solutions. New protocols, such as IPv6, RSVP, and RTP may facilitate the deployment of voice over data networks.

Based on years of reasearch, which began in 1975 for the senior author, the authors have generated two companion John Wiley texts, one covering voice over connection-oriented fast-packet transport technologies (*Delivering Voice over Frame Relay and ATM*) and the present text, covering voice over connectionless IP-based networks, including the Internet.

This book discusses the positioning of voice over IP on intranets and the Internet. It provides a review of compression and integration methods and some vendor and market information.

After an introduction in Chapter 1, a basic review of the IP technologies is provided in Chapter 2, which covers IP, IPv6, RSVP, RTP, MPOA, and Layer 3 switching. Chapter 3 discusses voice characteristics that can be utilized in packet networks. Chapter 4 discusses ADPCM as applied to packet-network environments. An overview of vocoder-based compression methods used in IP is provided in Chapter 5. Chapter 6 covers various proposals for delivery of voice in IP environments. Chapter 7 provides a practical application of voice over IP technology, while the appendix covers a commercial case study.

This book is aimed at technology and application developers, students, vendors, researchers, consultants, and corporate network planners.

Acknowledgments

The authors would like to thank Pushpendra Mohta, Vice President of TCG Cerfnet, for the support provided; Ben Occhiogrosso, President of DVI Communication, for enabling the senior author to do work on ARPAnet in the 1970s; and G. E. Minoli for developing the index for this book.

CHAPTER 1

Introduction and Motivation

1.1 Introduction

Data networks have progressed to the point that it is now possible to support voice and multimedia applications right over the corporate enterprise network and the intranet, for both on-net and off-net applications. Many companies have already deployed Asynchronous Transfer Mode (ATM)–based backbones that provide both broadband capabilities and Quality of Service (QoS)–enabled communications. Switching technology of both the ATM and the switched local area network (LAN) kinds has gone a long way in the past five years, providing higher-capacity, lower-contention services both across the enterprise campus network and across the enterprise regional, nationwide, and international networks.

A lot of industry effort has gone into supporting IP over ATM using a number of technologies, such as Classical IP over ATM (CIOA), LAN Emulation (LANE), and Multiprotocols over ATM (MPOA). In addition, other evolving services, such as Cisco's Tag Switching and NetFlows, Ipsilon's IP Switching, and the Internet Engineering Task Force (IETF) Multiprotocol Label Switching (MPLS) specification, also directly or indirectly provide improved support of IP services. In addition, QoS-supporting protocols, such as IPv6, Resource, Integrated Services Architecture (ISA), differentiated services in IPv4, and Real-time Transport Protocol (RTP), are now entering the corporate enterprise network (Reference [1] provides a treatment of the trends listed here).

At the same time, commercialized Internet use has exploded, as companies launch full speed ahead into Web-based commerce [2]. That large collection of backbones, access subnetworks, server farms, and hypertext information that is known as the Internet is acquiring ever-increasing importance, not only for the business community but also for the population at large. Access to information is proving increasingly valuable for education, collaborative work, scientific research, commerce, and entertainment. The advent of HTML-formatted, URL-addressable, and HTTP-obtainable information over the Internet—what is often called the World Wide Web (WWW or W3)—has generated a lot of attention of late. Nearly everyone in the United States has heard of or used the Web, whether for personal or corporate use. Now there is a movement afoot to make the transition to fully multimedia enabled sites that allow voice, video, data, and graphics to be accessed anywhere in the world. The issue so far, however, has been that voice and video, by and large, have been of the stored kind—namely, a one-way download of sound files that are played out in non–real time at the user's PC.

Given this extensive deployment of data networking resources, the question naturally presents itself, is it possible to use the investment already made to carry real-time voice in addition to the data? The desire to build one integrated network goes back to the 1970s, if not even earlier. The Advanced Research Projects Agency, with project DACH-15-75-C0135 (and many other projects with many other researchers), funded the senior author's work in 1975 to look at the feasibility of *integrated voice and data packet networks*. And Integrated Services Digital Network (ISDN) research started in Japan in the early 1970s (before the idea started to get some real attention in the late 1970s and early 1980s), with the explicit goal of developing and deploying integrated networks. However, a lot of the mainstream work has been in supporting voice and data over *circuit-switched* Time Division Multiplexed (TDM) networks. Only some early packet over data work, and then some Fiber Distributed Data Interface II (FDDI II) and Integrated Voice/Data LAN (IEEE 802.9) work, looked at voice support in a non-circuit-mode network. Even for ATM, the emphasis has been, until the past few years, on data services.

Now the idea of carrying voice over data networks is in full swing. Both the ATM Forum and the Frame Relay Forum have published specifications, and voice-supporting frame relay/ATM equipment is appearing. The work of these forums has focused on connection-oriented networks. However, connectionless IP-based networks are ubiquitous, and so there is a desire to carry business-quality voice over them. The major challenge in this regard is that IP networks do not yet support QoS features. Nonetheless, a plethora of *IP-phones* has already reached the market.

This book is one of two related Wiley books published by the authors. This book focuses on the IP telephony technology itself. Figure 1.1 depicts the various voice over data network technologies now evolving, including voice over IP (VOIP). Also note that IP can utilize a number of data link layer services, such as ATM and frame relay. Figure 1.2 depicts a possible scenario of voice over IP, as is addressed in this book.

After this introduction in Chapter 1, a basic review of the IP technologies is provided in Chapter 2, which covers IP, IPv6, RSVP, RTP, MPOA, and Layer 3 switching. Chapter 3 discusses voice characteristics that can be utilized in packet networks. Chapter 4 discusses adaptive differential pulse code modulation (ADPCM) as applied to packet network environments. An overview of vocoder-based compression methods used in IP is provided in Chapter 5. Chapter 6 covers various proposals for delivery of voice in IP environments. Chapter 7 covers a practical application of voice over IP technology, while the appendix provides a case study.

1.2 Drivers for Voice over IP

Besides the potential for savings on long-distance phone charges to communicate with friends or relatives, Internet phones already have a place in the business world. For example, one can leave Internet phones turned on and ready for calls throughout the day; the technology is useful for communicating with coworkers in other parts of the building and at other locations by simply dialing them up on

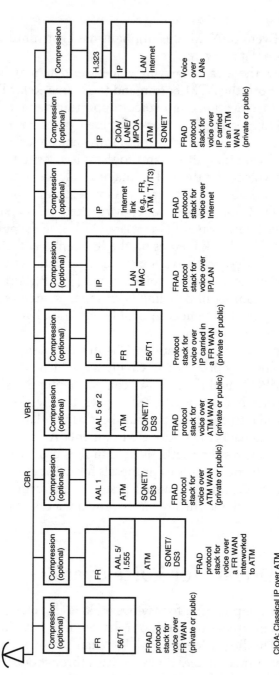

Figure 1.1
Voice over data networks.

4

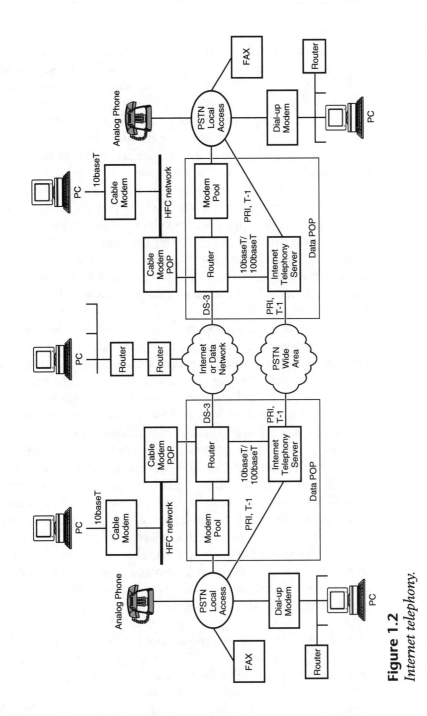

Figure 1.2
Internet telephony.

the Internet videophone. If they are at their desks, they can answer immediately. It can be a fine way to ask work-related questions without taking one's hands off the keyboard [3]. The technology is good for telecommuters, who can dial in to the office and see and speak to coworkers while getting a glimpse of the office from home [3, 4]. Similarly, it can be good for distance learning applications [5]. There are both market and business drivers for the introduction of voice telephony over IP at this time.

Increased deregulation means that both incumbent carriers (e.g., the vestiges of the regional Bell operating companies) and new carriers (e.g., competitive local exchange carriers, such as Teleport Communications Group) can enter the market with new services. At various times in the past twenty years, a variety of carriers were precluded from entering certain telecommunication service sectors. That is now rapidly changing as a consequence of the Telecommunications Act of 1996.

There is an exploding growth in data network investment, both by private organizations and by new and traditional carriers. The technology to carry voice over data networks is evolving, as noted in the introduction. There are economic advantages to end users in utilizing an integrated network, not only in terms of direct transmission costs, but also in reducing the network management costs of running separate and technologically different networks. That is the ultimate goal. In the meantime, many companies are, and will be for some time in the future, supporting the infrastructure and cost of multiple networks, including PSTN, private enterprise networks, wireless networks, intranets, business video networks, Internet access networks, and Internet-based Virtual Private Networks. Hence, the need to optimize the usage of all media components on all networks simultaneously, and to take advantage of pricing alternatives between networks, will become even more important as these networks proliferate in the corporate environment, and as the service providers offer increasingly competitive prices [6].

Business drivers also come into play. There are new revenue opportunities for Internet service providers (ISPs) in bundling voice service with Internet access. The interexchange carriers (IXCs) can avoid access charges. The local exchange carriers (LECs) can undercut the long-distance prices and offer InterLATA services without necessarily having to follow the traditional approach. Cable TV operators can bundle packet voice with cable services and perhaps find a better way to enter the telephony business without having to follow the classical *time-slot-interchange* method. All of these stakeholders can benefit by adding value to the network instead of just growing linearly to simply reach more physical points, and they can benefit by optimizing the economics of both packet-switched and circuit-switched networks.

In particular, the past few years have seen the emergence of reduced bit-rate voice compression algorithms that can increase the carrying capacity of a network by nearly tenfold (that is, by an order of magnitude) without the investment of additional resources in long-haul transmission facilities. The deployment, for example, of a network supporting near-toll-quality voice at 5.3 kbps rather than the twenty-five-year-old method of 64-kbps-per-call pulse code modulation (PCM) is not likely to be feasible in the context of an existing public switched telephone network (PSTN) because of the extensive embedded base of legacy equipment. Hence, if there is a desire to use the new compression algorithms and achieve a tenfold efficiency gain, then the IP route may be the way to go.

Voice over IP can be deployed in private enterprise networks, but some technology suppliers are concentrating on providing new solutions for carriers, consistent with the approach just outlined. Applications of the evolving VOIP technology include the following:

- Internet voice telephony
- Intranet and enterprise network voice telephony
- Internet fax service
- Internet videoconferencing
- Multimedia Internet collaboration
- Internet call centers
- PBX interconnection

It is worth noting that there has been a lot of progress recently in developing standards (with supporting equipment to follow) in the area of LAN/intranet-based multimedia (with compressed speech), as shown in Figure 1.3. These efforts will likely become the underpinnings of standards-based approaches to VOIP, while at present the market is seeing vendor-specific solutions.

Network	N-ISDN	PSTN	Iso-Ethernet IEEE802.9	Packet-switched	B-ISDN (ATM)	B-ISDN (ATM)
Multimedia standard	H.320	H.324	H.322	H.323	H.321	H.310
Audio/voice	G.711 (M) G.722 G.728	G.723.1 (M) G.729	G.711 (M) G.722 G.728	G.711 (M) G.722 G.728 G.723.1 G.729	G.711 (M) G.722 G.728	MPEG1 (M) G.711 (M) G.722 G.728
Audio rates, Mbps	64 48–64 16	5.3–6.3 8	64 48–64 16	64 48–64 16 5.3–6.3 8	64 48–64 16	$n \times 64$ 64 48–64 16
Video	H.261 (M)	H.261 (M) H.263 (M)	H.261 (M)	H.261 (M) H.263	H.261 (M)	H.262 (M) (MPEG-2) H.261 (M)
Data*	T.120	T.120	T.120	T.120	T.120	T.120
Multiplex	H.221 (M)	H.223 (M)	H.221 (M)	H.225.0 (M)	H.221 (M)	H.222.0 (M) H.222.1 (M)
Control	H.242 (M)	H.245 (M)	H.242 (M)	H.245 (M)	H.242 (M)	H.245 (M)
Signaling	Q.931	—	Q.931	H.225.0 (Q.931)	Q.931	Q.2931

(M) = Mandatory
*For example, Whiteboarding application

Figure 1.3
Evolution of voice over data networks via multimedia applications.

Naturally, there are going to be challenges in deploying IP-based voice services. Table 1.1 depicts some of these challenges and some potential ways around them.

1.3 Approaches for IP-Based Voice Systems

There have basically been two approaches to deploying voice over IP in networks:

1. *Desktop approach.* Each individual in the organization purchases VOIP-enabled terminals, which can be used to sup-

Table 1.1   Challenges and Quality Issues

Problem	Possible solution
PC too overloaded to run vocoder; processing delays too long	Use standard terminals and PBXs, and use a high-power Internet voice telephony processor.
Congested data networks	Use compression, in conjunction with echo cancellation and packet recovery technology. Move to ATM-based backbones and switched LAN segments.
Protocol limitations	Look to deploy IPv6, RSVP, and ATM.
Poor end-to-end network service	Upgrade to broadband, use switching, and use premium Internet services.
Limited routing and directory capabilities	Directory services are becoming available, for example, Bigfoot, Four11, Infospace, Internet Address Finder, Switchboard, WhoWhere?, and Microsoft's User Location Service (ULS).

port remote communications. This is in the vein of the Computer Telephony Integration (CTI) approach and the International Telecommunications Union—Telecommunications (ITU-T) H.323 terminal (as implied by the capabilities listed in Figure 1.3). In effect, this is similar to each user having a PC-based modem, a desk-resident fax machine, or a dedicated printer, rather than having a shared, network-resident server to support these functions.

2. *Shared approach.*   The VOIP capabilities are developed in an industrial-strength mode, using shared, network-resident servers (as implied by Figure 1.1).

The earlier approach is usually the first approach to market, but there are advantages in migrating up to the network-resident model. Figure 1.4 depicts what a VOIP server could look like.

As noted, voice compression is going to be a key enabling technology for new IP-based voice services. Digital Signal Processing (DSP) has progressed to the point where (in supporting 10 to 20 million instructions per second [MIPS]) good-quality voice is achieved. Recently adopted ITU-T standards, such as G.723.1, G.729, and G.729A, are discussed in some depth in the chapters that follow. In the past, voice analysis and synthesis using what is called *vocoder* technology produced a robotic-sounding voice, but this has changed dramatically during the 1990s. A lot of work has also gone into subjective testing of the voice to determine how

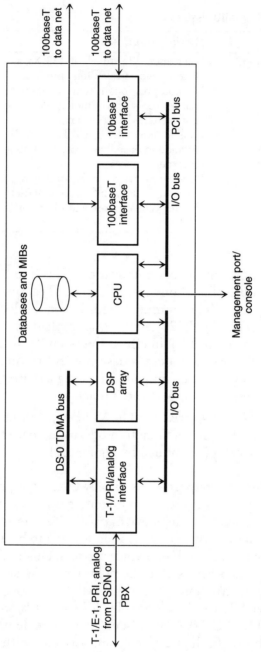

Figure 1.4
Typical voice over IP server.

10

good the proposed algorithms are. The most frequently used test in ITU-T SG12 is the *absolute category rating* (ACR) test. Subjects listen to about 8 to 10 s of speech material and are asked to rate the quality of what they heard. Usually a five-point scale is used to represent the quality ratings, such as 5 = excellent to 1 = bad. By assigning the corresponding numerical values to each rating, a *mean opinion score* (MOS) can be computed for each coder by averaging these scores. Typically, a test must include a selection of material (e.g., male and female utterances) [7]. Vocoder technologies are covered in Chapters 4 and 5.

Voice Servers Approach

Lucent Technologies has been a leader in the server-based approach to VOIP. In early 1997, it announced that IGC Communications would test its system for telephony over the Internet. IGC joins MCI, GTE, and France Telecom as the first companies to implement Lucent's recently announced Internet Telephony Server (ITS) for trial. The server can be installed on PSTNs to route telephone calls over data networks, such as the Internet. The technology is being positioned to the carriers as a means to offer cost-effective alternatives to traditional long-distance calling or to enhance their data offerings by adding voice service, creating a new revenue-generating or revenue-protecting opportunity. In addition to voice or fax services over the Internet, future applications of the ITS include phone-to-computer, computer-to-phone, and computer-to-computer connections. It will also enable audio conferencing, messaging, video conferencing, call center operations, and media collaboration over the Internet [8].

ITS is mentioned here as an illustrative technology. The ITS server functions at a user or system level, like a PBX Tie line. User selection of the IP network for voice or fax calling can be automated using PBX Least Cost Routing algorithms or can be dial-selected by users (e.g., by dialing 8 to access the IP/Internet). The use of the IP network could even be mandated through customer programming of PBX networking features. For example, customers could choose to have fax machines use only the Internet for intra-company correspondence, while allowing voice calls to use a combination of private or PSTN and intranet facilities. External fax correspondence could also use the intranet or Internet by using the tail-end hop-off networking feature of the PBX (or ISP) to escape from the data network at the closest point of presence to the terminating fax number. Also, remote users could access the ITS for voice and fax calls over the Internet from PC-net phones (IP-phones), allowing a single remote connection to be used for data, e-mail, voice mail, fax, and real-time voice calls. Such remote users might also receive all of the benefits of their host PBX or ISP service through remote access over the intranet or Internet [6]. As described by Lucent (see Figure 1.5),

> [T]o make a call, one of the users will simply pick up the phone as usual and dial the phone number of the second user. The PBX will route the call to its Internet Telephony Server (treating it as just another PBX Tie Line). The ITS will then make a "packet call" over the Internet to the distant ITS that will place the call through its associated switch. After the connection between the parties has been established, the rest of the phone operation will continue as if the call was going over the regular PSTN. Up to 24 sessions can take place simultaneously, each including either a single voice or fax call, per each T1 card in the ITS.
>
> The ITS uses a dynamic and transparent routing algorithm for its operation (e.g., no routing decisions on the part of the

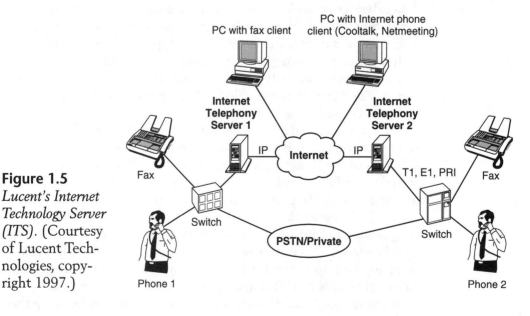

Figure 1.5
Lucent's Internet Technology Server (ITS). (Courtesy of Lucent Technologies, copyright 1997.)

customers are needed). In addition, if the quality of the "IP" network falls below pre-specified threshold, backup to PSTN is automatic. [6]

Another server on the market is Micoms V/IP Phone/Fax IP Gateway. The gateway utilizes ITU-T G.729 voice compression technology (see Chapter 5).

IP Voice and Video Phones

Internet phones and Internet videophones are entering the market, making it possible to talk to and see one or more remote parties over the Internet. Proponents make the case that personal computers (PCs) have always been the perfect vehicle for communication. Now, in conjunction with an ISP, one can use the PC to call anyone on the Internet (with the appropriate hardware and software) anywhere, anytime. For the time being, it does not cost any more to make these calls than the monthly ISP charges of $19.95, $14.95, or even $9.95. Some voice over Internet providers do not charge monthly access fees, but charge only on a per-minute basis.

At this writing there is a gamut of products on the market, including the following:

1. Audio-only Internet phones, such as Voxware Televox, 3rd Planet Publishing Digiphone, and Netscape CoolTalk
2. Videoconferencing systems
3. Internet videophones with audio and video transmission capabilities
4. Server-based products or higher-end videoconferencing products that cost between $5,000 and $10,000

Just looking at item 3 in the preceding list, there is an excess of a dozen hardware/software bundles and a dozen software-only solutions (three of which are free) at present, with many more expected to become available by the year 2000. Internet videophone bundles usually include everything one needs, including video capture card and camera (but typically lack a sound card, speakers, and, in a few cases, a microphone). The user can be up

Table 1.2   Key Software-Based Videophones

Smith Micro Software, Aliso Viejo, CA	*Audio Vision 2.0.* Not currently H.323 compliant, but support is under development. Requires manual configuration of components, such as microphone sensitivity and sound cards. Lacks volume control and has delay in voice and video response. Video images are grainy. Sells for $99.95 per user.
White Pine, Nashua, NH	*Enhanced CU-SeeME 2.11.* Works with the Macintosh as well as a PC. Has a small, nonobtrusive toolbar that acts as the program's main screen. When a call comes in, a small window appears to reveal the caller's identity and offers the option to accept or ignore the call. The video can be blurry, grainy, and delayed. Audio quality is good. Sells for $99 or $69 (Mac or PC) if purchased on the company's web site.
VocalTec, Northvale, NJ	*InternetPhone with Video 4-5.* Currently not H.323 complaint. Software sells for $49.95.
VDOnet, Palo Alto, CA	*VDOPhone 2.02.* This software is included with the majority of hardware bundles on the market. It is not H.323 compliant. Sells for $79 for two users.
NetSpeak, Boca Raton, FL	*WebPhone 3.0.* Not H.323 compliant. Has a tabbed address book that allows users to add entries alphabetically. Audio quality is choppy and the video is a little blurry. Sells for $49.95.

and running within an hour. Until very recently, Internet videophone solutions have tended to be incompatible (i.e., one could communicate with an Internet phone user only if he or she happened to be using the same software). While there are still several proprietary solutions, the emergence of the H.323 standard provides a foundation for audio, video, and data communications across IP-based networks, including the Internet. As previously implied, this standard allows multiple vendors to interoperate [3]. Tables 1.2, 1.3, and 1.4 depict some of the videophone systems available at present.

Table 1.3   Key Freeware-Based Videophones

IBM Internet Connection	*Phone 2.10.* Video image is grainy and the voice quality is poor.
Intel Internet Video	*Phone 2.0.* Video image is crisp and voice quality is good (little delay). Has a clean interface and the ability to enter just a coworker's IP address for an immediate connection. Volume and mute controls are included. Has directory service support. H.323 compliant.
Microsoft	*NetMeeting 2.0.* Supports Microsoft GUI. H.323 compliant. Easy to install. Audio transmission is good but not excellent.

Table 1.4 Current Hardware Bundles

US Robotics, Skokie, IL	*Bigpicture Video Camera and Capture Card.* Bundle includes a PCI video capture card, a Philips color PC video camera with focus control and a built-in microphone, and a copy of VDO-Phone. Priced at $249.95. *Bigpicture Video Kit.* Adds an ISA 33.6-kbps modem. Priced at $399.95.
Creative Labs, Milpitas, CA	*Video Blaster WebCam.* Includes a microphone and parallel port camera. Software includes Creative Video WebPhone (licensed from NetSpeak, the manufacture of WebPhone 3.0). Camera produces poor video quality and is slow because of the parallel processing limitation. Priced at $169.99.
Diamond Multimedia System Communications Division, Vancouver, WA	*Supra Video Phone Kit 3000.* Includes Philips Color PC Camera and high-quality Diamond Crunch IT 1001 capture card. Fast processing. Easy to install. Includes a Supra 33.6-kbps modem and VDOPhone software. Priced at $299.95.
Silicon Vision, Fremont, CA	*Grandma 2000 and InterVision Pro.* Includes a PCI card and Silicon Vision's own camera with a privacy door and a focus dial. Priced at $299.
Specom Technologies, Santa Clara, CA	*SuiteVISIONS.* Affordable Internet videophone solution. Bundle comprises a proprietary software solution and a color parallel camera. Reasonable clarity and speed of video transmission. Priced at $189.
AVerMedia Technologies, Freemont, CA	*AVer-TV-Phone.* Includes a PCI board and microphone that provide television, FM radio, video capture, and videoconferencing at an affordable price. Needs a composite camera that connects to the back of the card for video output. Bundles Smith Micro VideoLink software (currently not H.323 compliant). Package also includes a remote control for changing stations, channels, and volume. Priced at $199.
Winnov, Sunnydale, CA	*VideumConf Pro.* Combines two functions on one card (sound and video capture). Includes a slow ISA card and a high-quality Philips color camera with a built-in microphone and focus dial. Priced at $399.

1.4 The Future

It is expected that IP-based telephony is going to see continued penetration in corporate intranets, extranets, and the Internet in the next few years. This book, in conjunction with the companion Wiley texts [1, 9] should give planners enough information to begin to assess and evaluate the value of this evolving technology for their own environments.

References

1. D. Minoli and A. Schmidt. *Switched Network Services.* New York: Wiley, 1998.

2. D. Minoli and E. Minoli. *Web Commerce Handbook.* New York: McGraw-Hill, 1998.

3. L. Sweet. "Toss Your Dimes—Internet Video Phones Have Arrived." *ZD Internet Magazine* (August 1997): 57 ff.

4. O. Eldib, D. Minoli. *Telecommuting.* Norwood, MA: Artech House, 1995.

5. D. Minoli. *Distance Learning Technology and Applications.* Norwood, MA: Artech House, 1996.

6. Lucent Technologies. http://www.lucent.com/BusinessWorks/ internet/wap119a1.html.

7. R. V. Cox and P. Kroon. "Low Bit-Rate Speech Coders for Multimedia Communication." *IEEE Communications Magazine* (December 1996): 34 ff.

8. Lucent Technologies. http://www.lucent.com/press/0497/970416 .nsa.html.

9. D. Minoli and E. Minoli, *Delivering Voice over Frame Relay and ATM,* New York: Wiley, 1998.

CHAPTER 2

An Overview of IP, RSVP, Layer 3 Switching, and ATM Support

2.1 Introduction

IP-based networks are ubiquitous in the corporate landscape and in the Internet. Now developers and planners are looking at voice over IP for intranet and enterprise network applications, and at voice over the Internet for geographically dispersed applications [1]. Bandwidth efficiency and quality are the principal tradeoffs in this arena. Products for voice over IP are emerging because organizations have significant investments in private data facilities that have the capacity available to carry additional on-net traffic at what is perceived to be little initial incremental expense. Table 2.1 documents key technical requirements for the carriage of voice over an IP network. The issue, however, is that IP by itself has limited QoS support. Hence, one needs to look at other supplementary methods, such as ATM support of IP or RSVP.

The Internet now has millions of hosts connecting millions of people worldwide. The Internet provides connectivity for a wide range of application processes called *network services:* One can exchange e-mail, access and participate in discussion forums, search

17

Table 2.1   Basic Voice-Feature Requirements for Voice over Data Applications

Feature	Requirement
Compression. Sub-PCM compression significantly reduces the amount of bandwidth used by a voice conversation, while maintaining high quality.	Must have.
Silence suppression. The ability to recover bandwidth during periods of silence in a conversation makes that bandwidth available for other users of the network.	Must have.
QoS. Assuring priority for voice transmission is critical. This keeps delay, delay variation, and loss to a tolerable minimum.	Must have. Very little current support [type of service (TOS) is not generally implemented in routers]. There is a hope that the Resource Reservation Protocol (RSVP), which reserves resources across the network, will help. However, RSVP is only a protocol; intrinsic network bandwidth must be provided before a reservation can be made.
Signaling for voice traffic. Support of traditional PBXs and the associated signaling is critical.	Must have for real applications.
Echo control. Echo is annoying and disruptive. Control is key.	Must have for real applications.
Voice switching. Data network equipment can generally support on-net applications. Off-net is also critical. At the very least, the adjunct equipment must decide whether to route a call over the internal data network or to route it to the public switched telephone network.	Ability to route off-net is a must for real applications.

databases, browse indexes and sites, transfer files, and so forth. Use of the Internet for multimedia applications, including voice, is a relatively new development. The ability to carry voice (and fax) across an IP network or the Internet creates a cost-effective way to support intracorporate and intercorporate communications (see Table 2.2).

It is a well-known fact that ATM is a multimedia, multiservice, multipoint technology; hence, support of voice should be technically and theoretically more practical than over IP. ATM was designed from the start to be a multimedia, multiservice technology. ATM supports extensive QoS and service class capabilities, allowing time-sensitive traffic, such as voice, to be transported

Table 2.2 **Advantages of Voice over IP**

Advantage	*Approach*
Long-distance cost savings	By integrating voice, data, and fax over an IP enterprise network, a company can reduce long-distance charges for intracompany calls. By reducing the number of access lines, the organization can also reduce the FCC charges. Employees, regardless of location, can communicate with each other toll-free for as long as is wanted.
Reduced equipment investment	Companies generally lease or purchase separate equipment and facilities for voice support. With voice over IP, the cost of securing and servicing equipment is reduced, because all intracompany traffic, voice and data, is delivered over the same network.

across the network in a reliable, jitter-free manner, and ATM switches have been designed with effective traffic management capabilities to support the QoS and service classes needed for the various applications, including voice [2]. The issues, however, are: (1) ATM is not widely deployed and is relatively expensive (this being partially due to the increased throughput it supports), (2) many existing applications are IP-based, and (3) ATM should be able to support IP in an effective manner.

This chapter covers the following issues that will play a role in voice over data networks:

- IP and IPv6 [3, 4]
- IP over ATM
- Network layer switching technologies
- RSVP and RTP

2.2 Internet Protocol

The Role of the IP

TCP/IP is the name for a family of communications protocols used to support internetting in enterprise and interenterprise applications. Protocols include the Internet Protocol (IP), the Transmission Control Protocol (TCP), the User Datagram Protocol (UDP), and other protocols that support specific tasks, such as transferring files between computers, sending mail, or logging into another computer. TCP/IP protocols are normally deployed in layers, with each layer responsible for a different facet of the communications. Each layer has a different responsibility.

1. The *link layer* (sometimes called the *network interface layer*) normally includes the device driver in the operating system and the corresponding network interface card in the computer. Together they handle all the hardware details of physically interfacing with the cable.

2. The *network layer* (sometimes called the *Internet layer*) handles the movement of packets in the network. Routing of packets, for example, takes place here. IP provides the network layer in the TCP/IP protocol suite.

3. The *transport layer* provides a flow of data between two end system hosts for the application layer above. In the Internet protocol suite there are two transport protocols, TCP and UDP. TCP provides a reliable flow of data between two hosts. It is concerned with such things as partitioning the data passed to it from the application into appropriately sized frames for the network layer below, acknowledging received packets, and setting time-outs to make certain that the other end acknowledges packets that are sent. Because this reliable flow of data is provided by the transport layer, the application layer can ignore all those details. UDP, on the other hand, provides a much simpler service to the application layer. It sends packets of data called *datagrams* from one host to the other, but there is no guarantee that the datagrams will be delivered to the other end. Any desired reliability must be added by the application layer.

4. The *application layer* handles the details of the particular application. There are many common TCP/IP applications that almost every implementation provides:

   • Telnet for remote login
   • The file transfer protocol (FTP)
   • The Simple Mail Transfer Protocol (SMTP) for e-mail
   • The Simple Network Management Protocol (SNMP)
   • Others

In this architecture, TCP is responsible for verifying the correct delivery of data from the sender to the receiver. TCP allows a process on one end system to reliably send a stream of data to a process on another end system. It is connection-oriented: Before transmitting data, participants must establish a connection. Data can be lost in the intermediate networks. TCP adds support to detect lost data and to trigger retransmissions until the data is correctly and completely received.

IP is responsible for relaying packets of data [protocol data units (PDU)] from node to node. IP provides the basis for connectionless best-effort packet delivery service. IP's job is to move—specifically to route—blocks of data over each of the networks that sit between the end systems that want to communicate. IP provides for the carriage of datagrams from a source host to destination hosts, possibly passing through one or more gateways (routers) and networks in the process. An IP protocol data unit (datagram) is a sequence of fields containing a header and a payload. The header information identifies the source, destination, length, and characteristics of the payload contents. The payload is the actual data transported. Both end system hosts and routers in an internet are involved in the processing of the IP headers. The hosts must create and transmit them and process them on receipt; the routers must examine them for the purpose of making routing decisions and modify them (e.g., update some fields in the header) as the IP packets make their way from the source to the destination.

IP protocols are supported over a variety of underlying media, such as ATM, frame relay, dedicated lines, ISDN, Ethernet, Token Ring, and so forth. As IP networks have become ubiquitous, the business community has become sophisticated about utilizing IP networks as a cost-effective corporate tool, first in data communications and now for other real-time applications. Organizations favor networks based on IP because of the flexibility and vendor support. IP networks run under the most widely used network operating systems; they are scaleable to a large degree; and they enjoy extensive implementation across product lines (e.g., in the routers, PC clients, server switches, etc.). As noted, a relatively new IP application now in demand is toll-quality, low-bandwidth voice (and fax) transmission over IP networks.

Intranets use the same WWW/HTML/HTTP and TCP/IP technology used for the Internet. When the Internet caught on in the early to mid-1990s, planners were not looking at it as a way to run their businesses. But just as the action of putting millions of computers around the world on the same protocol suite fomented the Internet revolution, so connecting islands of information in a corporation via intranets is now sparking a corporate-based information revolution. Thousands of corporations now have intranets. Across the business world, employees from engineers to office workers are creating their own home pages and sharing details of their projects with the rest of the company.

IP Routing

One of the common ways to interconnect LANs and subnetworks at this time is through the use of *routers*. Routers are found at the boundary points between two logical or physical subnetworks. Routing is a more sophisticated—and, hence, more effective—method of achieving internetworking, as compared to bridging. In theory, a router or, more specifically, a network layer relay, can translate between a subnetwork with a physical layer protocol P1, a data link layer protocol DL1, and a network layer protocol N1 to a subnetwork with a physical layer protocol P2, a data link layer protocol DL2, and a network layer protocol N2. In general, however, a router is used for internetworking two networks or subnetworks that use the same network layer but have different data link layer protocols [5–7] (see Figure 2.1).

Routers have become the fundamental and the predominant building technology for data internetworking; however, ATM technology will likely impact the overall outlook. Routers permit the physical as well as the logical interconnection of two networks. Routers support interconnection of LANs over WANs using traditional as well new services, including frame relay and ATM. Some routers operate directly over synchronous optical network (SONET). They also are utilized to interconnect dissimilar LANs, such as Token Ring to Ethernet. With the introduction of ATM, however, the role of routers in enterprise networks could change. For example, devices enabling connectivity between locations based on router technology may, conceivably, no longer be obligatory elements—but the concept of routing (forwarding frames at the network layer of the protocol model) will certainly continue to exist. In addition, routers work well for traditional data applica-

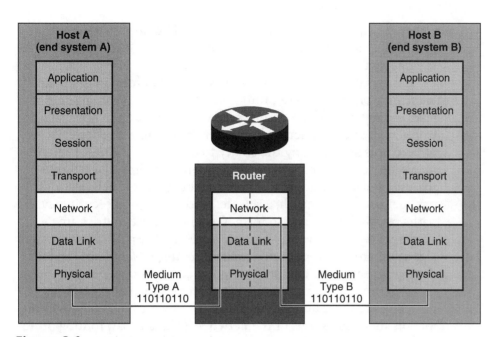

Figure 2.1
Protocol view of routers.

tions, but new broadband video and multimedia applications need different forwarding treatment, higher throughput, and tighter QoS control.

The use of routers allows the establishment of distinct physical and logical networks, each having its own network address space. Routing methodologies are becoming increasingly sophisticated as topologies become larger and more complex. There are a variety of protocols supported by various LAN subnetworks that need to interwork to make end-to-end connectivity feasible. The more common network layer protocols are IP, IPX, and AppleTalk, although the general direction is in favor of IP. Routers can be used to connect networks in building or campus proximity or to support wide area connections. The communication technology that can be used includes low-speed, high-speed, and broadband dedicated-line services, as well as low-speed, high-speed, and broadband switched services. Routing deals with techniques to move PDUs to distinguishable Layer 3 entities [7]. The issue of distinguishability relates to the address assignment, which is covered later on in this chapter.

There are two key underlying functions: (1) determination of optimal routes, and (2) movement (forwarding) of information through the internet.

Routers build their routing tables through information obtained via *routing protocols;* these protocols allow routers on an internet to learn about one another and to keep current about the optimal way to reach all attached networks. Routers interconnect different types of networks and embody the ability to determine the best route to reach the destination. Path determination is accomplished through the use of algorithmic metrics that are functions of such network parameters as path length, available bandwidth, path security level, path cost, path QoS, and so forth. Generally, these metrics are implemented in software. Values required by the path determination algorithm are stored in router-resident *routing tables* of appropriate depth; the entries of the table are populated through local, as well as remote, information that is circulated around the network. Routing protocols are the adjunct mechanism by which routers obtain information about the status of the network. That is to say, routing protocols are used to populate routing tables and to calculate costs.

Conceptually, routers operate by distributing, often through broadcast, advertisement PDUs that signal their presence to all pertinent network nodes. These advertisement PDUs also signal to the other routers destinations that are reachable through the advertising router or through links to neighbors. Routers communicate with other routers for the purpose of propagating the view of the network connections they have, the cost of connections, and the utilization levels.

A number of techniques are available to populate the routing tables, and thereby support routing of information PDUs. *Static routing* requires the network manager to build and maintain the routing tables at each router or at a central route server. This implies that once configured, the network paths used for the PDUs must not change. A router using static routing can issue alarms when it recognizes that a communication link has failed, but it will not automatically update the routing table to reroute the traffic around the failure. Static routing is, therefore, typically used in limited-distance internets, such as in a building's backbone or in a campus. *Dynamic routing* allows the router to automatically update the routing table and recalculate the optimal path, based on real-time network conditions (e.g., link failures, congestion, etc.).

Routers implementing dynamic routing exchange information about the network's topology with other routers. Dynamic routing capabilities are the most desirable, because they allow internets to adapt to changing network conditions.[1] Dynamic routing is nearly always used when internetworking across WANs. Dynamic routers regularly update the view of the entire network; this view also includes a map of devices operating at or below the network layer. Some dynamic routers also support traffic balancing. Special routing protocols are used to communicate across different administrative domains (such as an organization's intranet and the Internet).

To support effective communication, the exchange of appropriate routing and status information among routers is required. The routers exchange information about the state of the network's links and interfaces, and about available paths, based on different metrics. Metrics used to calculate optimal paths through the network include cost, bandwidth, distance, delay, load, congestion, security, QoS, and reliability. Routing protocols are used as the means to exchange this vital information. The three protocols commonly used in the TCP/IP context are RIP, IGRP, and OSPF. The process of reconfiguring the routing tables (the process called *convergence*) must occur rapidly so as to prevent routers with dated information from misrouting PDUs.

Two methodologies are used for information dissemination, *distance vector* and *link-state*. Routers that employ distance vector techniques create a network map by exchanging information in a periodic and progressive sequence. Each router maintains a table of relative costs (hop count or other weights, such as bandwidth availability) from itself to each destination. The information exchanged is used to determine the scope of the network via a series of router hops. After a router has calculated each of its distance vectors, it propagates the information to each of its neighboring routers on a periodic basis, say, once every 60 seconds.[2] If any changes have occurred in the network, as inferred from these vectors, the receiving router modifies its routing table and propagates it to each of its own neighbors. The process continues until all routers in the network have converged on the new topology. Distance vector routing was the early kind of dynamic routing. Distance vector protocols include RIP, IGRP, and DECnet Phase IV. Distance vector protocols can be implemented in a reasonably simple manner.

Routers using link-state protocols learn the topology of the internetwork infrastructure and update each other's tables by periodically flooding the network with link-state information. This information includes the identification of the links or subnetworks directly connected to each router, and the cost of the connection. Routers using the Open Shortest Path First (OSPF) algorithm send link-state information to all routers on the internet; in turn, these routers use the information to populate a table of routers and link and subnetwork connections. After this, each router calculates the optimal path from itself to each link; indirect paths are discarded in favor of the shortest path.

Link-state routing is a newer form of dynamic routing. Here, routers broadcast their routing updates to *all* routers within the administrative domain. Since routing information is flooded, rather than just sent between neighboring routers as is the case in distance vector environments, each router can develop a complete map of the network topology. Given the topology map, each router can then calculate the best path to each destination. Link-state routing may well be the preferred choice in the future because it requires less bandwidth than distance vector routing and converges much faster following a topology change. The higher processing requirement for link-state routing algorithms becomes less important as processor performance increases and the price per million operations per second continues to go down. Link-state protocols are indicated for rules-based routing and support of *type of service* or *quality of service* features. These protocols tend to be resistant to the creation of routing loops. In addition, they enjoy low overhead to support the routing function; bandwidth frugality is achieved through the use of more intensive computing resources and higher memory requirements for the router.

IP Datagrams

As noted, in a TCP/IP environment, IP provides the underlying mechanism to transfer information from one end system on one LAN to another end system on the same or a different LAN.[3] IP makes the underlying network transparent to the upper layers, TCP in particular. It is a connectionless protocol, where each IP PDU is treated independently. In this context, PDUs are also called *datagrams*. IP provides two basic services, addressing and fragmentation and reassembly of long TCP PDUs. IP adds no guarantees of delivery, reliability, flow control, or error recovery to the underlying network other than what the data link layer mechanism already provides. IP expects the higher layers to handle such functions. IP may lose PDUs, deliver them out of order, or duplicate them; IP defers these problems to the higher layers (TCP, in particular). Effectively, IP delivers PDUs on a *best-effort* basis. There are no network connections, physical or virtual, maintained by IP.

The format of an IP PDU is shown in Figure 2.2. It is 20 or more octets long. A partial discussion of the fields, their purposes, and their format follows.

The *VERS* field describes the version of the IP protocol, for example, Version 4. The LEN field is the length of the IP *header*, counted in 32-bit units.

The *Type of Service* field describes the quality of service requested by the sender for this IP PDU. It has the format:

Precedence|D|T|R|xxx

where Precedence is an indication of the priority of the IP PDU; D specifies whether this IP PDU can be delayed (0) or cannot be

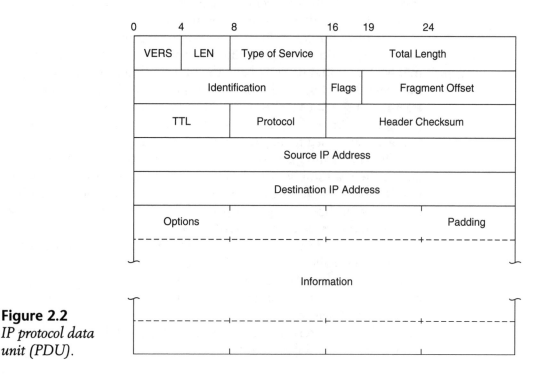

Information

Figure 2.2
IP protocol data unit (PDU).

delayed (1); T indicates the type of throughput desired (0 = normal, 1 = high); R specifies whether reliable subnetwork is required (1) or not (0); and xxx is reserved for future use. The precedence options are Routine (000), Priority (001), Immediate (010), Flash (011), Flash Override (100), Critical (101), Internetwork Control (110), and Network Control (111).

The *Total Length* field specifies the length of the entire IP PDU. Since the IP PDU is encapsulated in the underlying network frame (e.g., LLC/MAC), its length is constrained by the frame size of the underlying network. For example, as mentioned, the Ethernet limitation is 1500 octets. However, IP itself deals with this limitation by using *segmentation and reassembly* (SAR; also called *fragmentation and defragmentation*). IP does require, however, that all underlying networks be able to handle IP PDUs up to 576 octets in length without having to use SAR capabilities. Fragments of an IP PDU all have a header, basically copied from the original IP PDU, and segments of the data. They are treated as normal IP PDUs while being transported to the destination. However, if one of the fragments gets lost, the entire IP PDU is declared lost because IP does not support an acknowledgment mechanism; any fragments that have been delivered will be discarded by the destination.

The *Identification* field contains a unique number assigned by the sender to aid in reassembling a fragmented IP PDU (all fragments of an initial IP PDU have the same and unique identification number). The *Flags* field is of the form 0|DF|MF, where DF ("don't fragment") specifies if the IP PDU can be segmented (0) or not (1), and MF ("more fragments") specifies if there are more segments (1) or no more segments, the present one being the last (0).

The *Fragment Offset* field is used with fragmented IP PDUs and aids in the reassembly process. The value represents the number of 64-bit blocks (excluding header octets) that are contained in earlier fragments. In the first segment (or if the IP PDU consists of a single segment), the value is set to zero.

The *Time to Live* (TTL) field specifies the time in seconds that this IP PDU is allow to remain in circulation. Each IP gateway through which this IP PDU passes subtracts from this field the processing time expended on this IP PDU (each gateway is requested to subtract at least one unit from this counter). When the value of the field reaches zero, it is assumed that this IP PDU has been traveling in a loop, and it is therefore discarded.

The *Protocol* field indicates the higher-level protocols to which this gateway should deliver the data. For example, a code of decimal 6 (=00000110) means TCP; 29 is for ISO TP4; 10 is for BBN's RCC; 22 is for Xerox's IDP; 66 MIT's RVD; and so forth.

The *Header Checksum* field is a checksum covering the header only. It is calculated as the 16-bit ones complement of the ones complement sum of all 16-bit words in the header (for the purpose of the calculation, the Header Checksum field is assumed to be all zeros).

The *Source IP Address* field contains the 32-bit IP address of the device sending this IP PDU. The *Destination IP Address* field contains the destination for this IP PDU. The IP addresses consist of the pair

```
<network address><host address>
```

IP allows a portion of the host or device field to be used to specify a subnetwork (the network ID portion cannot be changed). Subnetworks are an extension to this scheme by considering a part of the <host address> to be a *local network address*, that is, a subnetwork address. IP addresses are then interpreted as

```
<network address><subnetwork address><host address>
```

Subnet masks are used to describe subnetworks; they tell devices residing on the network how to interpret the device ID portion of the IP address. An example is: 255.255.255.240 (also represented as /28) for an environment with 16 subnets each with 16 hosts—except for the first and last subnet, which have 15 hosts. The address-checking software in each device is informed via the subnet mask not to treat the device ID exclusively as a device identifier, but as a subnetwork identifier followed by a smaller device identifier. Naturally, since the address space is finite, there is a tradeoff between the number of subnetworks that can be supported and the number of devices on each subnetwork. The Internet community has adopted a scheme called Classless Internet Domain Routing (CIDR) that will preserve addresses by abandoning the old class rules. CIDR is expected to provide relief until the late 1990s, when a new scheme is required.

The *Options* field (which must be processed by all devices in the interconnected network, although not all devices must be able to generate such a field) defines additional specific capabilities. These include explicit routing information, recording routes traveled, and timestamping.

Support of Voice and Video in Routers

Even if new technologies such as those described later in this chapter (e.g., RSVP, RTP, IPv6, MPOA, and ATM) enter the market in a significant way, there will still be a large pool of enterprise networks based on traditional routers. Hence, support of such QoS metrics as delay, loss, jitter, and bandwidth in routers is important. Applications such as desktop conferencing, distance learning, mission-critical applications, voice, e-mail, and file transfer all compete for enterprise network resources. PDUs for all these applications show up in the routers and have to be appropriately handled, if QoS is to be secured.

QoS attention is being focused at the WAN level since, in general, there is adequate bandwidth at the LAN level. In addition, the move to switched Ethernet all but eliminates delays due to random access contention (however, queuing delays in campus routers remain to be addressed). Cisco Systems, who is the market leader for routers is approaching router-level QoS by using the following techniques (also see Figures 2.5 and 2.6)[4]:

- Smart queuing
    Priority queuing
    Custom queuing
    Weighted fair queuing
    Weighted Random Early Detection (WRED)
- Filtering and shaping
    Traffic shaping
    Frame relay traffic shaping

These techniques have been introduced in routers since the mid-1990s and are proving to be an initial first step in the direction of end-to-end QoS in both the Internet and in intranet. It is expected that in the coming years the protocols discussed in this chapter will become standard features in high-end routers.

IP Version 6 (IPv6)

The explosion of interest in Internet-based communication, the plethora of WWW sites being established on a daily basis, the introduction of electronic commerce [1], and the proliferation of networked resources all over the world may, in the next few years, exhaust the address space of IPv4. Therefore, in order to support an uninterrupted growth of the Internet while maintaining the current IP routing and addressing architecture, not only is a larger IP address space needed, but the assignments of addresses must also enable scaleable routing [8].

Although the 32-bit address mechanism in IPv4 can handle over 4 billion devices on about 16.7 million networks, the usable address space is more limited, particularly given the classification of addresses into Classes A, B, and C that exists for pre-CIDR applications. For example, an organization might have received a Class B address (i.e., the last 16 bits all represent hosts), but not made full use of it. Any time the administrator decides to subnet, a price must be paid in available devices. The total number of devices under subnets is always less than the number of devices without subnetting. That is the tradeoff for the ability to network more easily. The lost addresses are all zeros and all ones addresses for each subnet and the all ones and all zeros values for the subnet field itself. The price of subnetting varies with the number of subnet bits and the class of network used.

The IETF started to look at this problem in 1991. Part of its 1992 recommendation was to look at "bigger Internet addresses." IPv6 has a 128-bit address.[5] The group working on the protocol, sometimes known as the Simple Internet Protocol Plus Group, included the "working" IPv4 functions (though it included them in some different places in the IP header, or by different names), and removed (or made optional) infrequently used or "nonworking" functions. The following list depicts some highlights of IPv6 [9]. The protocol is described in RFC 1883; additional information on transition mechanisms can be found in RFC 1993 (see ds.InterNIC.net) [10, 11].

IPv6 Highlights

Priority. There are four bits of the datagram to indicate its priority relative to other datagrams traveling across the network.

The priority field first distinguishes among two broad types of traffic and then further refines the relative priorities within each traffic type. The broadcast distinction is between congestion-controlled and non-congestion-controlled traffic; it remains sensitive to congestion in the network. If the source detects congestion, it slows down, reducing traffic to the network. By slowing down, the system helps alleviate the congested situation.

Streamlined header format.   The IPv6 header is optimized for efficient processing. Superfluous fields have been eliminated, and all multibyte fields align on their natural boundaries.

Flow label.   The header now includes a flow label. Flow values may be assigned to particular streams of traffic with special quality-of-service requirements.

128-bit network addresses.   As needed for growth, IPv6 now supports 128-bit network addresses.

Elimination of header checksum.   IPv6 no longer has a checksum of its own header.

Fragmentation only by source host.   Intermediate routers can no longer fragment a datagram. Only the sending host can create fragments.

Extension headers.   IPv6 is much more flexible in its support of options. Options appear in extension headers that follow the IP header in the datagram.

Built-in security.   IPv6 requires support for both authentication and confidentiality.

The IPv4 address space problem is just one of the motivations behind IPv6. Some argue that today's IPv4 host implementations lack such features as autoconfiguration, network layer security, priority, and others. IPv6 is intended to address most of the inadequacies in the existing IPv4 implementations. These inadequacies require the introduction of a new network layer header (IPv6). IPv6 removes the Header field and the IP Header Checksum and changes the Time to Live field to become a Hop Count limit (see Figure 2.3). IPv6 is identified in the Ethertype field in the SNAP/LLC with the siglum 86dd hex instead of 0800 hex.

IPv6 supports datagram priority. Datagram-level priority values are placed in the priority field of the traffic's IP datagrams. For

Figure 2.3
IPv6 header.

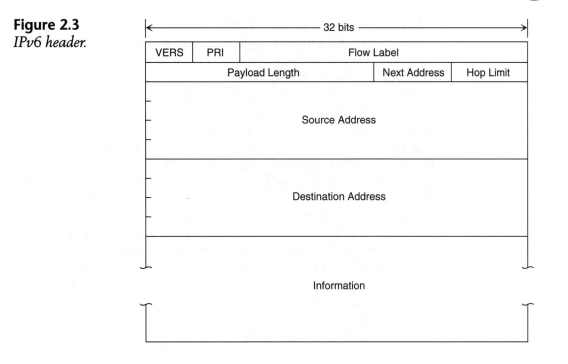

congestion-controlled traffic, IP defines seven specific priorities, as follows [9]:

0   No specific priority
1   Background traffic (e.g., news)
2   Unattended data transfer (e.g., e-mail)
3   Reserved for future definition
4   Attended bulk transfer (e.g., file transfer)
5   Reserved for future definition
6   Interactive traffic (e.g., remote login and windowing systems)
7   Control traffic (e.g., routing protocols and network management)

The second traffic type, non-congestion-controlled, does not adjust to congestion in the network. Such traffic sources include real-time audio, which cannot be delayed. IP reserves the priority values 8 through 15 for such traffic. For now, however, the IP standards offer no guidelines for specific assignment of these priorities. The source marks each datagram based on how willing it is to have the network discard that datagram. Lower priority values indicate a greater willingness to have a datagram discarded [9].

Real-time audio offers an example of how an application may use non-congestion-controlled priority. Many algorithms that digitize audio can tolerate the loss of some packets. In most cases, though, the algorithms have more difficulty reconstructing the audio when successive packets are lost. To reduce the probability of this happening, an audio application may vary the priority of its datagram. It might choose to alternate the priority between 8 and 9 with each datagram. Should the network have to discard two of the application's datagrams, it will try to discard two of priority 8 before any of priority 9. Note that there is no relative ordering between congestion-controlled and non-congestion-controlled traffic. A datagram of priority 8 (non-congestion-controlled), for example, has neither a lower nor higher priority than a datagram of priority 7 (congestion-controlled) [9].

2.3 IP over ATM

As a consequence of the popularity of IP implied in the previous section, one of the key considerations about ATM technology in recent years has been the support of IP. This requirement is driven by: (1) the desire to support the embedded base of applications and enterprise networks (including intranets), and (2) the desire to have access to the Internet, including virtual private networks (VPNs), over it. Beyond basic support of IP over ATM, the industry has also looked at ways to use the advantages of ATM to simplify IP-level Layer 3 PDU forwarding. In view of increased corporate dependence on information, including data, video, voice graphics, and distributed resources (Web access), users and planners want faster, larger, and better-performing networks—namely, higher speeds, scalability, and better performance and management.

Some of the challenges being addressed are [12]: (1) Support more than best-effort and constant-bitrate services on the same router-based network, (2) support circuitlike service via IP on a router-based network, and (3) support service levels, regardless of physical media and network discipline (e.g., ATM/LAN switching, traditional IP routing, and IP routing over ATM).

Classical IP over ATM is the method of moving LAN and intranet traffic over ATM that has been developed by the IETF. The IETF's specification is defined to provide native IP support over ATM and is documented in the following RFCs:

- RFC 1483: Multiprotocol Encapsulation over ATM Adaptation Layer 5
- RFC 1577: Classical IP and ARP over ATM
- RFC 1755: ATM Signaling Support for IP over ATM
- RFC 2022: Multicast Address Resolution (MARS) Protocol

These protocols are designed to treat ATM as virtual wire with the property of being connection-oriented, therefore, as with LAN Emulation (LANE), requiring unique means for address resolution and broadcast support. In the CIOA model,[6] the ATM fabric interconnecting a group of hosts is considered a network, called Non-broadcast Multiple Access (NBMA). A NBMA network is made up of a switched service like ATM or Frame Relay with a large number of end stations that cannot directly broadcast messages to each other. While there may be one Layer 2 network on the NBMA network, it is subdivided into several logical IP subnetworks (LISs) that can be traversed only via routers (see Figure 2.4).

One of the design philosophies behind CIOA is that network administrators started out building networks using the same techniques that are used today—that is, dividing hosts into physical groups, called *subnetworks*, according to administrative workgroup domains.[7] Then, the subnetworks are interconnected to other subnetworks via routers. A LIS in CIOA is made up of a collection of ATM-attached hosts and ATM-attached IP routers that are part of a common IP subnetwork. Policy administration, such as security, access controls, routing, and filtering, will still remain a function of routers because the ATM network is just fat wire.

In CIOA, the functionality of address resolution is provided with the help of special-purpose server processes that are typically located together. This is accomplished via software upgrades on legacy routers. Each CIOA LIS has an Address Resolution Protocol

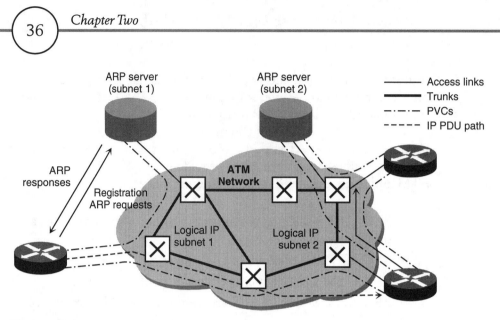

Figure 2.4
Classical IP over ATM model.

(ARP) server that maintains IP address–to–ATM address mappings. All members of the LIS register with the ARP server; subsequently, all ARP requests from members of the LIS are handled by the ARP server. IP ARP requests are forwarded from hosts directly to the LIS ARP server, using MAC/ATM address mapping that is acquired at CIOA registration. The ARP server, which is running on an ATM-attached router, replies with an ATM address. When the ARP request originator receives the reply with the ATM address, it can then issue a call setup message and directly establish communications with the desired destination.

One of the limitations of this approach is that CIOA has no understanding of ATM QoS. Also, CIOA has the drawback of supporting only the IP protocol because the ARP server is knowledge-able only about IP. In addition, this approach does little to reduce the use of routers, although it does have the effect of separating, to a degree, the data forwarding function from the IP PDU processing function. In effect, IP PDUs do not have to be examined at the end of each hop, but can be examined at the end of a virtual channel (VC) or virtual path (VP) that may consist of several hops. The challenge is how to identify (address) the VC in question to reach a specific remote IP peer—hence, the address resolution function.

The CIOA model's simplicity does reduce the amount of broadcast traffic and the number of interactions with various servers[8]; in addition, once the address has been resolved there is a potential that the data transfer rate may subsequently be reduced. However, the reduction in complexity does come with a reduction in functionality. Communication between LISs must be made via ATM attached-routers that are members of more than one LIS. One physical ATM network can logically be considered to be several logical IP subnetworks, but the interconnection across IP subnets, from the host perspective, is accomplished via another router. Using an ATM-attached router as the path between subnetworks prevents ATM-attached end stations in different subnetworks from creating direct virtual circuits between one another. This restriction has the potential to degrade throughput and increase latency. There are also questions about the reliability of the IP ARP server, in that the current version of the specification has no provisions for redundancy: If the ARP server were to fail, all hosts on the LIS would be unable to use the ARP. Finally, CIOA suffers from the drawback that each host needs to be manually configured with the ATM address of the ARP server, as opposed to the dynamic discovery allowed.

RFC 1577 specifies two major modifications to traditional connectionless ARP. The first modification is the creation of the *ATMARP message*, which is used to request addresses. The second modification is the *InATMARP message*, which inverts address registration. When a client wishes to initialize itself on a LIS, it establishes a switched virtual circuit to the CIOA ARP server. Once the circuit has been established, the server contains the ATM address extracted from the call setup message calling party field of the client.

The server can now transmit an *InATMARP request* in an attempt to determine the IP address of the client that has just created the virtual circuit. The client responds to the InATMARP request with its IP address, and the server uses this information to build its ATMARP table cache. The ARP table in the server will contain listings for IP-to-ATM pairs for all hosts that have registered and periodically refreshed their entries to prevent them from timing out. The ATMARP server cache answers subsequent ATMARP requests for the clients' IP addresses. Clients wishing to resolve addresses generate ATMARP messages that are sent to their servers and locally cache the replies. Client cache table entries expire and must be renewed every 15 minutes. Server entries for attached hosts time-out after 20 minutes.

Data transfer is done by creating a VC between hosts, then using Logical Link Control/Subnetwork Acess Protocol (LLC/SNAP) encapsulation of data that has been segmented by AAL 5. Mapping IP packets onto ATM cells using LLC/SNAP is specified in RFC 1483, Multiprotocol Encapsulation over ATM. RFC 1483 specifies how data is formatted prior to segmentation (the RFC documents several different methods; however, the vast majority of host and router implementations use the LLC/SNAP encapsulation, and LLC/SNMP specifies that each datagram is prefaced with a bit pattern that the receiver can use to determine the protocol type of the source). The advantages provided by the encapsulation method specified in RFC 1483 are that it treats ATM as a data link layer that supports a large maximum transfer unit (MTU) and that it can operate in either a bridge or a multiplexed mode. Because the network is not emulating an Ethernet or Token Ring, like LANE, the MTU has been specified to be as large as 9180 bytes. The large MTU can improve the performance of hosts attached directly to the ATM network.

As noted, multicast support is also of interest. CIOA provides multicast support via the Multicast Address Resolution Server (MARS). The MARS model is similar to a client/server design because it operates by requiring a multicast server to keep membership lists of multicast clients that have joined a multicast group. A client is assigned to a multicast server by a network administrator at configuration time. In the MARS model, a MARS system, along with its associated clients, is called a *cluster.* The MARS approach uses an address resolution server to map an IP multicast address from the cluster onto a set of ATM endpoint addresses of the multicast group members.

2.4 Multiprotocol over ATM (MPOA)

MPOA can be viewed as solving the problems of establishing connections between pairs of hosts that cross administrative domains (i.e., IP subnets) and enabling applications to make use of a network's ability to provide guaranteed QoS [14, 15]. For some time, manufacturers have been releasing products that separate switching from routing and allow applications to designate their required QoS. MPOA supports intersubnet cut-through in enterprise networks. The MPOA working group of the ATM Forum is chartered with developing a standard approach to forwarding Layer 3 protocols, such as IP or Novell's IPX, transparently over ATM backbones. Building upon LANE,[9] MPOA allows ATM backbones to support legacy Layer 3 protocols and their applications. MPOA will also allow newer Layer 3 protocols and their applications, such as packetized video applications using IP's RSVP, to take advantage of ATM's QoS features over the same ATM backbone. With MPOA, end systems (user clients and corporate servers) can all be just one hop away. In effect, the routing is relegated to the edge of the network. This unbundles the data-forwarding function from the IP PDU processing function. The following list gives some highlights of MPOA [16]. Figure 2.5 depicts the operation of MPOA.

MPOA Highlights

- Designed primarily for LANs and campuses, it replaces a collapsed backbone with a *distributed* or virtual router.
- LAN switches and other edge devices become the virtual router's I/O ports, the route server is the central processor, and ATM switches are the backplane.

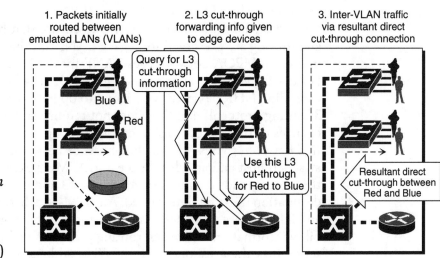

Figure 2.5
Distributed Net-Flow switching MPOA operation description.
(Courtesy of Cisco Systems, copyright 1997.)

- Workstations and servers belong to virtual subnets.
- PDUs destined within virtual subnets are bridged at Layer 2 using LANE.
- PDUs destined between virtual subnets are sent to the route server, which forwards them to the destination device. Simultaneously, the route server downloads Layer 3 information to the source device, and the Next Hop Routing Protocol (NHRP) determines the ATM address of the destination. Subsequent PDUs between the same source and destination cut through the ATM backbone directly, bypassing the route server.

MPOA enables the separation of the route calculation function from the actual Layer 3 forwarding function. This provides three key benefits: (1) integration of intelligent Virtual LANs (VLANs), (2) cost-effective edge devices, and (3) an evolutionary path for clients from LANE to MPOA. In the MPOA architecture, routers retain all of their traditional functions so that they can be the default forwarder and continue to forward short flows as they do today. Routers also become what are commonly called the *MPOA server* or *route server* and supply all the Layer 3 forwarding information used by MPOA clients, which include ATM edge devices as well as ATM-attached hosts. Ultimately, this allows these MPOA clients to set up direct cut-through ATM connection between VLANs to forward long flows without having to always employ an extra router hop [14, 15].

A design desiderata of MPOA is to ensure that both bridging and routing are preserved for legacy LANs and the VLAN topology in use. An MPOA network uses LANE for the bridging function. For the Layer 3 forwarding function, MPOA is adopting and extending NHRP. NHRP is designed to operate with current Layer 3 routing protocols and thus does not require any replacement or changes of those protocols. In order to set up a direct ATM connection between two ATM-attached hosts or between an ATM-attached host and an edge device, the ATM address of the exit point that corresponds to the respective Layer 3 address of the desired destination must be determined. An ATM-attached host can send an NHRP query to an MPOA server that has been getting reachability information from such routing protocols as OSPF. The MPOA server may then respond with the ATM address of the exit point or

ATM-attached host used to reach the destination Layer 3 address, or it may forward the query to other MPOA severs if it does not know the answer. Ultimately, the MPOA server that is serving the client that can reach the destination Layer 3 address will know the answer and reply. Once the source receives the reply, it can set up a direct cut-through ATM connection [14, 15].

2.5 Network Layer Switching

Besides CIOA and MPOA, there are other ways to use ATM in an IP environment.[10] Layer 3 switching, also known as *IP switching*, in all its forms, has two goals: (1) to find a way for internetworks (especially the Internet) to scale economically, and (2) to bring effective QoS support to IP [16]. Some approach the scaling challenge with faster routers and higher-speed lines. Several vendors have launched superrouter initiatives and have announced IP over SONET interfaces. Many researchers and developers, however, believe that solutions based on switched technologies like ATM have much more potential. Switching can replace latency-prone, processing-intensive Layer 3 hops with more efficient Layer 2 connections.

The approaches to IP support over ATM covered thus far evolved in the mid 1990s. The late 1990s have seen the emergence of various schemes to address several limitations of traditional IP routing, including: (1) the need for meshed or near-meshed physical networks, (2) the requirement to perform Layer 3 processing at the endpoints of each link (in effect collapsing data forwarding and transmission, IP processing, and topology discovery into a single, obligatory function at each link endpoint), (3) the relative complexity of Layer 3 processing, (4) the duplication of Layer 2 and Layer 3 functionality (e.g., addressing), and (5) the relatively poor use of improved data link layer technologies (e.g., ATM) by IP.[11]

To address these concerns, a number of vendor-specific as well as standards-based solutions have been proposed and/or are under development or deployment. Notable vendor-specific solutions include Cisco's NetFlow and Tag switching technology and Ipsilon's IP Switching technology. Standards-based solutions include MPOA (already discussed) and Multiprotocol Label Switching (MPLS), which is the evolving specification for cohesive Layer 2 and Layer 3 switching and routing.

When Ipsilson Networks introduced the IP Switching concept in 1996, the announcement attracted a lot of attention, although the ATM Forum and the IETF were already working on ways to route IP over ATM. Ipsilon offered the argument that the emerging standards were too complex, that interoperability and scalability might suffer, and that its IP Switching was simpler and more robust. At this writing, the idea of generic IP switching, the forwarding and routing function that seeks to directly and cohesively switch and forward frames without having to do Layer 3 processing unless absolutely needed, has become well accepted. Some vendors (e.g., Cisco) advance their own "optimized solutions" (e.g., Tag switching and NetFlows) for large internetworks, but still support MPOA for smaller networks. The industry is now working toward a standard (MPLS).

The ability to switch data based on very fast hardware table lookups on the MAC or ATM addresses leads to very fast and reliable networks. However, these technologies also pose problems in scalability and complexity that are seen by large ISPs or in large enterprise networks. High degrees of scalability can be difficult to achieve with a Layer 2 switched network because the address space is, in some cases, nonhierarchical. Their combination is difficult to find with a pure Layer 2 switched network, so network managers have traditionally used network layer protocols, like IP, to fill that void. Of the problems introduced by large Layer 2 networks, some of the more pressing concerns have to do with smoothly integrating Layer 2 switching with Layer 3 switching.

The goals of network layer switching are to provide new means for interworking Layer 2 and Layer 3 technologies. The body of work in the field of network layer switching can be subdivided into two categories, based on the level of granularity that is applied when mapping IP traffic to ATM virtual circuits. These models are called *flow-based* versus *topology-based*. From a high-level view of network switching, one can think of the flow-based models as building a network out of routers or switching devices in which unique ATM virtual circuits are created for each IP *conversation*, where *conversations* are synonymous with a file transfer or WWW session. In the topology proposals, the routers or switching devices use their ATM fabrics to create ATM virtual circuits that can carry all of the traffic destined between pairs of subnetworks or IP routes.

Regardless of the technical approach, the goals of network layer switching are similar because network layer switching's fundamental motivations are to remove excess computational processing done during PDU transmission by clearly dividing routing from forwarding and then removing routing from the process whenever possible. In both the flow-based and the topology-based models, the ATM switch must be aware of IP and be capable of participating in IP routing protocols. However, the processes of forwarding and routing still maintain a clear division. Once the control process (i.e., routing) has detected either a route or a flow, it removes itself from the communication path and employs high-speed forwarding from the ATM fabric.

Cisco's NetFlow and Tag Switching Technology

Cisco has been the first major player to address the issue of Layer 3 cut-through, via its NetFlow and tag switching technology. This technology supports flow-oriented switching for multiple protocols. The approach is to "learn once—switch many times." Cisco has positioned tag switching as a LAN technology and NetFlow as a WAN technology—fundamentally they are similar in concept.

Tag switching is Cisco's answer to Ipsilon's IP switching, and it is positioned for networks with 30 to 40 backbone routers. Tag switching utilizes traditional routing protocols to identify and maintain paths. The novelty is that all paths leading to the same destination (e.g., an IP subnet) are assigned the same *tag*. The Tag Distribution Protocol (TDP) maintains tables in each node that relate tags to destinations. As PDUs enter the network, a router handles Layer 3 processing and assigns each one a tag; at subsequent nodes, which can be routers, ATM switches, or frame relay switches, Layer 3 processing is bypassed and PDUs are forwarded based only on their tags. Routing hops are eliminated from the interior of the network [16]. Hence, this approach enables a form of cut-through, in that the routing decisions are ostensibly relegated to the edge of the network.

A *flow* is a unidirectional sequence of packets between a given source and destination. Issues related to flows are: what is used to define a NetFlow; what determines the start of a NetFlow; what determines the end of a NetFlow; and how one does time-out on a NetFlow entry. NetFlow granularity can be defined in terms of application (application layer applications, such as Telnet and FTP), transport layer protocols (e.g., TCP and UDP), network layer IP parameters (e.g., IP address), and data link layer protocols (e.g., Ethernet and Token Ring).

The IP header contains a protocol field (the tenth byte) that can be used to define a flow (e.g., the protocol could be ICMP, TCP, UDP, etc.). In turn, the UDP and TCP headers contain port numbers that define the nature of the data being carried (e.g., port 53 for DNS, port 520 for RIP, port 161 for SNMP, port 23 for Telnet, port 21 for FTP, and port 80 for WWW). Hence, NetFlow granularity can be defined at the TCP/UDP source or destination port, IP protocol type, and IP source or destination address. The NetFlow flow can start with a TCP SYN flag and terminate with a TCP FIN flag.

A router has various kinds of memory, specifically packet memory and system memory. With NetFlow enhancements to the router, a NetFlow cache is allocated. An incoming frame is first copied to packet memory. Normally, IP processing takes place to determine the route; that is, the destination address is removed from the PDU and the routing table is consulted, so that the PDU can be sent to the exit interface. In a NetFlow-enabled router, when a new frame arrives there may be no match in the NetFlow switching cache. Hence, the PDU is copied to the system buffer for processing. *A lookup in the Layer 3 network address table is undertaken to see where the frame should be routed.* The NetFlow switch cache is initialized and the frame is sent to the exit interface. For the next frame, it is copied to packet memory, but a match is found in the NetFlow switching cache. This implies that the frame can now be sent directly to the output interface without having to go through the additional IP routing processing, specifically frame deenveloping and routing table lookup, which can be relatively demanding in terms of resources.

Tag switching is applicable at the campus network level, while NetFlow is positioned at the WAN level. Tag switching addresses the throughput, scaling, and traffic engineering issues of corporate enterprise networks. It permits a graceful evolution of routing and is intended to allow integration of ATM and IP. Tag switching combines Layer 3 routing with label-swapping forwarding (such as is available on Layer 2 ATM and Frame Relay networks). The simplicity of Layer 2 forwarding offers high performance; the separation of forwarding for long flows and routing aids the evolution of routing (see Figure 2.6).

Forwarding is based on a label-swapping mechanism, as well as a control component that is used to maintain and distribute bindings. The router maintains a tag forwarding information base (TFIB), whose entries include the incoming tag and one or more subentries, such as outgoing tag, outgoing interface, and outgoing MAC address. The TFIB is indexed by the incoming tag; TFIB may be per box or per incoming interface. The forwarding algorithm works as follows: (1) extracts the tag from the incoming frame; (2) finds the TFIB entry with the incoming tag equal to the tag on the frame; (3) replaces the tag in the frame with the outgoing tags; and

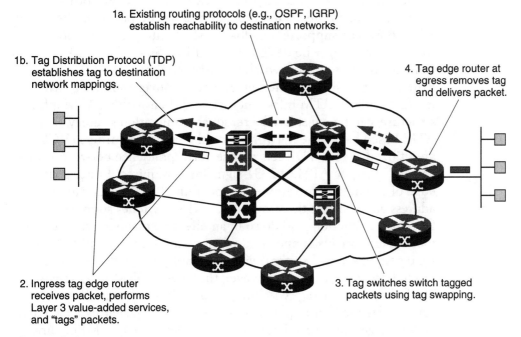

1a. Existing routing protocols (e.g., OSPF, IGRP) establish reachability to destination networks.

1b. Tag Distribution Protocol (TDP) establishes tag to destination network mappings.

4. Tag edge router at egress removes tag and delivers packet.

2. Ingress tag edge router receives packet, performs Layer 3 value-added services, and "tags" packets.

3. Tag switches switch tagged packets using tag swapping.

Figure 2.6
Tag switching operation. (Courtesy of Cisco Systems, copyright 1997.)

(4) sends the frame to the outgoing interface. In working this way, the label-swapping mechanism is really like an ATM switch. Note that the forwarding algorithm is network layer–independent. The TPD is used to distribute tag bindings to neighbors; the protocol sends information only if there is a change in the routing table and the device does not have a label.

Because tags correspond to destinations rather than source-destination pairs or traffic flows, tag population grows at order N rather than N^2; this makes scaling feasible in large enterprise networks and in the Internet. Tags are allocated in advance; therefore, there are no performance penalties to short-lived flows or to the first PDU of long-lived flows.

PDUs carry the tag between the IP datagram and its Layer 2 envelope. (With IPv6, tags will be included in the Layer 3 flow label field.) Each router examines the tag and sends the PDU directly to the output port, bypassing normal routing processing. This implies that tag switching can be used without having to immediately convert the physical network to ATM. Performance improvements in the 10 to 20 percent range are possible. The use of ATM, however, supports broadband. Most enterprise networks today can no longer be designed with T1 (1.544-Mbps) links, especially in the presence of switched 10-Mbps Ethernet, 100-Mbps Ethernet, and Gigabit Ethernet. Hence, a conversion to tag switching first without ATM infrastructure, and then with an ATM infrastructure, can be considered a reasonable migration strategy. In an ATM-based backbone network, virtual channel identifiers (VCIs) are utilized as tags. TDP sets up the correspondence between routes and VCI tags; no ATM Q.2931 signaling is required. Routers at the edge of the network examine the incoming PDU's IP destination address and assign it the proper VCI. ATM switches support the forwarding function, and do so in an effective manner. The internetwork itself remains connectionless, since there are no end-to-end (end system–to–end system) virtual circuits, and switches route around network failures. However, the issue of ATM interworking is not fully solved by tag switching, because PDUs from different sources destined for a specific destination end up sharing a VCI and cells may get interleaved, which is a problem in ATM. MPLS aims to address this issue.

Figure 2.7 compares NetFlow and tag switching with IP switching and some other current proposals [18].

Requirement	NetFlow switching	Cabletron SFVN	3Com Fast IP	Bay IP Autolearn	Ipsilon IP switching
Standards-based	Yes	No, VLSP	No, uses dNHRP	Yes (ARP Proxy)	No, uses IFMP
Multiprotocol support	Yes	No	No	No	No
VLAN aware	Yes	Yes	Yes	Yes	No, coexistence
Scalability	Yes	Limit to 20 switches	Layer 2 switch path only	Processor-based	Limited by number of VCs
Seamless migration	Yes	End station changes	3Com adapters required	New chassis, no network redundancy	Routed backbone only
Cells and frame based	Yes	Frame only	Yes	Ethernet only	ATM only
Layer 4 security	Yes	No	No	No	Yes

Figure 2.7
Layer 3 switching approaches.

IP Switching

IP switching is a proprietary (nonsanctioned by ATM Forum or IETF) networking technology advanced by Ipsilon Networks that combines the control of IP routing with ATM's speed, scalability, and quality of service to deliver millions of IP packets per second throughput to intranet and Internet environments.[12] Ipsilon took what they call a "fresh" look at the problem. The company wanted to "make IP go fast, but also to create a complete paradigm shift." IP switching implementations have already propagated from network interface cards to edge systems, telecommunications devices, and backbone, campus, and workgroup switches.

An IP switch implements the IP protocol stack directly onto ATM hardware, allowing the ATM switch fabric to operate as a high-performance link layer accelerator for IP routing. An IP switch delivers ATM at wire speeds while maintaining compatibility with existing IP networks, applications, and network management tools.

Using intelligent IP switching software, an IP switch dynamically shifts between store-and-forward routing and cut-through switching based on the needs of the IP traffic, or flows. An IP switch automatically chooses cut-through switching for flows of longer duration, such as file transfer protocol (FTP) data, Telnet data, hypertext transmission protocol (HTTP) data, and multimedia audio and video. It reserves hop-by-hop store-and-forward routing for short-lived traffic, such as domain name server (DNS) queries, simple mail transfer protocol (SMTP) data, and SNMP queries. The majority of the data is switched directly by the ATM hardware without additional IP router processing, achieving relatively high throughput.

IP switching utilizes the same topology and the same routing protocols as conventional routers, but replaces Layer 3 hops with Layer 2 switching. The N^2 problem of multiprotocol encapsulation (RFC 1483) goes away, and network performance improves. Each Ipsilon IP switch comprises a router (called an IP switch controller) and an ATM switch. The router exchanges topology information with other IP switches and provides Layer 3 store-and-forward services, while the ATM switch forwards cells at broadband speed. The software can recognize flows (a flow being a coherent stream of PDUs between the same source and destination). The IP switch analyzes each flow and classifies it as short- or long-lived.[13] Short-lived flows (e.g., SNMP queries, WWW URLs, and DNS packets) are routed by traditional IP-level methods over default VCs and incur normal router latency. Longer flows, such as file transfers, are assigned separate VCs that bypass the IP-level routing processing, and so can be forwarded at much higher speeds [16].

In an IP-switched network, all hosts and switches communicate through a common set of cooperative protocols—the Ipsilon Flow Management Protocol (IFMP; IETF RFCs 1953 and 1954) and the General Switch Management Protocol (GSMP; IETF RFC 1987)—to optimize short- and long-lived conversations between a sender and a receiver. Routing decisions need be made only once. As soon as longer-lasting flow data has been identified and cut through, there is no need to reassemble its ATM cells into IP packets at intermediate switch points. Thus, traffic incurs minimal latency, and throughput remains optimized throughout the IP-switched network. End-to-end cooperation also enables QoS implementation, since with cut-through switching, policies naturally span administrative boundaries. Hence, flows can be utilized to support flow-binded QoS: By analyzing IP headers, the IP switch can relate individual flows to performance requirements and can request ATM VCs with the proper type of service. Flows emanating from a time-critical application (if they can be identified in the same manner, e.g., port number, IP address, etc.) might receive highest priority, while ordinary file transfers would run at low priority [16].

Multiprotocol Label Switching (MPLS)

The Multiprotocol Label Switching (MPLS) Working Group has recently been charted by the IETF to develop a label-swapping standard for Layer 3 switching. The group started with Cisco's tag switching and IBM's nearly identical Aggregate Route-based IP Switching (ARIS). As was noted, the issue of ATM interworking is not fully solved by tag switching, because cell and PDU inter-leaving occurs when the tag is identified with the VCI. At this writing, two schemes are being considered by MPLS to address the issue [16]:

1. The ATM switch merges multiple VCs into a single VC without interleaving. If two PDUs arrive at the switch simultaneously, the switch buffers cells from one PDU until the other PDU leaves. This approach may require additional hardware in the ATM switch to buffer colliding PDUs. Cisco reportedly plans to use the buffer approach as it adds tag switching to the BPX ATM switch.

2. The network grows a tree upward from the egress point using ATM virtual path (VP) labels, one VP per egress point. By convention, each source point uses a different VC within the VP. Using VCIs inside the VP, the destination switch can sort out interleaved cells from separate sources. Although more VCs are used in this method, the amount of state information is still order N, where N is the number of destinations. This approach needs no new hardware. Ascend reportedly has chosen this approach. A standard is expected to emerge within a year or so at this writing.

2.6 RSVP and Integrated Services Architecture (ISA)

This section covers support of QoS in IP networks. To support real-time services in an IP environment, the Resource Reservation Protocol (RSVP) has recently been advanced as the signaling protocol to enable network resources to be reserved for a connectionless data stream.[†] (*See* Notes.) Real-time Transport Protocol (RTP) is also covered. These techniques come into play in voice over IP scenarios, where: (1) the planner is seeking a more powerful engine at Layer 2, specifically ATM, to secure better performance; or (2) a non-ATM-based approach to QoS is sought and employed. The ultimate goal is to develop the capability to use MPOA-based networks, which already have the advantages of using ATM and enabling route cut-through, as well as being able to hook into the IP application (via RSVP) to support QoS at the same time.[14]

The traditional network service on the Internet is *best-effort* packet transmission. In this service, packets from a source are sent to a destination, with no guarantee of timely delivery. For those applications that require a guarantee of delivery, the TCP protocol will trade packet delay for correct reception by retransmitting those packets that fail to reach the destination. For such traditional computer-communication applications as FTP and Telnet, in which correct delivery is more important than timeliness, this service is satisfactory. However, a new class of applications that use multiple media (voice, video, and computer data) has begun to appear on the Internet. Examples are voice over the Internet and intranets, video teleconferencing, video on demand, and distributed simulation. While these applications can operate to some extent using best-effort delivery, trading packet delay for correct reception is not an acceptable trade-off. Operating in the traditional mode for these applications results in reduced quality of the received information and, potentially, inefficient use of bandwidth [19].

To support QoS-sensitive applications, such as voice and video, intranets and the Internet need to provide differentiated quality of service. These graduated service levels will, in turn, also be important for data applications—for example, for legacy SNA traffic or for newer mission-critical time-sensitive applications that have heretofore received the same treatment in intranets and the Internet as bulk file transfers. To remedy this QoS problem, the IETF is developing a real-time service environment in which multiple classes of service are supported in IP-based networks. This environment will extend the existing best-effort service model to meet the needs of multimedia applications with real-time constraints. Table 2.3 depicts some of the industry development efforts underway [19]. To make QoS on IP networks a reality, these specifications

Table 2.3   **Working Groups Looking at Integrated Services Internet**

Group	*Purpose*
Integrated Services (Int-Serv) group	Defining a new IP service model called Integrated Services Architecture (ISA), including a set of services suited to a range of real-time applications
Resource Reservation Protocol (RSVP) group	Defining a resource reservation protocol by which the appropriate service for an application can be requested from the network
Internet Streams Protocol V2 (ST-II) group	Updating RFC 1190, a stream-oriented Internet protocol that provides a range of service qualities
IETF IP over ATM working group and the ATM Forum Multiprotocol over ATM (MPOA) group	Defining a model for protocols to make use of the ATM layer, specifically MPOA and MPLS

have to be broadly implemented by technology and service providers. The eventual extent of such implementation remains to be understood at this writing.

QoS guarantees in IP-based networks can be achieved in two possible ways:

1. In-band, where carriers and ISPs can provide a priority mechanism to packets of a certain type. This could be done, for example, with the TOS field in the IPv4 header, or the Priority field in the IPv6 header. The tag or MPLS label is another way to identify to the router or IP switch that special treatment is required. If routers, switches, and end systems all used or recognized the appropriate fields, and the queues in the routers or switches were effectively managed according to the priorities, then this method of providing QoS guarantees could be called the simplest. This is because no new protocols would be needed, and the carrier's router can be configured in advance to recognize labels of different types of information flows.

2. Out-of-band signaling mechanisms. This includes ATM signaling for different classes of services (e.g., in a CIOA environment), but RSVP is more characteristic of the IP environment.

With RSVP the end user can request services based on QoS. It should be immediately noted, however, that RSVP only reserves, and does not provide, bandwidth. As such, it augments existing unicast and multicast routing protocols, IP in particular; in turn, IP may well have to rely on ATM (say, via CIOA or MPOA) to obtain bandwidth. By contrast, ATM provides a connection-oriented service, where resource reservations for QoS support are made at connection setup time, using a UNI and a NNI signaling protocol. Given the industry's interest and the likelihood of deployment, a discussion of RSVP and ancillary constructs follows.[15]

Integrated Services Model

The IETF is currently developing an *integrated service model* that is designed to support real-time services on the Internet and in enterprise internets. The model defines the architecture of RSVP service guarantees. The Integrated Services Architecture (ISA) uses a setup protocol whereby hosts and routers signal QoS requests pertaining to a flow to the network and to each other.

The integrated service model starts with a flow-based description of the problem being solved. A *flow* is a single data stream from a single sending application to a set of receiving applications. Aggregated flows form a *session*, which is a homogeneous stream of simplex data from several senders to several receivers. An example of a flow is the data being sent from a TCP source to a TCP destination (the reverse is a separate flow). Each TCP stream is one of a series of successive steps in moving information from a sender to a receiver. In this case, the flow identifiers are the source and destination IP addresses, the IP transport protocol identifier (e.g., UDP or TCP) and the port number [20].

As noted in Table 2.3, the QoS development effort has been divided between two working groups, the RSVP group (RSVP) and the Integrated Services group (Int-Serv). When building an IP network that supports QoS, the RSVP specification is the mechanism that performs QoS requests, this being analogous to *ATM signaling.* The Integrated Services specifications aim to document what capabilities are available to QoS-aware applications; this is analogous to *ATM traffic management.*

Just like the ATM service classes, the IETF has defined service categories in ISA, as follows [21]:

- *Guaranteed service.* This service allows the user to request a maximum delay bound for an end-to-end path across a packet network. Service is guaranteed to be within that delay bound, but no minimum is specified. This is analogous to ATM's Constant Bit Rate (CBR). Real-time applications can make use of this service. Leaky-bucket, reserved-rate, and weighted fair queuing are used for application control. The underlying transport mechanism can be, among others, ATM (CBR or VBR-rt).

- *Controlled load service.* This service provides a small set of service levels, each differentiated by delay behavior. It supports three relative levels, but without particular numerical values of delay associated with them. This service provides a best-effort end-to-end capability with a load baseline. Applications sensitive to congestion can make use of this service. Leaky-bucket methods are used for application control. The underlying transport mechanism can be, among others, ATM (VBR-nrt or ABR with a minimum cell-rate support).

- *Best-effort service.* This baseline (default) represents the service that can be achieved over the Internet or intranets without any QoS modifications. This service provides a best-effort end-to-end capability. Legacy applications can make use of this service. The underlying transport mechanism can be, among others, ATM [Unspecified Bit Rate (UBR) or Available Bit Rate (ABR) with a minimum cell-rate support].

ISA requires work for each Layer 2 technology. Hence, the IETF is utilizing different subgroups to look at Ethernet, Token Ring, and ATM. Utilizing ISA methods, the Internet can be redesigned for real-time applications (e.g., real-time video). However, the overall performance efficiency at the network level remains to be understood (i.e., how many customers can be supported over a given router or link).

RSVP Mechanisms

The RSVP signaling protocol uses resource reservation messages from sources to destinations to secure QoS-based connectivity and bandwidth [22, 23]. Along the path between the source and the target, the resource requests are used to obtain permission from admission control software to use available local resources (e.g., buffers, trunks, etc.) to support the desired QoS. Then, resource requests reestablish the reservation state, thereby committing the reservation. When the desired request cannot be fulfilled, a request failure message is generated and returned to the appropriate party. In cases where the reservation messages are transmitted but are lost somewhere in the network, the end stations may assume that a request was accepted and may begin to transmit information to a destination that, in fact, has no resources reserved; that information will likely be dropped by the routers. In order to allow a host to determine if an RSVP message was successful, the host can, if desired, explicitly query the network for state information. See the following list for a snapshot of the features of RSVP.

RSVP highlights
- Supports the ability of entities to signal their desired quality of service.
- Not a routing protocol.
- Assumes the prior existence of network layer routing support via protocols IGRP, BGP, and so forth.
- Requests for state information, but does not help provide it.
- Soft, not hard state.
- Not an admission-control or packet-scheduling application.
- Receiver-oriented *protocol receivers* send QoS requests upstream toward senders; this works particularly well in multicast environments (i.e., a receiver can best determine the acceptable quality of a video conference and/or if additional costs are justified).
- Supports two reservation styles for use in multisender sessions:

    Distinct reservations.   Separate reservations for each sender
    Shared reservations.   Shared by multiple senders

- Applications have the ability to request different reservation styles depending upon the type of service or economic considerations.

Multicasting is an evolving application that needs to be supported. RSVP is designed to support heterogeneity of QoS if there are multiple receivers in a multicast session: Each receiver can get a different QoS by either merging requests or using different QoS layers. Because RSVP is a receiver-driven protocol, it has the capability to scale to a large number of recipients. There is a merging function in RSVP to reduce the number of messages traveling upstream. It should be clear that from a functional perspective RSVP is similar to ATM signaling: With RSVP, a user can provision a network connection with a carrier or ISP that utilizes a single physical connection, but over which it can provide dynamic quality of service.

Some of the RSVP nomenclature follows. *Flow* is the term used in RSVP, MPOA, MPLS, switching routers, and so forth to describe a sequence of PDUs with the same QoS requirements. Typically, flows are segregated by the pair of IP destination address and port number. A *session* designates flows with a particular destination IP address and port; in this manner a session can be identified and provided with special QoS treatment. RSVP utilizes two terms to describe traffic categories: (1) The *flowspec* is the information contained in the reservation request pertaining to QoS requirements for the reservation in question, and (2) the *filterspec* specifies the flows received or scheduled by the host. *Adspec* (Advertised Specification) is a set of modifiable parameters used to describe the QoS capability of the path between the source and the destination [24, 25].

RSVP work in support of first-generation Internet-based multimedia tools started in 1991 at Lawrence Berkeley National Laboratories and at Xerox's Palo Alto Research Center. Design desiderata were efficient use of Internet resources, scalability, support of unicast and multicast, and ability to coexist with TCP/IP. The following three components are used by end systems (hosts) to determine and signal QoS:

1. The setup protocol used by routers or hosts to signal QoS into the network
2. A traffic model or specification (the flowspec) that defines the traffic and QoS characteristics of flow data leaving a source
3. Traffic controls (shaping mechanisms) that measure traffic flow leaving a host or router to ensure that it does not exceed the preagreed QoS

RSVP uses IP as the basic method of carrying the signaling messages; this facilitates broad application, since, for example, ISP's networks are IP-based. However, RSVP produces a simplex reservation—that is, the end stations are only specifying resource reservations for one direction at a time; hence, two reservation requests are needed if bidirectional quality of service is desired. As noted, if an RSVP reservation is successful there is no acknowledgment from the network, as would be the case with an ATM call request for a switched virtual channel (SVC). This design decision was made to keep the protocol simple, but it could pose problems when interworking with ATM. RSVP messages can be passed from router to router and processed only by routers that support RSVP; as was covered for IPv6, in the case where the PDUs cross non-RSVP-capable routers, the messages are ignored.

RSVP can also be used in conjunction with ATM. In the ATM environment one can use the RSVP protocol to interface directly with the application. Here, below the RSVP layer, there is an interface with traffic-shaping software provided by the ATM layer. In this context, the application developer utilizes the RSVP protocol as a generic mechanism for requesting QoS: The RSVP signaling message is translated into an ATM signaling message requesting the establishment of virtual circuits with the desired QoS. The RSVP-application construct allows independent software design without worrying about lower-layer protocols. This topic is revisited in the "Interworking with ATM" subsection, following.

RSVP Message Exchange

Implementations of the RSVP protocol are similar to those of client/server models. The specification identifies messages exchanged and determines which sequences are supported. The RSVP protocol also defines several data objects, which carry resource reservation information. There are five basic message types (see Table 2.4) used in RSVP, and each message type carries several subfields.

The operation of RSVP is defined by the exchange of RSVP messages that contain information objects. Reservation messages flow downstream from the senders to notify receivers about the pending content and what associated characteristics are required to adequately accept the material. Reservations flow upstream toward

Table 2.4   RSVP Messages

Message type	Function
PATH	Sent by the source to specify that a resource exists and, optionally, which parameters should be used when transmitting.
RESV	Transmission of a message in hopes of reserving resources.
CONFIRMATION	Sent by a receiver, this optional message signals successful resource reservation.
TEARDOWN	Deletes an existing reservation.
ERROR	Indicates an abnormal condition, such as a reservation failure.

the senders to join the multicast distribution tree and/or to place QoS reservations. The information flows in RSVP can be categorized as follows [24]:

1. *RSVP data generated by the content source specifying the characteristics of its traffic (sender TSpec) and the associated QoS parameters (sender RSpec).* This information is carried, unmodified, by interconnecting network elements in a RSVP SENDER_TSPEC object to the receivers. An RSVP Adspec is also generated by the content source that carries information describing properties of the data path, including the availability of specific QoS services.

2. *RSVP data generated by the interconnecting network elements (i.e., ATM switch and IP routers) that is used by receivers to determine what resources are available in the network.* The QoS parameters that can be reported help the receivers determine available bandwidth, link delay values, and operating parameters. As in the sender's RSVP data, an RSVP Adspec can be generated by the interconnecting network elements that carries a description of the available QoS services (the SENDER_TSPEC contains information that cannot be modified, while the Adspec's content may be updated within the network).

3. *RSVP data generated by the receiver specifying the traffic characteristics from both a packet description (receiver TSpec) and a resource perspective (receiver RSpec).* This information is placed into an RSVP FLOWSPEC and is carried upstream to interconnecting network elements and to the content source. Along the path toward the sender, the FLOWSPEC may be modified by routers because of reservation merging.

Interworking with ATM

A discussion of ISA cannot be divorced from a discussion of ATM. Concurrent with the IETF's efforts, the ATM Forum is developing ATM networking that similarly provides real-time networking support. The use of ATM in the Internet as a link layer protocol is already occurring, and both the IETF and the ATM Forum are producing (or have already produced) specifications for IP over ATM. There is interest in interworking the two systems, so that better use can be made of ATM in support of voice and other applications. This subsection briefly examines how these somewhat dissimilar technologies can be internetworked.

ATM was initially developed as a replacement for the current telephone network protocols, but more recently has been developed as a data link layer protocol for computer communications. As it was developed from the beginning with telephone voice applications in mind, a real-time service environment is an integral part of the protocol. With the approval of UNI 3.1/4.0 by the ATM Forum, the ATM standards now have several categories of service. Given the wide acceptance of ATM by the long-distance carriers, the use of ATM in the Internet is, if not guaranteed, highly likely. The question now becomes how we can successfully interface between the real-time services offered by ATM and the new, integrated service environment soon to be available in the IP protocol suite [19]. CIOA standards assume no real-time IP protocols. Most researchers and planners are of the opinion that ATM should, if possible, be used as more than a leased-line replacement. While it is possible for the Internet to be overlaid on CBR PVCs, this is unlikely to be the most efficient way to use ATM services as they are offered by carriers or as they appear in LANs.

When an IP PDU that is somehow QoS-aware is passed from a packet-switched network interface to an ATM network, it must cause some type of connection setup message to occur in the ATM network. The difficulty involved in this is determining what ATM traffic class is appropriate for the IP data stream and, once the correct traffic class has been selected, determining what parameters should be used in the ATM signaling message.

In comparing the IETF's and the ATM Forum's traffic and QoS descriptions, the network planner may notice some differences as well as some similarities, especially in the traffic descriptors. The IP traffic description contained in the TSpec uses the same parameters that correspond to VBR's Sustainable Cell Rate (SCR) and Maximum Burst Size (MBS). Therefore, the TSpec uses the same parameters that are values of the second leaky bucket implemented in ATM's policing mechanism. Analogously to ATM's Peak Cell Rate (PCR), the TSpec also supports a peak rate parameter. The IETF's model contains three service classes, listed earlier, whereas the ATM Forum has defined five categories. Therefore, there are several possible mappings that can be supported when converting RSVP to ATM signaling, or vice versa. In ATM some classes also require specification of peak cell rate, whereas peak rates are not currently included in the IP traffic characterizations; it may be possible to use incoming interface speeds to determine an approximate peak rate.

The challenge is: Given traffic in a particular IP service class with certain QoS parameters, how should it be sent across an ATM network in such a way that it both meets its service commitments and makes efficient use of the ATM network's resources? One of the functions that must be performed in order to carry IP traffic over an ATM network is, therefore, a mapping from the characterization of the traffic as supplied to IP to a characterization that is acceptable for ATM [19]. Some of the possible mappings between ISA and ATM are as follows:

- Guaranteed service by and large equates to the ATM Constant Bit Rate (CBR) service. The values of PCR, SCR, and Minimum Bit Rate (MBR) can be mapped directly from the TSpec to the RSVP Reservation Request Receiver TSpec; the only "guess" needs to be the value of the Cell Transfer Delay (CTD).

- Controlled delay service has explicitly specified values of delay that can be mapped to ATM's real-time Variable Bit Rate (VBR) service category. It would also be possible to utilize ATM's CBR; however, the CBR category does not yield much statistically multiplexing gain and therefore is not optimal for Internet traffic.

- Best-effort service can be mapped to ATM services like UBR or ABR, or non-real-time VBR. The most common choice today is UBR in conjunction with Early Packet Discard.

2.7 Real-time Transport Protocol (RTP)

There has been a flurry of activity in the recent past in the development of real-time protocols. These protocols are called *real-time* because they are used when there are tight constraints on the quality of service that must be delivered in the network (e.g., the total transit delay or interpacket arrive time must be bounded). The following key primary protocols have been developed to support real-time delivery of information:

- *Real-time Transport Protocol (RTP).*   A real-time end-to-end protocol utilizing existing transport layers for data that has real-time properties. (RFC 1889, Jan. 1996.)
- *RTP Control Protocol (RTCP).*   A protocol to monitor the quality of service and to convey information about the participants in an ongoing session.[16] It provides feedback on the quality of the information transmitted so that modifications can be made and on total performance. (RFC 1889, Jan. 1996.)
- *Real-Time Streaming Protocol (RTSP).*   A transport layer protocol designed for controlling the transmission of audio and video over the Internet (this protocol is not further discussed here—see Reference [24]).

RTP provides end-to-end delivery services for data with real-time characteristics, such as interactive audio and video. Those services include payload type identification, sequence numbering, timestamping, and delivery monitoring. Applications typically run RTP on top of UDP to make use of its multiplexing and checksum services; both protocols contribute parts of the transport protocol functionality. However, RTP may be used with other suitable underlying network or transport protocols. RTP supports data transfer to multiple destinations using multicast distribution, if provided by the underlying network [26]. RTP provides transport of data with an inherent notion of time, and it also provides a means for transmitting real-time data because it, unlike the legacy transport layer protocol, has been optimized for such tasks. RTP has been developed with flexibility and scalability in mind and is now being used as the core protocol real-time transport on both pure IP-network and hybrid MPOA systems.

RTP by itself does not address resource reservation and does not guarantee QoS for real-time services. Specifically, RTP does not provide any mechanism to ensure timely delivery or provide other quality-of-service guarantees, but relies on lower-layer services to do so. (The functions of quality-of-service guarantees and delivery are the responsibility of RSVP and network support of QoS-based services.) It does not guarantee delivery or prevent out-of-order delivery, nor does it assume that the underlying network is reliable and delivers packets in sequence. The sequence numbers included in RTP allow the receiver to reconstruct the sender's packet sequence, but sequence numbers might also be used to determine the proper location of a packet—for example, in video decoding—without necessarily decoding packets in sequence [26].

The data transport is augmented by a control protocol (RTCP) to allow monitoring of the information delivery in a manner scaleable to large multicast networks and to provide minimal control and identification functionality. Like RTP, RTCP is designed to be independent of the underlying transport and network layers [26].

While RTP is primarily designed to satisfy the needs of multi-participant multimedia conferences, it is not limited to that particular application. Storage of continuous data, interactive distributed simulation, and control and measurement applications may also find RTP applicable.

RTP is intended to be malleable to provide information required by a particular application and will often be integrated into the application processing rather than being implemented as a separate layer. RTP is a protocol framework that is deliberately not complete[17] [26]. RTP's primary role is to act as a simple, improved, scaleable interface between real-time applications and existing transport layer protocols; RTP does not dictate which transport layer protocol is used. (The protocol is independent of the underlying transport and network layer, although, as noted, UDP is typically utilized.)

RTP provides functions that allow transport protocols to work in a real-time environment and provides functionality just above the transport layer. The underlying network is assumed to be any IP network; this implies that in all likelihood, but not with certainty, a packet will arrive at its destination. Due to the nature of packet switching (including frame relay and ATM), variable delay is to be expected. In addition, due to packet switching and routing, packets may arrive out of order. The protocol also contains definitions of which component should perform which specified function. The RTP component carries individual real-time data streams with a source identifier and payload type, time, and sequencing information. The feedback component monitors application performance and conveys information about the session (i.e., information about participants).

The following lists provide a snapshot of RTP and a glossary of key concepts and terms. In a nutshell, when packets arrive at the destination the sequence number of each packet is examined to determine the correct sequencing of data and also to record the fraction of lost frames. The RTP packet's timestamp is used to determine the interpacket gap. The timestamp value is set by the source as it encodes the data and transmits the packet into the network. As packets arrive at the destination, the change in interpacket gap can be examined, and during playback this information can be used to regenerate the contents at the same rate as they were encoded. By utilizing buffering at the receiver, the source can attempt to pace the outgoing traffic independently of the jitter introduced by the packet network [24].

RTP Highlights

- Designed to provide end-to-end delivery services for temporally sensitive data with support for both unicast and multicast delivery.
- Can be carried inside of a UDP payload.
- Provides data source and payload type identification that is used to determine payload contents.
- Provides packet sequencing that is used to confirm correct ordering at the receiver.
- Provides timing and synchronization that is used to set timing at the receiver during content playback.
- Provides monitoring that is used to facilitate diagnosis or feedback to the sender on the quality of data transmission.
- Supports integration of heterogeneous traffic that is used to merge multiple transmitting sources into a single flow.

RTP Glossary

contributing source (CSRC)   A source of a stream of RTP packets that has contributed to the combined stream produced by an RTP mixer (see **mixer**). The mixer inserts a list of the SSRC identifiers of the sources that contributed to the generation of the particular packet into the RTP header of that packet. This list is called the *CSRC list*. An example application is audioconferencing, where a mixer indicates all the talkers whose speech was combined to produce the outgoing packet, allowing the receiver to indicate the current talker even though all the audio packets contain the same SSRC identifier (that of the mixer).

end system   An application that generates the content to be sent in RTP packets and/or consumes the content of received RTP packets. An end system can act as one or more synchronization sources in a particular RTP session, but typically acts only as one.

mixer   An intermediate system that receives RTP packets from one or more sources, possibly changes the data format, combines the packets in some manner, and then forwards a new RTP packet. Since the timing among multiple input sources will not generally be synchronized, the mixer will make timing adjustments and generate its own timing for the combined streams. Thus all data packets originating from a mixer will be identified as having the mixer as their synchronization source.

monitor   An application that receives RTCP packets sent by participants in an RTP session, in particular the reception reports, and estimates the current quality of service for distribution monitoring, fault diagnosis, and long-term statistics. The monitor function is likely to be built into the applications participating in the session, but may also be a separate application that does not otherwise participate and does not send or receive the RTP data packets. These are called *third-party monitors*.

non-RTP means   Protocols and mechanisms that may be needed in addition to RTP to provide a usable service. In particular, for multimedia conferences, a conference control application may distribute multicast addresses and keys for encryption, negotiate the encryption algorithm to be used, and define dynamic mappings between RTP payload type values and the payload formats they represent for formats that do not have a predefined payload type value. For simple applications, e-mail or a conference database may also be used. The specification of such protocols and mechanisms is outside the scope of this text.

RTCP packet   A control packet consisting of a fixed header part similar to that of RTP data packets, followed by structured elements that vary depending upon the RTCP packet type. Typically, multiple RTCP packets are sent together as a compound RTCP packet in a single packet of the underlying protocol; this is enabled by the length field in the fixed header of each RTCP packet.

RTP packet   A data packet consisting of the fixed RTP header, a possibly empty list of contributing sources (see **contributing source**), and the payload data. Some underlying protocols may require an encapsulation of the RTP packet to be defined. Typically, one packet of the underlying protocol contains a single RTP packet, but several RTP packets may be contained if permitted by the encapsulation method.

RTP payload   The data transport by RTP in packets; for example, audio sample or compressed video data. The payload format and interpretation are beyond the scope of the RTP specification.

RTP session   The association among a set of participants communicating with RTP. For each participant, the session is defined by a particular pair of destination transport addresses (one network address plus a port pair for RTP and RTCP). The destination transport address pair may be common for all participants, as in the case of IP multicast, or may be different for each, as in the case of individual unicast network addresses plus a common port pair. In a multimedia session, each medium is carried in a separate RTP session with its own RTCP packets. The multiple RTP sessions are distinguished by different port number pairs and/or different multicast addresses.

synchronization source (SSRC)   The source of a stream of RTP packets, identified by a 32-bit numeric SSRC identifier carried in the RTP header so as not to be dependent upon the network address. All packets from a synchronization source form part of the same timing and sequence number space, so a receiver groups packets by synchronization source for playback.

Examples of synchronization sources include the sender of a stream of packets derived from a signal source, such as a microphone, a camera, or an RTP mixer (see **mixer**). A synchronization source may change its data format (e.g., audio encoding) over time. The SSRC identifier is a randomly chosen value meant to be globally unique within a particular RTP session; the binding of the SSRC identifiers is provided through RTCP. If a participant generates multiple streams in one RTP session—for example, from separate video cameras—each must be identified by a different SSRC.

translator   An intermediate system that forwards RTP packets with their synchronization source identifiers intact. Examples of translators include devices that convert encodings without mixing, replicators from multicast to unicast, and application-level filters in firewalls.

transport address   The combination of a network address and port that identifies a transport-level endpoint; for example, an IP address and a UDP port. Packets are transmitted from a source transport address to a destination transport address.

2.8 RTP Control Protocol (RTCP)

The previous section highlighted that RTP is a simple protocol designed to carry real-time traffic and to provide a few additional services that are not present in existing transport protocols like UDP: With RTP, receivers can utilize the timestamp along with sequence numbers to better synchronize sessions and improve playback. As a companion to RTP the IETF has designed the RTP Control Protocol (RTCP), which is used to communicate between the sources and destinations. RTCP is not used to establish QoS parameters with the ATM switch; instead, it is oriented toward state information.

RTCP is based on the periodic transmission of control packets to all participants in the session, using the same distribution mechanism as the data packets. The underlying protocol must provide multiplexing of the data and control packets, for example, by using separate port numbers with UDP. RTCP performs four functions [26]:

1. The primary function is to provide feedback on the quality of the data distribution. This is an integral part of the RTP's

role as a transport and is related to the flow and congestion control functions of other transport protocols. The feedback may be directly useful for control of adaptive encodings, but experiments with IP multicasting have shown that it is also critical to get feedback from the receivers to diagnose faults in the distribution. Sending reception feedback reports to all participants allows one who is observing problems to evaluate whether those problems are local or global. With a distribution mechanism like IP multicast, it is also possible for an entity such as a network service provider that is not otherwise involved in the session to receive the feedback information and act as a third-party monitor to diagnose network problems.

2. RTCP carries a persistent transport-level identifier for an RTP source called the *canonical name* (CNAME). Since the SSRC identifier may change if a conflict is discovered or a program is restarted, receivers require the CNAME to keep track of each participant. Receivers also require the CNAME to associate multiple data streams from a given participant in a set of related RTP sessions, for example, to synchronize audio and video.

3. The first two functions require that all participants send RTP packets; therefore, the rate must be controlled in order for RTP to scale up to a larger number of participants.

4. A fourth, optional function is to convey minimal session control information, for example, participant identification to be displayed in the user interface. This is most likely to be useful in loosely controlled sessions where participants enter and leave without membership control or parameter negotiation. RTCP serves as a convenient channel to reach all the participants, but it is not necessarily expected to support all the control communication requirements of an application. A higher-level session control protocol may be needed.

2.9 ATM QoS Mechanisms

ATM's claim to fame is its support of QoS. This is done via expansive use of resource sharing techniques, so that communications resources (specifically, broadband communication channels) are available on a per-VC basis, without having to allocate the maximum number of resources, which would grow linearly on the number of VCs or ports. ATM is a statistical multiplexing technology par excellence; yet, the statistical multiplexing is done is such an intelligent way that QoS is guaranteed to the user. Statistical multiplexing allows higher utilization of resources based both on allocating unused bandwidth to those that need it and on the intrinsic higher efficiency of pooled traffic.[18] Furthermore, the judicious use of overbooking also increases efficiency. The good news is that not only have standards been developed (e.g., UNI 3.1 and UNI/TM 4.0), but that *switches have been brought to the market* by many vendors that support these standards, as described in Reference [27]. In general, support of QoS implies *buffer management*; in addition to algorithmic resources, this implies the presence of relatively large buffers. Besides the photonics (specifically, long-reach lasers), the bulk of the cost in an ATM switch is in memory.

Traffic management allows ATM networks to have well-behaved operations in terms of predictable performance matching the expected (negotiated) level, thereby minimizing congestion and maximizing efficiency. ATM's QoS support is useful not only in pure ATM networks, but also in IP/RSVP-based networks that rely on ATM for Layer 2 transport. Today applications are not QoS-aware, but new voice, video, multimedia, and CTI applications may be developed with QoS in mind.

In spite of the benefits, QoS and the switches' approach to supporting it (e.g., dropping cells) have to be clearly understood, because some applications, such as TCP, may not operate well in a scenario of high cell loss; the cell loss naturally depends on the class of service that is selected (with CBR having the lowest and UBR having the highest).

QoS is achieved by managing the traffic intelligently. There are controls for the rate at which the traffic enters the network, at the VC level. The parameters used by ATM (specifically from the ATM layer pacing mechanism) to do traffic management are obtained at SVC or PVC setup time [28].

In ATM, the host signals its requirements to the network via the signaling mechanism. Each ATM switch in the path uses the traffic parameters to determine, via the Call Admission Control (CAC) mechanism, if sufficient resources are available to set up the connection at the requested QoS level. In private networks the Private Network Node Interface (P-NNI)[19] protocol is responsible for determining if the required resources are available across the network (end-to-end). The CAC is used in each individual switch to determine if locally controlled resources are available, consistent with the request of the SETUP message. If the switch does have resources to support the call-request, it then reroutes the message to the next switch along a possible best path to the destination.[20]

To convey QoS requests, there has to be a capability for the end system to signal to the connecting ATM switch its requirements. In turn, this switch must propagate that request across the network. The former is done via User-Network Interface (UNI) signaling (e.g., ATMF UNI 4.0); the latter is done via NNI signaling (e.g., PNNI 1.0) [24, 29]. The signaling mechanism whereby the various QoS parameters are coded into the SETUP message supplements the *QoS Class* procedures defined in ATMF UNI 3.1 and ITU-T I.356, briefly discussed in the following. It is worth noting that many switches and carriers actually support UNI 3.1 (rather than UNI 4.0) at this writing. In practice, however, many networks will continue to offer discrete, class-based values for services, although the "vocabulary" is now available for the user to communicate the QoS values to several digits of precision. The specification indicates that "implementations capable of stating QoS in terms of individual numeric parameter values may do so using the procedures defined in UNI Signaling 4.0 and PNNI 1.0; implementations must at a minimum support QoS indication via *QoS classes*."

An important requirement of QoS is to exactly define measurements, cell events, outcomes, and so forth and to have a reference model. For example, a *lost cell outcome* is defined as the situation when no cell is received corresponding to the transmitted cell within a specified time *Tmax*. Another important point is that quantitative values for performance objectives are not defined in the specifications; rather, the document specifies means to *measure* or *estimate* the values of defined performance metrics.[21] It is understood why no numbers were specified: No one wanted to commit to some specific goal. This is not the case with other transmission standards. For example, ANSI and Bellcore standards define exact jitter bit error rate (BER) values, and so forth for DS1 lines, DS3 lines, and so forth. The consequence of this is that the *VBR service from one carrier may be different from the service obtained from another carrier*, even though the name of the service is the same. Somewhat mitigating this possibility for inconsistency is that carriers may all use a few kinds of switches (say, Cisco LS1010, Fore ASX1000, etc.). Hence, to a degree there may be some derivative commonality.

It is to be understood that the measurement of the network performance on a VC is likely to be different from the negotiated objective at any given time. This is because (1) the negotiated objective is the worst case of network performance that the network will allow, including peak intervals (hopefully, the QoS measures will exceed these numbers in many cases); and (2) transient events may cause the measured performance to be worse that the negotiated objective (if and when a measurement is taken over a small time base).

QoS commitments are probabilistic in nature; therefore, both users and carriers have to realize that statements like "guaranteed QoS" are actually incorrect. The stated QoS is only an approximation of the performance that the network plans to offer over the duration of the connection. Specifically, since there is no limit to the length of the connection and the network makes resource decisions based only on information available at the time the connection is established, the actual QoS may well vary over the course of time. Transient events such as intermittent physical trunk failure, higher transient bit error rate (e.g., for circuits over microwave links), and even bursts of traffic from other sources when the UPC parameters (including switch-specific "fudge knobs") are not properly set by the switch administrator, can all impact QoS. Thus, the ATMF TM 4.0 document indicates that "QoS commitments can only be evaluated over a long period of time and over multiple connections with similar QoS commitments." Although this implies that in the long term the QoS is met, it could also mean temporary problems with real-time traffic such as voice, particularly if CBR services are not used.

Quality of Service Parameters

The ATMF TM 4.0 supports the following six QoS parameters:

- Peak-to-peak cell delay variation (ptpCDV)
- Maximum cell transfer delay (MaxCTD)

- Cell loss ratio (CLR)
- Cell error ratio (CER)
- Severely errored cell block ratio (SECBR)
- Cell misinsertion rate (CMR)

The first three can be negotiated as part of the call setup, while the last three are more network-intrinsic. Negotiation may entail specifying one or more of the parameters in question; also, the QoS could be set up differently for the two directions (or multiple legs) of a VC. By definition of call setup, QoS can be established on a per-call per-VC basis. In the network, QoS support is achieved by appropriate dynamic routing of the connection or by implementation-specific mechanisms. What may well fit in this last category is the current tendency of carriers to overengineer the network to make sure that QoS can be achieved and sustained. It should be noted, however, that carriers may provide a small set of discrete choices for the negotiable parameters, rather than accept a continuum of request values. For example, there may be a low (10^{-9}), medium (10^{-8}) and high (10^{-7}) CLR to choose from, and so forth.

Maximum cell transfer delay and peak-to-peak cell delay variation (both of which are negotiable) have to be defined very exactly, also using the reference model (as done in ATMF TM 4.0 [30]). Table 2.5 depicts some of the dependability measures that can be defined by formula.

Table 2.5   Dependability QoS Metrics

$$CLR = \frac{\text{Lost cells}}{\text{Total transmitted cells}}$$

$$CER^* = \frac{\text{Errored cells}}{\text{(Successfully transferred cells + Errored cells)}}$$

$$SECBR = \frac{\text{Severely errored cell blocks}}{\text{Total transmitted cell blocks}}$$

$$CMR = \frac{\text{Misinserted cells}}{\text{Time interval}}$$

*CLR is negotiable in UNI 4.0; the other metrics are not negotiable.

A service agreement for ATM services involves a traffic contract.[22] The user's traffic is described via traffic parameters, specifically the following:

- Peak Cell Rate (PCR)
- Sustainable Cell Rate (SCR)
- Maximum Burst Size (MBS)
- Minimum Cell Rate (MCR)

QoS Classes

As noted, carriers may support only a QoS-class service level (i.e., select from a menu), rather than a continuum of values for the parameters in question. Also, various parameters may be bundled, to arrive at classes, as follows:

Gold package	ptpCDV < 250 ms	MaxCTD = 30 ms	CLR = 10 in 1 billion
Silver package	ptpCDV < 350 ms	MaxCTD = 40 ms	CLR = 10 in 0.1 billion
Bronze package	ptpCDV < 450 ms	MaxCTD = 40 ms	CLR = 10 in 0.01 billion

According to the standards (e.g., ITU-T Recommendations I.150 and Q.2931), a user of an ATM connection (a VCC or a VPC) is provided with one of a number of QoS classes supported by the network. It should be noted that a VPC may carry VC links of various QoS classes; here the QoS of the VPC must meet the most demanding QoS of the VC links carried. The QoS class associated with a given ATM connection is indicated to the network at the time of connection establishment and will not change for the duration of that ATM connection.

QoS class (the reader may think of these as packaged menus) can have specified performance parameters (called *Specified QoS class*) or no specified performance parameters (called *Unspecified QoS class*). A Specified QoS class specifies a set of performance parameters and the objective values for each performance parameter identified. Examples of performance parameters that could be in a QoS class are all or a subset of the following: cell transfer delay, cell delay variation, and cell loss ratio.

Within a Specified QoS class, at most two cell loss ratio parameters may be specified. If a Specified QoS class does contain two cell loss ratio parameters, then one parameter is for all CLP=0 cells and the other parameter is for all CLP=1 cells of the ATM connection. As presently foreseen, other performance parameters besides the cell loss ratio would apply to the aggregate cell flow of the ATM connection. A QoS class could contain, for example, the following performance parameters: maximum cell transfer delay, a cell delay variation, and a cell loss ratio on CLP=0 cells. The performance provided by the network should meet (or exceed) performance parameter objectives of the QoS class requested by the ATM endpoint.

A *Specified QoS* class provides a quality of service to an ATM connection in terms of a subset of the ATM performance parameters discussed in the preceding. For each Specified QoS class, there is one specified objective value for each performance parameter. Initially, each network should define objective values for a subset of the ATM performance parameters for at least one of the following Service Classes from ITU-T Recommendation I.362 in a reference configuration that may depend on propagation delay and other factors[23]:

Service Class A	Circuit Emulation and Constant Bit Rate Video
Service Class B	Variable Bit Rate Audio and Video
Service Class C	Connection-Oriented Data Transfer
Service Class D	Connectionless Data Transfer

The following Specified QoS Classes are currently defined:

Specified QoS Class 1.   Supports a QoS that will meet Service Class A performance requirements. Specified QoS Class 1 should yield performance comparable to current digital private line performance.

Specified QoS Class 2.   Supports a QoS that will meet Service Class B performance requirements. Specified QoS Class 2 is intended for packetized video and audio in teleconferencing and multimedia applications.

Specified QoS Class 3.   Supports a QoS that will meet Service Class C performance requirements. Specified QoS Class 3 is intended for interoperation of connection-oriented protocols, such as Frame Relay.

Specified QoS Class 4. Supports a QoS that will meet Service Class D performance requirements. Specified QoS Class 4 is intended for interoperation of connectionless protocols, such as IP or SMDS.

In the *Unspecified QoS* class, no objective is specified for the performance parameters. However, the network may determine a set of internal objectives for the performance parameters. In fact, these internal performance parameter objectives need not be constant during the duration of a connection. Thus, for the Unspecified QoS class, there is no explicitly specified QoS commitment on either the CLP=0 or the CLP=1 cell flow. Services using the Unspecified QoS class may have explicitly specified traffic parameters. An example application of the Unspecified QoS class is the support of a best-effort service (i.e., UBR). For this type of service, the user selects the Best-Effort Capability, the Unspecified QoS class, and only the traffic parameter for the PCR on CLP=0+1. This capability can be used to support users that are capable of regulating the traffic flow into the network and to adapt to time-variable available resources.

References

1. D. Minoli and E. Minoli. *Web Commerce Handbook.* New York: McGraw-Hill, 1998.

2. D. Minoli and J. Amoss. *IP over ATM.* New York: McGraw-Hill, 1998.

3. D. Minoli and A. Alles. *LAN, ATM, and LAN Emulation,* Norwood, MA: Artech House, 1997.

4. D. Minoli. *Internet and Intranet Engineering.* New York: McGraw-Hill, 1997.

5. D. Minoli. *Telecommunication Technology Handbook.* Norwood, MA: Artech House, 1991.

6. D. Minoli. *Designing Broadband Networks.* Norwood, MA: Artech House, 1993.

7. R. Perlman. *Interconnections: The Theory of Bridges and Routers.* Reading, MA: Addison-Wesley, 1991.

8. Cisco Systems. Internet Protocol Version 6. http://www.cisco/warp/public/732/ipv6/ipv6_wp.html.

9. S. A. Thomas. *IPng and the TCP/IP Protocols.* New York: Wiley, 1996.

10. ARG. *Hands-on Internetworking with TCP/IP.* Morristown, NJ, Spring 1997.

11. IPng. http://playground.sun.com/ipng; ftp://ftp.parc.xerox.com:/pub/ipng; and majordomo@sunroof.eng.sun.com.

12. J. McQuillan. *The NGN Executive Seminar.* New York, March 20, 1997. Business Communications Review.

13. A. Schmidt and D. Minoli. *MPOA.* Greenwich, CT: Prentice-Hall/Manning, 1998.

14. D. Minoli and A. Alles. *LAN, ATM, and LAN Emulation Technologies.* Norwood, MA: Artech House, 1997.

15. D. Minoli and A. Schmidt. *Client/Server Over ATM.* Greenwich, CT: Prentice-Hall/Manning, 1997.

16. R. B. Bellman. "IP switching—Which Flavor Works For You?" *Business Communication Review* (April 1997): 41–46.

17. D. Minoli and A. Schmidt, *Switched Network Services.* New York: Wiley, 1998.

18. N. Walker. "The Emergence of Gigabit Ethernet." Networkers Conference, Los Angeles, CA, May 1997.

19. Request for Comments 1881: Integration of Real-Time Services in an IP-ATM Network Architecture. http://sunsite.auc.dk.RFC/rfc/raf1821.html. August 1995.

20. Fred Baker. "Lies, Damned Lies and RSVP." *Business Communications Review* (March 1997): 30 ff.

21. R. Braden, D. Clark, and S. Shenker. Request for Comments 1633: Integrated Services in the Internet Architecture: an Overview. June 1994.

22. R. Braden, L. Zhang, S. Berson, S. Herzog, and S. Jamin. Resource Reservation Protocol (RSVP)—Version 1 Functional Specification, Internet Draft. www.ietf.org://draft-ietf-rsvp-spec-14.txt or ftp://mercury.lcs.mit.edu/pub/intserv/drafts/draft-ietf-rsvp-spec-13.txt. May 1996.

23. J. Wroclawski. The Use of RSVP with IETF Integrated Services, Internet Draft. ftp://mercury.lcs.mit.edu/pub/intserv/drafts/draft-ietf-intserv-rsvp-use-01.txt. October 1996.

24. A. Schmidt and D. Minoli. *MPOA*. Greenwich, CT: Prentice-Hall/Manning, 1998.

25. D. Zappala. "RSVP Protocol Overview." http://www.isi.edu/div7/rsvp/overview.html.

26. H. Schulzrinne, S. Casner, R. Frederick, and V. Jacobson. Request for Comments 1889: RTP: A Transport Protocol For Real Time Applications. http://www.globecom.net/(nocl,sv)/ietf/rfc/rfc1889.shtml. 1996.

27. D. Minoli and J. Amoss. *Broadband and ATM Switching Technology*. New York: McGraw-Hill, 1998.

28. N. Giroux. "ATM Traffic Management for Efficient Multi-Service Networks." Network & Service Management for ATM. ICM-sponsored conference, Chicago, IL, August 1997.

29. D. Minoli and G. Dobrowski. *Signaling Principles for Frame Relay and Cell Relay Services*. Norwood, MA: Artech House, 1994.

30. The ATM Forum. Traffic Management Specification 4.0, af-tm-0056.000. April 1996.

Notes

[1] Dynamic routing mechanisms can coexist in networks that use static routing on certain routers.

[2] More pedantically, periodic updates are not a property of distance vector routing; they are the mechanisms of choice over unreliable links. Broadcast is used to provide reliability through retransmission.

[3] This section is reduced from a more extensive treatment in Dan Minoli, *1st, 2nd, and Next-generation LANs* (New York: McGraw-Hill, 1993).

[4] Information from Cisco Materials, including Networker's 1997 CD-ROM.

[5] Preserving the current IP routing and addressing architecture while increasing the total size of the IP address space is just one possible way of supporting growth of the Internet; however, it is not the only possible way. If the restriction on uniqueness of IP addresses within a private internet is relaxed, then the size of an internet (for example, the Internet) would

no longer be bound by the size of the available IP address space. This would change the current architecture, but it would also allow the continued use of IPv4 without constraint by the size of the IPv4 address space. One technology that supports connectivity in the presence of nonunique addresses is Network Address Translation (NAT; RFC 1631). NAT technology allows each organization connected to the Internet to reuse the same block of addresses (for example, the addresses defined in RFC 1918), while requiring only a small number (relative to the total number of addresses used by the organization) of globally unique addresses for external connectivity. The case can be made that the use of NAT devices represents a significant departure from the current IP routing and addressing architecture. However, widespread deployment of mediating gateways indicates that the traditional IP-level connectivity may not be that crucial and that the connectivity provided by such gateways could be sufficient [8].

[6] This section is based on Reference [13].

[7] As was discussed earlier, however, this need not be an obligatory imperative in the future.

[8] By reducing communication that would be required in LANE with the LECS, LES, and BUS, the time required for address resolution can be reduced.

[9] The ATM Forum's LANE specification defines how existing LAN-resident applications can operate unchanged over ATM networks. It also specifies how to communicate between an ATM internetwork and Ethernet, FDDI, and Token Ring LANs.

[10] Some of the techniques discussed in this section, for example, tag switching, do not mandate ATM but can make use of it if available.

[11] This section is based on Reference [17].

[12] This section is based on Ipsilon Networks promotional material, used with permission, and on personal communication with J. Doyle of Ipsilon.

[13] Ipsilon estimates that longer flows constitute more than 80 percent of internetwork traffic.

[14] RSVP is a general-purpose signaling protocol and could be used to map resource reservations to ATM signaling messages.

[15] Some have also suggested the use of ST-II; this topic is not treated further here.

[16] The latter aspect of RTCP may be sufficient for loosely controlled sessions—that is, where there is no explicit membership control and setup—but it is not necessarily intended to support all of an application's control communication requirements. (This functionality may be fully or partially subsumed by a separate session-control protocol.) [26]

[17] RTP is intended to be tailored through modifications and/or additions to the header as needed. Therefore, a complete specification of RTP for a particular application will require one or more companion documents, such as: (1) a profile specification document, which defines a set of payload type codes and their mapping to payload formats (e.g., media encodings); and (2) payload format specification documents, which define how a particular payload, such as an audio or video encoding, is to be carried in RTP.

[18] For example, pooling the tellers at a bank and merging the queue into one queue is more efficient than having multiple servers and multiple queues behind them. Similarly, pooling the voice, video, and data traffic is intrinsically more efficient than having separate networks because of the teletraffic/queuing principles.

[19] PNNI is used for global QoS support in a private ATM network. This is accomplished via hierarchical, link-state, source-based QoS-driven routing, where the information is propagated using the ATMF UNI signaling mechanism (rather than, for example, being based on the Broadband ISDN User Part of the Common Channel Signaling System No. 7).

[20] The PNNI interswitch routing protocol is used to identify the shortest path between the current location and the destination; the switch then computes the probability of successfully completing the call (based on available resources to supported the requested QOS) over all available paths. The path with the highest likelihood for completion is selected.

[21] The only exception to this is the Circuit Emulation Service, where jitter, wander, and BER values are specified by the ATMF.

[22] Formally, the negotiated characteristics of a connection. The traffic contract at the public UNI consists of a connection traffic

descriptor and a set of QOS parameters for each direction of the connection. The connection traffic descriptor consists of parameters such as PCR, SCR, MBS, and MCR, along with the Cell Delay Variation Tolerance and the conformance definition used to unambiguously specify the conforming cells in the connection. Refer to Reference [30] for more discussion and definition.

[23] As noted, though, the standards do not specify the numerical values of these parameters. This discussion only makes the point about the structure of the QOS request (i.e., that it ought to be based on a predefined menulike mechanism).

[†] RSVP consists of the following RFCs:

RSVP proposed standards	RFC 2205 *Resource ReSerVation Protocol (RSVP)—Version 1 Functional Specification* (Sept., 1997).
	RFC 2206 *RSVP Management Information Base using SMIv2* (Sept., 1997).
	RFC 2207 *RSVP Extensions for IPSEC Data Flows* (Sept., 1997).
	RFC 2210 *The Use of RSVP with IETF Integrated Services* (Sept., 1997).
	RFC 2208 *Resource ReSerVation Protocol (RSVP)—Version 1 Applicability Statement* (Sept., 1997).
	RFC 2209 *Resource ReSerVation Protocol (RSVP)—Version 1 Message Processing Rules* (Sept., 1997).
RSVP mailing list	The RSVP mailing list is rsvp@isi.edu. To join the list, send a request to majordomo@isi.edu.
RSVP WG co-chairs	Bob Braden (braden@isi.edu) and Lixia Zhang (lixia@parc.xerox.com).

CHAPTER 3

Issues in Packet Voice Communication

3.1 Introduction

Packet-switched IP networks have established themselves as an attractive option in a wide variety of data communication environments. To the present, circuit-switched networks have been the principal mechanism for transmitting human speech on a real-time conversational basis. However, because of perceived economic and technical benefits, digital voice techniques and corresponding network architectures have received considerable attention in the recent past. These benefits range from noise and crosstalk immunity to data and voice compatibility, security, bandwidth conservation, integrated networking, new service synergies, and network management cost reductions, among others.

To briefly illustrate the pervasiveness of digital techniques, consider the widely used interoffice digital transmission carriers and digital switching of the PSTN; the plethora of voice analysis/synthesis technology and standards now emerging; digital telephone sets and next-generation PBXs; IP phones; and Computer Telephony Integration (CTI).

During the past decade or so, the interest in integration started with a move to support simple digitized voice (i.e., supporting

PCM-encoded voice in a circuit-based network such as ISDN) and moved to packetized voice over packet/IP networks and the use of compressed voice.

To fully exploit the benefits intrinsic in voice codification, these techniques must be coupled with a network concept that allows real-time sharing of resources and guaranteed availability. A number of configurations and related models have been presented in the literature. The natural network construction for digital voice appears to be a packet-switched IP arrangement; packet voice, for example, has been considered in conjunction with packet radio networks and processing satellites via random packet-access schemes, in addition to the standard use for telephonic communication. The common goal of the models is to distill the cost-performance trade-offs obtained by integration. Some of the key parameters to be quantified for voice call in this network environment are blocking probability, end-to-end packet delay, interpacket mean and variance gap time, end-to-end packet loss probability, header overhead, and throughput. Similar or related factors need to be studied for the data section of the network, if any. Concention here is on delay as the performance parameter of interest.

Network transmission adds corruptive effects—noise, delay, echo, jitter, and packet loss—to the speech signal. Subjective studies have been conducted to access the impact of these effects. Many customers may be willing to tolerate degradation in some or all the listed criteria, if other benefits, notably transmission cost reduction, could be achieved. The sharing of transmission and switching facilities between data and voice, and the apparent gain in capacity obtained by interpolating several conversations on the basis of the on/off statistics of voice, appear to ensure such cost reduction. In view of this flexibility in customer performance requirements, the network designer may construct cost-effective architectures if analytical relations interconnecting some or all of the preceding criteria can be attained.

Research is under way to develop such design techniques so that, with the cost-performance trade-offs as a tool, system optimizations can be performed with the characteristics of the terminals, the network topology, and the protocol all considered jointly. Furthermore, assessments can be made of the relative merits of packet switching, circuit switching and hybrid alternatives for handling speed traffic and, ultimately, for mixed data and speed traffic.

This chapter covers some classical issues for the support of voice in general packet networks. The reader not interested in some level of queuing machinery may wish to skip Sections 3.4 and 3.5. The models presented in this chapter are not to be interpreted as the only applicable models; in fact, there is quite an extensive literature on this topic. The models presented are simply some of the work that the senior author has undertaken over the years [1–56].

Scope

Consideration here is restricted to the modeling, analysis, and design of packet-switching networks carrying only real-time speech packets; thus, the presence of network control traffic is ignored. Any switch or router design considerations are further ignored, and ideal switch or router behavior is assumed.

Section 3.2 of this chapter contains a discussion of packetized speech traffic models, and Section 3.3 discusses performance criteria. These traffic models and performance criteria are significant because these are the environmental conditions that provide reasons why packetized speech network design differs from the data case. In general, speech traffic has a more regular and predictable arrival pattern than data; so, intuitively, one would expect the network design to be able to capitalize on this by achieving higher facility utilization with speech than is possible with data. On the other hand, network performance criteria for speech will be more stringent and, in particular, will require a regularity and consistency that is not required for data transmission. A queuing model for a single link carrying packetized speech data is presented, and its solution is used to study the end-to-end performance of the system under consideration. This is, of course, the simplest possible network, but it has sufficient complexity to reveal many of the issues that will be present in more general links and networks. A fully connected network with only direct routing would consist of links of this type. Multilink hopping will generally be less viable with speech traffic because of tight delay constants; however, these will be encountered in typical intranets and corporate enterprise networks. Also briefly outlined is how the steady-state distribution of the queuing delay experienced on the typical link of the packetized speech network can be obtained. Finally, the results and implications of this link model for a packetized speech network are addressed; some results on the optimal packet length are presented.

As discussed in Chapter 4, there are two major techniques used in speech analysis, waveform coding and vocoding. *Waveform coding* attempts to reconstruct the facsimile of the input wave by sampling and digitizing its amplitude-time domain at regular time intervals. *Vocoding* methods generally attempt to model some key characteristic of the power-frequency domain (e.g., the sequence of local maxima, called *formants*) and resynthesize the speech at the remote end. Vocoding is a lossy compression method.

Summary of Results

The major results reported in this chapter are as follows:

1. A unified treatment of speaker behavior models is presented.
2. An analysis of the relationship between a variety of protocols and performance criteria is presented.
3. Closed form and computational schemes for obtaining the steady-state delay distribution are presented.
4. The delay distribution is shown to be approximately exponential; the single parameter characterizing the distribution is obtained as a function system parameters.
5. The delay dependencies on packet size are obtained. A closed-form expression for optimal packet size is reported. It is indicated that a network serving low-bandwidth terminals (e.g., vocoders) requires very small packets (20 to 50 bytes) whereas a network for high-bandwidth terminals (e.g., PCM) operates best with somewhat longer packets (60 to 70 bytes).
6. The effects of finite buffers to sustain excellent performance, even high utilization, are presented.
7. The transient behavior of the system is analyzed. Transient performance degradation is shown to be of limited duration.

3.2 Traffic Models

Although the generation process is given only cursory attention in most of the published models, detailed scrutiny of such input is required for any further analysis.

Introduction

The statistical analysis of speech patterns has attracted attention for the past half century. As a product of such study, several models for telephonic speech patterns have emerged. In general, to obtain a better fit to empirically measure data, the models must grow correspondingly in sophistication and complexity.

The major realization of the investigation has been that a Markov process, with an appropriate number of states, describes speech mechanics well. This section describes, in an organized fashion, various models that can be used to study speech behavior in a statistical sense. Some of the models have been studied in the literature; others have been developed to fill in the trade-off gaps between model complexity and correspondence with the empirical data. A short discussion of the relative merits and weaknesses of each model is given.

The accuracy of a model is its ability to predict the length of the ten speech events described in the following subsection. The most sophisticated models can accurately predict the distribution of all of these events. The less sophisticated models can predict the distribution of only a few events, particularly the talkspurt length and the pause length. However, it is these events that are of the most interest for our traffic models for network statistics. These simpler models yield more tractable analytical formulations. These models are applicable to waveform coding methods with silence suppression.

Speech Events

The following ten events are relevant to speech patterns:

1. Talkspurt
2. Pause
3. Doubletalk
4. Mutual silence
5. Alternative silence
6. Pause in isolation
7. Solitary talkspurt
8. Interruption
9. Speech after interruption
10. Speech before interruption

Consider two speakers, *A* and *B*. The major events are defined as follows:

1. *Talkspurt, Pause.*   The technique of obtaining on/off speech patterns is summarized as follows. A flip-flop is set each time speech (full-wave rectified and unfiltered) from speaker *A* crosses a threshold. This flip-flop is examined and cleared every 5 ms, with the output being a one if the threshold was crossed, zero otherwise. The resulting string of ones (spurts) and zeros (gaps) is examined for short spurts; all spurts less than 15 ms are erased. After this has been done, all gaps less than 200 ms are filled in to account for momentary interruptions, such as those due to stop constants. The resulting on/off pattern consists, by the definition used here, of talkspurts and pauses. An identical procedure is used for speaker *B*. (Note that this definition of talkspurt is not universal; other investigators use alternate definitions.)

2. *Doubletalk.*   A time when speech is present from both *A* and *B*.

3. *Mutual silence.*   A time when silence is present from both *A* and *B*.

There is a slight divergence from the approach employed in the literature, in that a packetized talkspurt is considered: namely, instead of considering a Markov process, a Markov chain is used. Furthermore, the chain is assumed to be homogenous (time invariant). The existence of a device or software algorithm that can test a speech packet for an energy threshold is presumed. The definition of talkspurt is as follows: A contiguous sequence of nonempty packets from a single talker constitutes a talkspurt. A packet is considered to be nonempty if it exceeds the energy threshold. Thus, any pause duration less than one packet's timelength will most likely be swallowed up in the discrete packetization, and the talkspurt will be considered not to have been interrupted by a pause. Pauses of up to two packets in length could be swallowed up, depending on the time phasing of the pause (see Figure 3.1).

Speaker Models

A time-slotted environment in which the speech takes place is assumed. That is, a clock divides the time axis into segments, during

Figure 3.1
Packet stream for an actual speech wave.

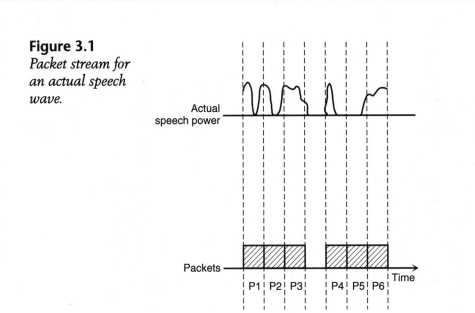

each of which a speaker generates an empty or nonempty packet, depending on whether the threshold energy was exceeded during that time period. These time segments will be called *frames*. Note that this specifically excludes voice-actuated synchronization. In the transmitted speech signal, it is assumed that empty packets mean a nonempty packet. The usual simplifying assumption that only one member of the speaker-listener pair changes speech activity states during a frame is made.

Six-State Markov Chain Model (Brady Model)

The Markov chain-state-transition diagram is depicted in Figure 3.2*a*. A possible sequence of events is depicted in Figure 3.2*b*. Observe that a talkspurt for *A* is made up of any concatenation of states 1, 2, and 3.

Although this six-state model is of interest because of its excellent predictive ability for the ten events, there exist simpler models that, although they cannot accurately describe certain events in the dynamics of a conversation, still yield accurate talkspurt and pause lengths.

Four-State Markov Chain Model

By collapsing states 2 and 3 into a single state, and similarly collapsing states 4 and 5 into a single state, we obtain the four-state chain

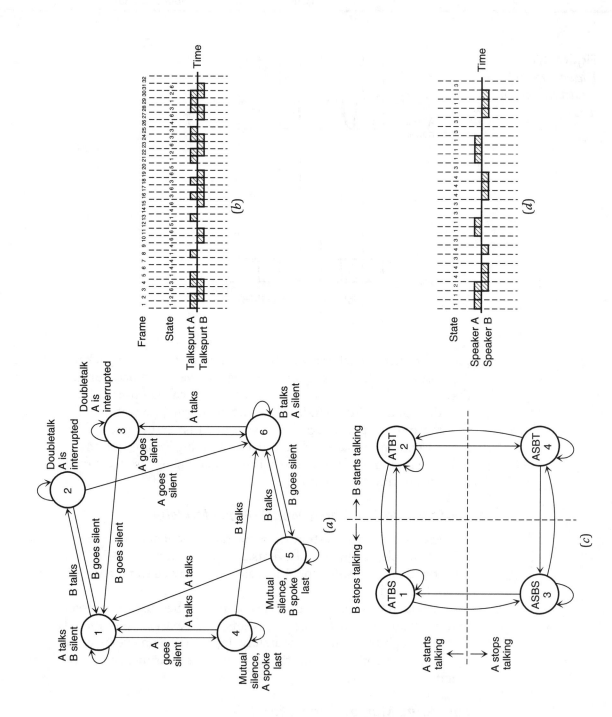

86

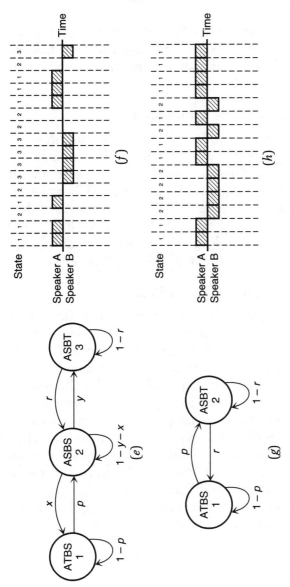

Figure 3.2
Speech origination models (XYTS = X talks, Y silent): (a) six-state model for speech pattern; (b) representative conversational sequence of events—shaded areas indicate a nonempty packet issued by the speaker; (c) four-state Markov chain model; (d) example of four-state model event sequence; (e) three-state model with transition probabilities; (f) example of a three-state model event sequence; (g) two-state model; (h) example of a two-state model event sequence.

87

depicted in Figure 3.2c. Figure 3.2d shows one of the possible events.

Observe that now a talkspurt from A consists of the concentration of states 1 and 2 only. This model predicts talkspurt length and pause length well, but does not provide an accurate fit to empirical data for doubletalk.

Three-State Markov Chain Model

By ignoring the possibility of doubletalk altogether—namely, by eliminating state 2 in the previous model—a model is produced that can predict talkspurt length and silence length distribution but cannot represent doubletalk (see Figures 3.2e and 3.2f). Note that the talkspurt is characterized by a single state, and the silence period of a particular talker is characterized by two states. With this model, the talkspurt length is geometrically distributed, but the silent-period length is not. This is also true of the empirical data.

Two-State Markov Chain Model

As a final simplification, an elementary two-state chain can be assumed. This can still model the talkspurt length fairly reasonably, but it does not model the silence length well. This chain is obtained by eliminating the possibility for mutual silence; namely, state 2 in the previous chain. Thus, speakers A and B alternate their turns, speaking with no pauses or response-time silences (see Figures 3.2g and 3.2h). The talkspurt length and the silence length are both geometrically distributed (only the former is realistic). In view of its simplicity, this model has been investigated further and applied to this link model analysis. The other models could also be used with a slight increase in computational effort.

It is easily shown that in this case the probability (there are k packets input at the nth frame, and m pairs of terminals are active) is

$$\binom{m}{k}[P_1^{(n)}]^k[P_2^{(n)}]^{m-k}$$

where

$$P_1^{(n)} = P_1^{(0)}p_{11}^{(n)} + P_2^{(0)}p_{21}^{(n)}$$
$$P_2^{(n)} = P_1^{(0)}p_{12}^{(n)} + P_2^{(0)}p_{22}^{(n)}$$

and

$$P_{AB}^n = \begin{bmatrix} p_{11}^{(n)} p_{12}^{(n)} \\ p_{21}^{(n)} p_{22}^{(n)} \end{bmatrix}$$

$$= \begin{bmatrix} \dfrac{p}{r+p} + r\dfrac{(1-r-p)^n}{r+p}, & \dfrac{r}{r+p} - r\dfrac{(1-r-p)^n}{r+p} \\[2ex] \dfrac{p}{r+p} - p\dfrac{(1-r-p)^n}{r+p}, & \dfrac{r}{r+p} + p\dfrac{(1-r-p)^n}{r+p} \end{bmatrix}$$

One can also obtain

$$\lim_{n\to\infty} \text{prob } (k \text{ packets from } m \text{ speakers at frame } n)$$

$$= \binom{m}{k} \left(\frac{p}{r+p}\right)^k \left(\frac{r}{r+p}\right)^{m-k}$$

Thus, it is observed that the steady-state arrival process is a binomial process. This is clearly due to the fact that each speaker's behavior is an independent Bernoulli trial, with probability $p/(r+p)$ of supplying a nonempty packet. This result can be used to easily compute the steady-state traffic statistics; it has, in fact, been used in the model in Section 3.4.

The steady-state traffic can be used in studying long-term network behavior but the nth-step unconditional probabilities would be needed for any investigation of network transient behavior.

Other Models

For the purpose of studying network behavior, the most significant aspect of the traffic models for a speaker is the resulting distribution of the length of the stream consecutive packets (i.e., talkspurt length). In comparing the implications of the previous models with empirical data, it can be noticed that, although the empirical distribution talkspurt length is closer to the geometric that the models predict, the most significant discrepancy is an underprediction of the frequency of short talkspurts.

An intuitive conjecture is that a speaker operates in at least two models: one where he or she is the *controlling* speaker, and the other where he or she is merely issuing short utterances to *reinforce* the speech he or she is receiving. Thus, any one of the previous models can be extended to include two distinct states for A talking, B silent. In Figure 3.2g the two-state chain can be augmented to a four-state chain by introducing two such new states, one for each speaker. One state has a high probability for speech to be continued into the next frame, and the other state has a much lower continued speech probability. Thus, each active speaker can be in a *long-burst* or *short-burst* mode.

Call Origination Model

Thus far, the behavior of a population of m terminals, where m is fixed, has been considered. This section addresses the issue of the call origination process.

Let M be the maximum number of speakers that can access the packet switch under consideration; let $m^{(n)}$ be the number of off-hook terminals (i.e., active terminals) at frame n.

Two issues need to be addressed:

1. The statistical behavior of $m^{(n)}$
2. The length (holding time) of a typical call.

While specific answers can be given only with exact data from the community of users for which the network is intended, mathematical models that capture the *flavor* of the phenomenon (rather than the exact numbers) are easily constructed.

The speech-originating process will be modeled by a more complex Markov chain that drives the imbedded speaker models. Figure 3.3 illustrates the technique for the two-state model. Let the new chain be denoted by $Y_i^{(n)}$. Note that the holding time (i.e., the time the $Y_i^{(n)}$ is in a state greater than or equal to 1) is geometrically distributed in each case, because $Y_i^{(n)}$ remains in state 0 with probability $1 - s\alpha$, where s is the number of states in the speech chain and α is the probability of a transition from an on-hook state to each of the off-hook states. This is consistent with the memoryless holding-time standard assumption.

It is clear that by appropriately selecting the parameter Ω the conversation can be made statistically longer or shorter; also, the

Figure 3.3
Call-origination model interfaced to a two-state speech model.

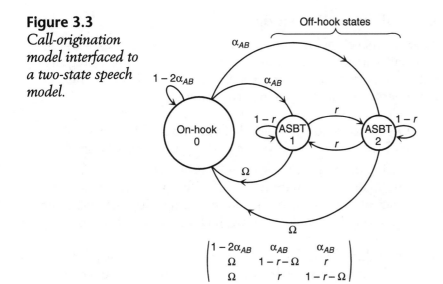

$$\begin{pmatrix} 1-2\alpha_{AB} & \alpha_{AB} & \alpha_{AB} \\ \Omega & 1-r-\Omega & r \\ \Omega & r & 1-r-\Omega \end{pmatrix}$$

α_1, Ω very small

number of transitions to the off-hook state, namely, the number of calls the pair *A-B* is likely to make in a time interval *t* can be controlled.

3.3 Performance Criteria

Well-documented subjective testing and measurements have established ranges of transmission network corruptive effects on speech where these effects are either: (1) not perceptible, (2) perceptible but tolerable, or (3) not tolerable.

Estimates for the boundaries between these regions are available, although further investigation into combinations of effects is needed. The *not-perceptible* range is easy to deal with. The *not-tolerable* range is slightly deceptive, in that it will not usually result in a disruption of the conversation unless sustained for an unacceptable period of time. Fortunately, it is only in the not-tolerable range that speaker behavior leads to unstable degradation (shouting, heavy doubletalking, no information transfer, etc.). In the middle range, the speakers eventually begin to act to produce more efficient information transfer (fewer interruptions, etc.); thus, speaker models based on ideal network performances will tend to be conservative in estimating the degree of corruptive effects.

Results of Subjective Studies

Packetized speech belongs to the category of real-time data traffic. Consistent with this classification, it has stringent delivery requirements with respect to loss or error. Generally speaking, the delivery requirements can be divided into two categories:

1. Owing to the psychological effects induced by delay, the end-to-end average network delivery time must be small.
2. Owing to the psychological effects induced by *glitching* (gaps due to delay fluctuation, noise, buffer overflow losses and other protocol discarding and misaddressing), the end-to-end variation of the delivery time, including losses, must be small.

In other words, the human listener in a conversation has limited tolerance to both the average delay and the fluctuation of delay. It is thus apparent that the network designer must control not only the first moment of the delay (mean), but also the second moment (variance). This latter requirement is formally established in the "Smoothness Criteria" subsection.

End-to-End Delay

The overall end-to-end delay can be written as

$$D(t) = V + h + d(t) + B$$

where V is the delay due to the speech analog-digital conversion, h is the delay due to the packetizing period (equivalent to the packet timelength), $d(t)$ is the network delay at time t, and B is the waiting time at the receiver end. The precise value of V depends on the terminal technology and is usually small compared with the other terms; it will be ignored in the sequel. Therefore, if $D = h + d$, D represents the total end-to-end delay before the application of any receive-end buffering. The overall delay $D(t)$ should not exceed 200 ms, the value of delay that has been shown to be commercially acceptable. When the delay reaches 800 ms, adverse psychological factors impede normal telephonic conversation. A delay of 200 to 800 ms is conditionally acceptable for a short portion of the conversation, when the occurrences of such delays are rare and far apart. In other words, there is a well-established range of acceptable delay, and temporary degradation is admissible, as long as such degradation occurs with low probability and short duration. Particular applications usually require more stringent constraints. As noted in Chapters 4 and 5, delays in the 100 to 200 ms range are now the typical goal; during the 1980s researchers were willing to consider longer delays.

Glitching

Studies have been conducted in which speed is temporarily segmented and temporarily interrupted at constant (deterministic) rates, and in which speech is manipulated according to some random process. The following results have been shown:

- In interrupted speech (equivalent to loss or discard of packets):

  Intelligibility decreases to very low values (10 percent) as the packet size approaches 0.25 s.

  Intelligibility increases to 80 percent as packet size approaches 0.020 s.

- In segmented speech (equivalent to waiting for late packets):

  For fixed active-speech segment length, intelligibility increases as the silence period decreases.

  For fixed silence length, intelligibility decreases as the active-speech segment length decreases.

Curing suggestions, such as short packets and interleaving, have been suggested.

Owing to the high redundancy of the speech signal, speech losses as high as 50 percent can be sustained with marginal degradation if such loss occurs for very small (e.g., 20 ms) segments. This concept might be employed to control total network traffic in case of congestion. Thus, the acceptable packet loss rate is a function of packet size. Under certain speech encoding techniques, such as vocoding, the packets themselves may be composed of self-contained speech elements, called *parcels*, the selective discarding of which could be used as a traffic throttle. With PCM, for example, if an eight-level quantification is used, each 8-bit character can be considered a parcel.

Smoothness Criteria

The reconstructed continuous speech delivered to a listener by a packet-switched IP network contains gaps due to the statistical fluctuation of the network load and the consequent fluctuation of the network delay and loss performance. The gap structure perceived by the listener will be not only a function of these fluctuations but also a function of the network policy or protocol at the receiver end for dealing with these gaps. This section shows the importance of obtaining the delay distribution, or at least the second moment of delay. For data traffic, the mean delay has usually been the only design criterion.

Waiting for Late Packets

Consider an A talkspurt, that is, a segment of continuous active speech between a speaker-listener pair A-B with a consecutive stream of nonempty packets issued by speaker A. Assume that a frame i ($i = 1, 2, \ldots$), a packet issued by A, experiences delay D_i, where D_i are identically (but not independently) distributed for all i. Then, for a fixed packet time length h, $a_i = ih$ is the time when A issues packet i, and $b_i = D_i + ih$ is the time when B receives packet i. Note that, as defined here, h is identical to the packetizing delay in the previous delay formula. Let f_i be the temporal fluctuation between packets $i - 1$ and i, as received by B. More precisely (see Figure 3.4),

$$f_i = D_i - D_{i-1} + \min(0, f_{i-1}) \qquad \text{for } i = 1, 2, \ldots$$

with the initial condition $D_0 = 0$, $f_0 = 0$.

Figure 3.4
*Unlimited waiting
protocol.*
$f_1 = 1 - 0 + 0 = 1,$
$\quad Z_1 = 0, G_1 = 1$
$f_2 = 2 - 1 + 0 = 1,$
$\quad Z_2 = 0, G_2 = 1$
$f_3 = 6 - 2 + 0 = 4,$
$\quad Z_3 = 0, G_3 = 4$
$f_4 = 1 - 6 + 0 = -5,$
$\quad Z_4 = G_4 = 0$
$f_5 = 3 - 1 - 5 = -3,$
$\quad Z_5 = -3, G_5 = 0$

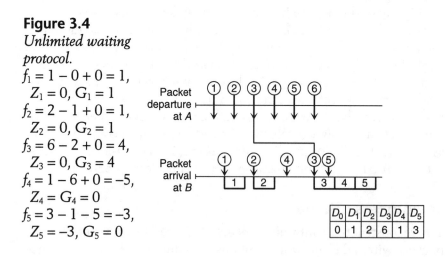

Then f_i represents the a posteriori lateness of the ith packet relative to the lateness of the $(i-1)$st packet. Because $0 \le D_i \le \infty$, the range of f_i is $-\infty \le f_i \le \infty$. If $f_i \le 0$ corresponding to the ith packet arrival not later than the earliest time that an in-order delivery to B can be made, no temporal disruption results, provided that adequate buffering facilities exist at the receiver end. For this protocol the reconstructed speech is simply

$$G_i = \max (f_i, 0) = \begin{cases} f_i & \text{if } f_i > 0 \\ 0 & \text{if } f_i \le 0 \end{cases}$$

That is, gaps are introduced only when f_i is positive.

Clearly, the network should be designed such that the distribution of G_i is acceptable from a performance point of view. After long algebraic manipulation, one arrives at

$$\text{prob} (G_i > K_\alpha) \le \frac{2\sigma_D{}^2 (1 - \rho_D)}{K_\alpha{}^2} < \frac{\sigma_D{}^2}{K_\alpha{}^2}$$

where $\sigma_D{}^2$ is the variance of the end-to-end delay, and ρ_D is the correlation in deliveries.

Thus, for any performance criteria where one wishes to control the tail of the gap distribution, given K_α, one can impose constraints on $\sigma_D{}^2$ so that the probability of gaps exceeding K_α can have arbitrarily small probability. Note that K_α itself can be made arbitrarily small, certainly sufficient in an engineering sense, but that it cannot be made strictly zero. Thus, one can ensure the constraint

$$\text{prob} (G_i > K_\alpha) \le \alpha$$

by satisfying

$$\sigma_D{}^2 \le \frac{\alpha K_\alpha}{4}$$

Note that as α decreases, the amount of area $\sigma_D{}^2$ allowed in the tail must decrease. Also, as the cutoff point for the tail K_α decreases, the needed $\sigma_D{}^2$ decreases.

Limited Waiting for Late Packets

Under the protocol in the preceding subsection it is shown that the gaps in the reconstructed speech are

$$G_i = \max{(f_i, 0)}$$

If the designer of the network could control the variance of the delay, then the tail of the gap distribution would also be controlled. The variance, however, cannot be completely controlled or, in general, reduced to any arbitrary value. Therefore, an alternative protocol must be sought to prevent long gaps.

Waiting indefinitely for late packets at the receiver end (say, by buffering subsequent packets) implies not only a long gap in the reconstructed speech until such late packets arrive, but also temporal distortion of the consecutive spoken material from that point on. Also, such a protocol implies no recovery from lost or misaddressed packets. To avoid these complications, a protocol can declare missing, and subsequently ignore, a packet whose lateness exceeds a certain preset limit S. Such an action is called a *discard*. Assume that $(J-1)h \leq S \leq Jh$, where J is a positive integer. By substituting a period of silence of length Jh whenever a packet does not arrive in time, the temporal distortion of the overall speech string can be bounded by a predetermined value. Note that $J = 1$, for example, implies a temporal distortion of at most S and a gap of at most h before the protocol is reapplied to the next packet. In this case, a single packet arrives infinitesimally before the discard decision, in which case the packet is still delivered. Further improvement can be obtained if the silent period following rejection is aborted on the arrival of the next packet, but this alternative has not yet been investigated here. It can be shown that under this protocol the gap structure can again be controlled by controlling σ_D, but σ_D need not be made small as for the protocol in the preceding subsection.

Receiver-End Buffering

The limited waiting period S can be regarded as a delay-variance reduction technique, wherein temporal gaps due to a single packet are prevented from exceeding S, paying for it with a glitch silence of length Jh. An additional protocol strategy can be employed to reduce the gap variance by buffering packets at the receiver end so that their total delay to the receiver is at least some minimum quantity. What is sacrificed with this technique is an increase in the average delay in return for the improved smoothness.

This modification involves buffering at the receiver end those packets whose delay does not exceed a certain appropriately chosen value w. These packets would be stored for an amount of time equal to $w - D_i$.

3.4 Link Model

So far, the input to the system and the requirements to be satisfied in delivering the input traffic to its destinations have been discussed. The system to accomplish such transfer is now described.

Introduction

This section considers a distributed population of digital voice terminals and a network of packet switches (or routers) interconnected by a topology of (usually high-capacity) links. Terminals are homed to a specific packet switch or router. Communication between remote terminals takes place via the appropriate backbone packet switches or router, which are used for entry, exit and store-and-forward relay operations.

The objective of this network model is to obtain end-to-end delay, the percentage of lost packets, the amount of glitching, and so forth. The discussion initially looks at a single link on a channel and draws appropriate conclusions. Later, the analysis is extended to a network of tandem links and then to a more general network.

Model Description

The discussion begins by identifying the underlying assumptions and introducing some descriptive notation.

Traffic

Given any pair of speakers *A-B*, consider any one of the traffic models of Section 3.2, interfaced to the call origination model. Let $P_i^{(n)}$ be the vector of unconditional probabilities of speaker i being in state 0, 1, 2, 3, . . . at frame n; for example:

$$P_i^{(n)} = [P_{i,0}^{(n)}, P_{i,1}^{(n)}, \ldots P_{i,s}^{(n)}]$$

This discussion is concerned only with some of the elements of this vector, namely $P_i^{(n)}$, the probability that speaker A supplies a packet at frame n, given that the pair A-B is off-hook. Then

$$P_i^{(n)} = \frac{\displaystyle\sum_{j/i\,\text{talks}} P_{i,j}^{(n)}}{\displaystyle\sum_{j=1} P_{i,j}^{(n)}}$$

Queue Operation

1. m terminals accessing the packet switch or router under consideration are off-hook and are engaged in infinitely long conversation.

2. Each terminal has two buffers for potential packets, and so it can start building the next packet after completion of one. Before the new one is completed, the old one must be cleared or it will be overwritten. This implies a constraint on the processor.

3. A scheduled arrival of potential packets is assumed; namely, terminal T_i, generated completed empty or nonempty packets at times $rh + i\Delta, r = 0, 1, 2, \ldots$, where Δ is a parameter, possibly dynamically adjustable, of the entry switch or router. Although such synchronization is impossible to arrange immediately following the off-hook condition, it can be accomplished in subsequent frames by appropriately clipping speech or adding silence. This needs to be done only once.

4. The appropriate buffer of T_i is processed at time $rh + i\Delta$. If occupied by a nonempty packet, the contents of the buffer are placed on a queue for transmission. The queue itself operated in a first in, first out (FIFO) mode.

5. It is assumed that τ_i, the speaker behavior, is independent of the queue backlog.

It is clear that $h \le m\Delta$ must be met to preserve the real-time requirement (avoid extra delay or packet loss) at the entry node caused by the processor falling further and further behind in its cynical scan for packets requiring transmission. Summarizing the preceding assumptions, it is seen that a packet joins the output transmission queue at time $rh + i\Delta$ with probability $P_i^{(r)}$. The time period h between the possible successive submissions of a packet by a particular terminal will still be referred to as a frame (see Figure 3.5).

Link Parameters

The following parameters influence the link performance:

m = Number of off-hook users accessing the switch
B = Rate at which the digital voice terminal supplies bits, bps
C = Capacity of the transmission link, bps
P = Speech content per packet, bits
$h = \dfrac{P}{B}$ = Timelength of speech carried in a packet, s
ϕ = Packet overhead in header and so forth, bits
s = Number of states in the speech model, as discussed in Section 3.2
p = Steady-state probability that a speaker will issue a packet in a frame; determinable, in general, from s and the speech model state transition parameters $(p = \lim_{r \to \infty} P_i^{(r)})$

For formulation simplicity, it is assumed that s, B, P, ϕ, and, therefore, h are also identical for all terminals. From the preceding model parameters, it follows that the transmission service time for

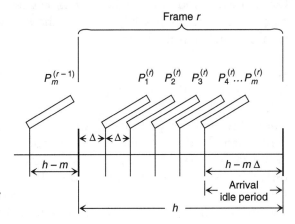

Figure 3.5
Probabilistic queue arrival sequence.

a packet is the constant μ obtained by dividing the total packet length in sets by the line capacity, namely, $\mu = (P + \phi)/C$. An expression for line utilization ρ can be stated in terms of the preceding parameters:

$$\rho = \frac{Pm[B + |P|\phi]}{C} = \frac{PmB}{C}\left[1 + \frac{\phi}{P}\right]$$

Outline of Queue Solution

Thus, it is assumed that at any instant $i\Delta$ ($i = 0, 1, 2, \ldots$, with Δ an integer number of time units) a packet joins the queue with probability p. Namely, if $\tau_i = 1$ if a customer arrives at $i\Delta$ and 0 otherwise, then

$$\text{prob } (\tau_i = 1) = p$$
$$\text{prob } (\tau_i = 0) = 1 - p$$

Assume that the service time per packet is given by

$$\text{prob } (S = j) = S_j \qquad j = 1, 2, 3, \ldots$$

This is slightly more general then the constant server problem stated previously. Note that Δ can certainly be made an integer for all practical purposes by appropriately choosing the underlying unit—say, seconds, milliseconds, microseconds, and so forth. The utilization of the system is $\rho = pE(S)/\Delta$.

Using the method of embedded Markov chains, consider the amount of unfinished work W_n just after the nth potential arrival point (not actual arrival). Then

$$W_0 = 0$$
$$W_{n+1} = \max (0, W_n - \Delta) + \tau_{n+1}S$$

Under the assumption that W_n and τ_{n+1} are statistically independent—namely, the arrival behavior is independent of the queue statue—W_n ($n = 0, 1, 2, \ldots$) is a Markov chain. Because the queue is assumed empty at time zero, W_n can take only values $j = 0, 1, 2, \ldots$

Assuming that $\rho < 1$, so that a steady state exists, and letting

$$W = \lim_{n \to \infty} W_n$$

$$\pi_{j,n} = \text{prob} \ (W_n = j)$$

$$\pi_j = \lim_{n \to \infty} \pi_{j,n}$$

the following steady-state recurrence relations are obtained:

$$\pi_0 = (1 - p) \sum_{i=0}^{\Delta} \pi_i$$

$$\pi_Q = \left(ps_Q \sum_{i=0}^{\Delta} \pi_i \right) + \left(\sum_{i=0}^{Q-1} ps_{Q-i} \pi_{\Delta+i} \right) + (1 - p) \pi_{\Delta+Q}$$

$$Q = 1, 2, 3, \ldots$$

Let $\psi_\pi(Z)$ be the generating function of the π's and $\psi_s(Z)$ the generating function of the server's discrete distribution.

Then, by the usual technique,

$$\psi_\pi(Z) = \frac{[p\psi_s(Z) + 1 - p] \sum_{i=0}^{\Delta-1} (Z^\Delta - Z^i) \pi_i}{Z^\Delta - [p\psi_s(Z) + 1 - p]}$$

Note that at this point there are Δ unknowns $(\pi_0, \pi_1, \ldots, \pi_{\Delta-1})$ in the generating function. Evaluating $\psi(Z)$ at $Z = 1$ obtains

$$\sum_{i=0}^{\Delta=1} (\Delta - i) \pi_i = \Delta - pE(S)$$

$\Delta - 1$ other equations are needed to obtain the first $\Delta \pi$'s.

Even without the evaluation of these Δ unknowns, an expression for the expected amount of unfinished work can be obtained. In fact,

$$E(W) = \psi_\pi'$$

$$= \frac{[\Delta - pE(S)] \ [\Delta - 1 + 2pE(S)] - \{\Delta(\Delta - 1) - pV(S) - pE(S)[E(S) - 1]\} \sum_{i=0}^{\Delta-1} i(\Delta - i) \pi_i}{2[\Delta - pE(S)]}$$

of interest here is the delay U, seen at steady state by an incoming customer. Clearly,

$$U = \max(W - \Delta, 0) + S$$

Thus,

$$\begin{aligned}E(U) &= E[\max(W - \Delta, 0)] + E(S)\\&= E(W) - pE(S) + E(S)\end{aligned}$$

With a constant server, it can be shown that the mean of the distribution (mean waiting time for link, plus transmission) is

$$E(U) = \left[\frac{0.75 - \dfrac{\rho}{2}}{1 - \rho} \right]\mu$$

so that

$$E(U) = \left[\frac{p + \phi}{C} \right]\left[\frac{P\left(0.75 - \dfrac{mB}{4C}\right) - \dfrac{mB\phi}{4C}}{P\left(1 - \dfrac{mB}{2C}\right) - \dfrac{mB\phi}{2C}} \right]$$

Generally speaking, the delay distribution is also a function of five parameters driving the model, namely: (1) the line capacity C, (2) the packet length P, (3) the overhead ϕ, (4) the digitization bit rate B, and (5) the number of simultaneous users m. To obtain such distribution, the Δ unknowns previously mentioned must be obtained. This can be done with the aid of the following three propositions.

Let

$$\psi_\pi(Z) = \frac{M(Z)N(Z)}{D(Z)}$$

Proposition 1: $D(Z) = Z^\Delta - p\psi_s(Z) - 1 + p$ has exactly Δ roots inside or on $|Z| = 1$.

Proposition 2: $N(Z) = \sum\limits_{i=0}^{\Delta-1}(Z^\Delta - Z^i)\pi_i$ has exactly Δ roots on $|Z| = 1$.

Proposition 3: No root of $M(Z) = p\psi_s(Z) + 1 - p$ coincides with a root of $D(Z)$.

Thus, it follows that the zeros Z_i of $D(Z)$, $|Z_i| \leq 1$ must coincide with the zeros of $N(Z)$; more specifically, because $D(Z)$ has Δ zeros inside or on the unit disk, the $\psi(Z)$ converges at least inside the unit disk, it follows that the zeros of the denominator are also the zeros of the numerator. Thus, there are exactly Δ equations for the determination of the Δ unknowns $\pi_0, \pi_1, \ldots, \pi_{\Delta-1}$.

3.5 Results

This section studies the following for the steady-state situation: the delay distribution faced by a typical packet, both for the case of infinite buffer capacity and the finite case; the effect of the speech model on the delay and on the utilization of the line; and, finally, the determination of optimal packet lengths, with respect to a specific performance criterion, as a function of the number of users, the overhead, the digitization rate, and the capacity of the transmission line. The model is also used to address some transient issues via numerical solution.

Properties of the Delay Distribution

As indicated previously, the general interest here is in studying the characteristics of the delay distribution. A concentration of probability around the delay mean necessarily implies a related concentration of probability near zero for the gap structure.

A distribution with a high-probability tail is poor, in the sense that one must pay a high price in terms of network control and clack facility utilization to ensure a certain performance confidence. Packet speech is particularly vulnerable to high-probability tails in the delay distribution, because the value of its information is perishable. If a network is not designed properly—say, with much hopping (e.g., too many router links) and a very high utilization of line capacity—the variance may be such that one would be forced to wait several seconds before ensuring that the fraction of the packets needed for fidelity are received. This would violate the tight delivery-time requirements previously described.

As a first-order approximation, the end-to-end variance can be taken as the sum of the links variances (and is bounded by $L^2 \sigma_M^2$ where L is the number of links and σ_M^2 is the largest link variance).

Therefore, the variance of the end-to-end delay can be directly related to the variance of the delay on a single link. A key issue is, what is the single-link-delay distribution for a packet voice network?

Figure 3.6 shows the distribution of total delay for five values of ρ for the case $P = 800$, $\phi = 200$, $C = 50$ kbps, $B = 5$ kbps, and a symmetric two-state speaker model. Naturally, as the utilization increases, the distribution becomes more dispersed. Figure 3.7 shows the expected value and the 95th percentile with the mean as predicted from an $M|M|1$. In terms of concentration of probability, the distributions under consideration are comparable to exponential distribution for the cases of $\rho = 0.813$ and $\rho = 0.938$. The agreement is excellent. From this observation it appears that the single-link-delay distribution can be approximately characterized with one parameter, its expected value.

For the infinite-buffer case, the following conclusions can be made:

1. The exponential distribution accurately fits the actual delay distribution.

2. As a consequence of good exponential fit, the 95th, 99th, and 99.9th percentiles of the model's total delay distribution are comparable to those of the exponential distribution (in the number of standard deviations).

Figure 3.6
Typical total delay distributions:
(a) $\rho = 0.563$,
m = 9
(b) $\rho = 0.688$,
m = 11
(c) $\rho = 0.813$,
m = 13
(d) $\rho = 0.875$,
m = 14
(e) $\rho = 0.938$,
m = 15

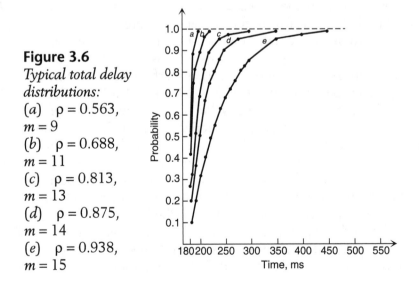

Figure 3.7
Expected delay as a function: (a) E(D) for M|M|1, (b) $K_{0.95}$, and (c) E(D).

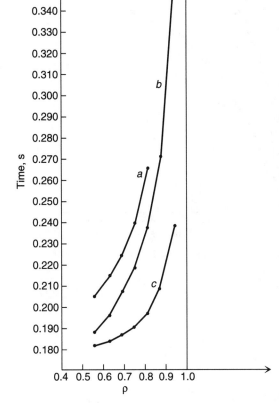

The model delay has an accumulation of probability at an initial point, indicating the possibility of finding a server idle; this feature is not captured by the exponential random variable.

On the other hand, the finite-buffer case reduces the expected delay and contracts delay distribution as compared to the infinite-buffer case, at the expense of blocking some packets. The "Finite-Buffer Case" subsection addresses this issue in more detail.

To point out the peculiarities of the delay distribution (Figure 3.8) for a voice environment, compare the results of the present model to an M|D|1 model (representative of packet radio, random-access schemes); an M|M|1 model (representative of a data packet switched network); and also against the well-known G|G|1 heavy traffic approximation (see Figure 3.9).

Figure 3.8
Comparison between model delay distribution and exponential approximation:
(a) ρ = 0.813,
(b) ρ = 0.938.

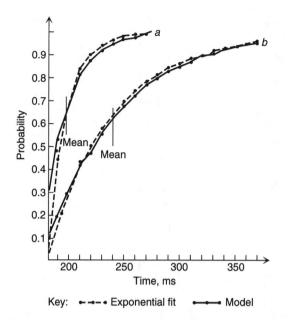

Figure 3.9
*Comparison of approximations, where P = 0.5, f = 110, ϕ = 110, B = 2000, C = 10,000, m = 5, and ρ = 0.95: (a) Model, (b) G|G|1, heavy traffic, (c) M|D|1, and (d) M|M|1. (*NOTE: *Only the dots should be compared.)*

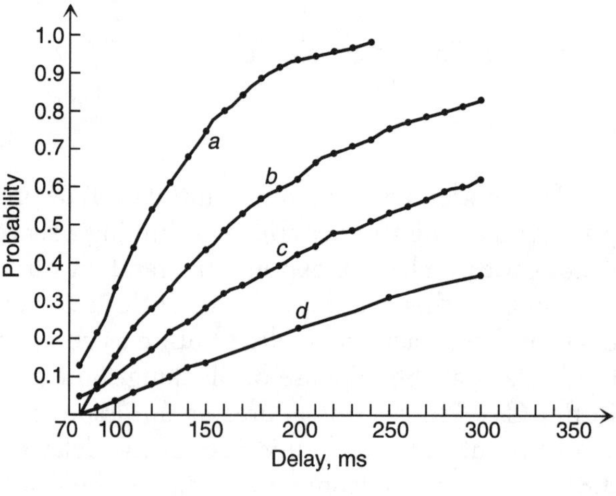

106

As anticipated, the other models turn out to be conservative in that these distributions imply a larger mean value and a higher probability tail.

Finite-Buffer Case

This finite-buffer case is interesting from an engineering point of view. First, there is the issue of how many buffers to provide at a packet switch; second, what is the buffer overflow probability, given that a fixed number of buffers is provided? The modified version of the model in the "Outline of Queue Solution" subsection can be employed to successfully address and answer these issues.

The examples in the "Properties of the Delay Distribution" subsection were rerun with two, three, and four buffers, and the results were analyzed.

Figure 3.10 shows a plot of some of these results. The delay distributions for finite-buffer cases are contrasted with the infinite-buffer situation. Finite-buffer situations have a delay distribution that is much less dispersed; the long tail of the delay distribution is

Figure 3.10
Comparison between the delay distribution for infinite- and finite-buffer facilities, where P = 112, f = 800, ϕ = 200, m = 13–15, B = 5000, C = 50,000, h = 0.16, and μ = 0.02: (a) k = 2, 2 buffers; (b) k = 4, 4 buffers; (c) k = ∞, infinite buffer.

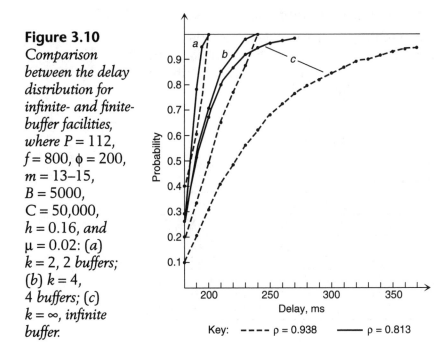

Key: ---- ρ = 0.938   ——— ρ = 0.813

cut off. This has the beneficial effect of improving the performance of those packets that are not blocked, at the expense of dropping a few packets. Table 3.1 compares the mean and the 95th percentile of those packets that are successfully delivered; the improvement effect previously mentioned can be seen, particularly for high utilization. Note that now the largest possible delay is $K\mu + h$, where K is the number of buffers.

Not yet shown is the probability that a packet is blocked; this is expected to increase as the number of buffers decreases. The significant observation is that such probability is low, even when the number of buffers is small. Table 3.2 depicts results that are typical for any model parameter selection. Thus, even at $\rho = 0.938$, four buffers are sufficient to guarantee that 95 percent of the packets are not blocked.

Effect of Speech Models

Thus far the speaker model has been kept frozen with respect to two factors: (1) the number of states in the speech chain, and (2) the transition matrix of the speech chain.

Transition Matrix Changes for the Two-State Model

Because of the symmetry requirement, the steady-state distribution is invariant under changes in the transition matrix. This follows, quite simply, because the steady-state distribution of the arrival process can be shown to be

$$P(Z^{(\infty)} = k) = \binom{m}{k}\left(\frac{1}{2}\right)^m$$

Table 3.1   Effect of Finite Buffer

	Buffer size							
	$K = \infty$		$K = 4$		$K = 3$		$K = 2$	
Utilization	$E(D)$	$K_{0.95}$	$E(D)$	$K_{0.95}$	$E(D)$	$K_{0.95}$	$E(D)$	$K_{0.95}$
0.563	0.182	0.188	0.182	0.188	0.182	0.188	0.182	0.188
0.688	0.187	0.207	0.187	0.205	0.187	0.203	0.185	0.190
0.813	0.197	0.238	0.194	0.226	0.191	0.213	0.186	0.196
0.938	0.239	0.357	0.203	0.234	0.196	0.216	0.188	0.198

Table 3.2 Fraction of Packets Not Blocked

	$K = \infty$	$K = 4$	$K = 3$	$K = 2$
$\rho = 0.563$	1.0	1.0	1.0	0.9995
$\rho = 0.688$	1.0	0.9996	0.9967	0.9653
$\rho = 0.813$	1.0	0.9905	0.9738	0.9139
$\rho = 0.938$	1.0	0.9557	0.9275	0.8653

for a two-state chain. Changes in the transition matrix affect only the transient behavior unless the symmetry requirement is eliminated.

Three-State Speaker Model

A brief investigation of a three-state speaker model was undertaken. It has already been indicated that the two-state model is very conservative, predicting more traffic than actual. The average number of packets per frame supplied by a population of m users under the two- and three-state model are $m/2$ and $mx/(2x + p)$, respectively, where the three-state transition matrix is

$$\begin{pmatrix} 1 - p & p & 0 \\ x & 1 - 2x & x \\ 0 & p & 1 - p \end{pmatrix}$$

Typical values of the transition and probabilities are $p = 0.1$, a high tendency to continue speech, once initiated; and $x = 0.46$, a high tendency to break away from mutual silence. Thus, for m terminals, $0.46m$ packets would be expected, compared with $0.5m$ for the two-state model. With the assumption of a three-state speech model, 10 percent more users can be accommodated (if $x = 0.23$, the model could accommodate 20 percent more speakers). The delay distribution for the examples of the "Finite-Buffer Case" subsection have been obtained for the three-state model and are depicted in Figure 3.11 for infinite buffers. Observe that the delay distribution is fairly similar to the distribution obtained with a two-state model at the same utilization. Compare $\rho = 0.733$, $s = 3$; $\rho = 0.845$, $s = 3$; and $\rho = 0.813$, $s = 2$.

The effect of buffer size is similar to that described for the finite-buffer case. For the three-state speaker model, with the same value of m, fewer packets arrive at the packet switch, and so the number of buffers necessary for acceptable operation is the same or

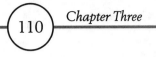
Figure 3.11
Comparison between the delay distribution for a two-state speech model and a three-state speech model, where P = 800, φ = 200, m = 13–15, B = 5000, C = 50,000, h = 0.16, and μ = 0.02:
(a) three states, m = 13, ρ = 0.733
(b) two states, m = 13, ρ = 0.813
(c) three states, m = 15, ρ = 0.845
(d) two states, m = 15, ρ = 0.938

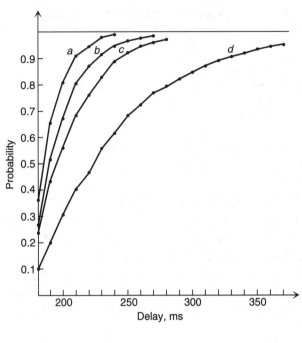

reduced. In addition, the three-state speaker model has little or no effect on the steady-state output distribution, reflecting only the change in utilization. The explicit dependence of $E(D)$ on ρ, h, and μ continues to hold.

Optimal Packet Length

Figure 3.12 depicts the convexity of the total delay experiences by a voice packet (packetization plus network delay), when plotted against the packet length P. Figure 3.13 shows an actual curve where the mean total delay and the 0.01 and 0.05 percentiles are shown.

From these curves, it is obvious that the designer must be careful in selecting the appropriate packet length if the delay is to be optimized. This model has been used in Reference [8] to show that $P_{opt} = L(1 + F)/(1 - L)$ and

Figure 3.12
Convexity of total delay against packet length: (a) link delay, (b) packetizing delay, and (c) total delay.

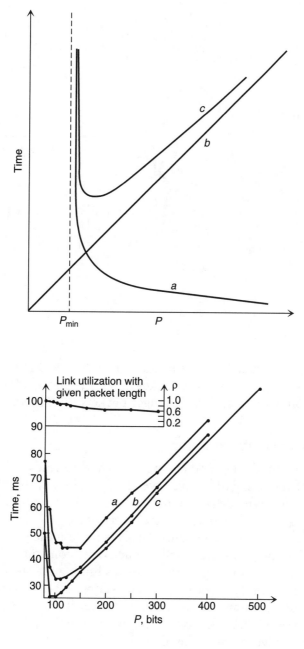

Figure 3.13
Representative optimization curve for the packet length: (a) $K_{0.01}$, (b) $K_{0.05}$, and (c) $E(D)$.

$$E(D)|_{P=P_{opt}} = \frac{\phi}{B} \frac{\left(\frac{L}{1-L}\right)(F+1)^2 \left[A\left(\frac{0.75 - \frac{L}{2}}{1+L}\right) + 1 \right] + (F+1)A\left[\frac{0.75 - L}{1-L} - \frac{L}{1-L}\right] - \frac{A}{2}}{F}$$

where

$$F = \sqrt{\frac{1 - \left[1 - \frac{A}{2} \frac{(0.5 - L)}{L} \right]}{\left(\frac{1 + A\left[0.75 - \frac{L}{2} \right]}{1 - L} \right)}}$$

and

$$A = \frac{B}{C} \qquad L = \frac{mA}{2}$$

Detailed analysis of this formula indicates that vocoder technologies usually require short packet lengths (150 to 400 bits), while PCM can operate at slightly longer packets (600 bits).

Transient Behavior

The model at hand can be employed to study the transient behavior of the single link. This reveals the time duration of degraded performance when a bad state is entered, that is, an unusual period of high speech activity in one direction.

The basic procedure involves finding the steady-state delay, then perturbing the speaker activity in one direction.

The basic procedure involves finding the steady-state delay, then perturbing the speaker activity states and observing the effect on the system. As an extreme, at a particular frame, every terminal is forced to supply a packet by restarting each speaker Markov chain in state 1 (active) with probability $(1/2)^m$. On average, we would expect it only every $(0.5)^{-m}$ frames; for $m = 20$, this is about one in 1 million frames; in other terms, for a frame length of 0.11 second, this transient would occur once every 30 hours, on the average.

This perturbation overloads the system for a period of time, causing a related increase in the delay faced by a typical incoming packet. Figure 3.14 shows the instantaneous expected delay as a function of time for various examples. The following observations can be made:

1. The maximum delay perturbation caused by the transient is very dependent on the steady-state link utilization and the speaker behavior parameter r (r is the probability that the speaker continues to speak).
2. The duration of the transient is a function of r only. As r decreases the more frame-to-frame correlation increases ($r = 0.15$, $r = 0.1$, $r = 0.08$) and the duration of the transient increases. The transient dies off rather rapidly (2 to 3 s) for typical values of r, $r \geq 0.08$.
3. Finite buffer size has a damping effect on the transient. This behavior is intuitive. The system becomes overloaded: If the

Figure 3.14
Transient behavior:
(a)   9 users,
$r = 0.1$, $\rho_\infty = 0.536$
(b)   11 users,
$r = 0.08$, infinite
buffers, $\rho_\infty = 0.688$
(c)   11 users,
$r = 0.1$, infinite
buffer, $\rho_\infty = 0.688$
(d)   11 users,
$r = 0.15$, infinite
buffer, $\rho_\infty = 0.688$
(e)   11 users,
$r = 0.1$, finite
buffer, $\rho_\infty = 0.688$
(f)   13 users,
$r = 0.1$, $\rho_\infty = 0.813$

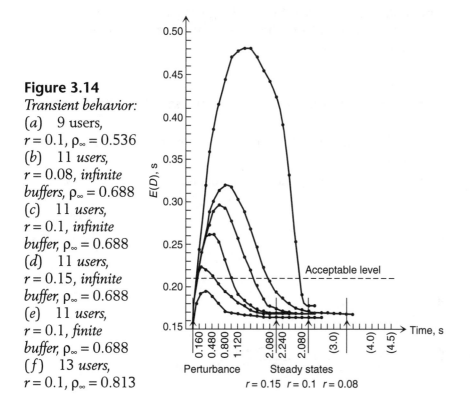

buffer is infinite, there is no other way to unload but to pump the packets out the line; in the case of a finite buffer, an unloading takes place when the packets are blocked, because there is no room in the buffer. The packet-blocking rate for this example immediately follows the overload (Figure 3.15).

Typical transient delay distributions are shown in Figure 3.16, and Figure 3.17 depicts the overload situation. Note that utilization is temporarily pushed over 1.

Because packet voice networks would be designed to be driven at high utilization, designers must guard against transients, or at least be aware of their effect.

3.6 Conclusion

A methodology is needed for the design of packet voice networks. Such networks differ from the packet data case in the following fundamental respects:

- Regularity of input traffic
- More complex performance criteria (smoothness and error tolerance)
- Performance criteria imposed on a worst-case and end-to-end basis
- Different set of applicable protocols

Figure 3.15
Transient blocking rate for a four-buffer system.

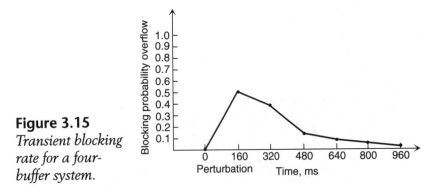

Figure 3.16
Transient delay distribution: (a) frames 7 to 11, and (b) frames 12 to 20.

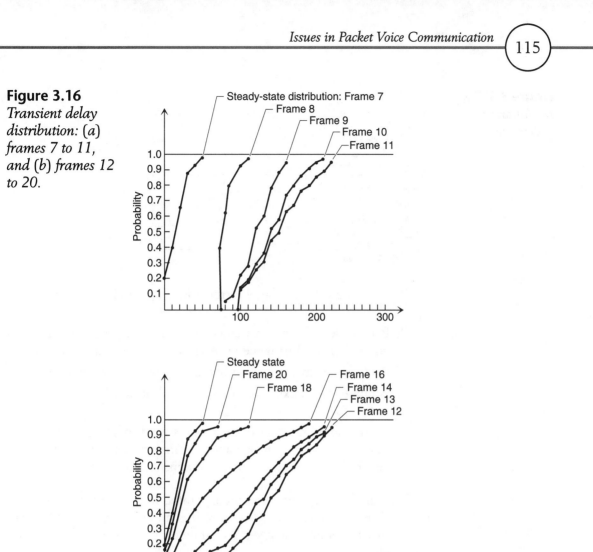

A single-link situation has been modeled and implemented with a computer program. The link model can accept a wide variety of speech models and system parameters and yields the complete steady-state or transient distribution of delay.

Some of the important facts learned from the studies are as follows:

1. Standard approximations are overly conservative in that they predict poorer performance than can be actually attained.

Figure 3.17
*Instantaneous
utilization.*

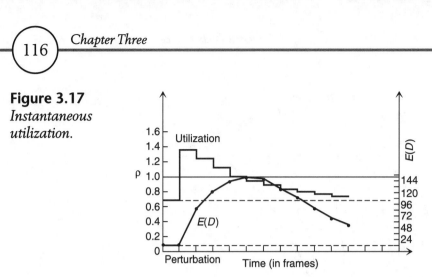

2. The single-link delay distribution is approximately exponential.
3. Percentile delay performance criteria track very well with
equivalent performance criteria placed on the mean delay.
4. A closed-form expression for the mean delay is obtained.
5. A closed-form expression for optimal packet length is
obtained.
6. Only a small number of buffers is found to be necessary to
sustain adequate performance. A small number of buffers
also reduces the transient excursions and durations.

The single-link model was incorporated into a tandem-link
model. Implementation and study of this model gives results for the
situation when a link must service an incoming line as well as local
terminals.

Based on the results already obtained, a foreseeable methodology for general network design for packet voice can be outlined as
follows:

1. Interactively set topology, link parameters, and system
parameters.
2. Using closed-form analytical approximations for link delay
behavior, obtain an optimal routing pattern.
3. Evaluate performance results using the detailed link model.
4. Return to step 1 until satisfied that the network is the cheap-
est one that satisfies all the design criteria.

References

1. D. Minoli. "Issues in Packet Voice Communication." *Proceedings of IEE* 126 (8): 729–740.

2. D. Minoli. "Packetized Speech Networks. Part 1: Overview." *Australian Electronics Engineer* (April 1979): 38–52.

3. D. Minoli. "Packetized Speech Networks. Part 2: Queueing Model." *Australian Electronics Engineer* (July 1979): 68–76.

4. D. Minoli. "Packetized Speech Networks. Part 3: Delay Behavior and Performance Characteristics." *Australian Electronics Engineer* (August 1979): 59–68.

5. D. Minoli. "General Geometric Arrival, Constant Server Queuing Problem with Applications to Packetized Voice." *ICC 1978 Conference Record* 3: 36.6.1–36.6.5.

6. D. Minoli and E. Lipper. "Mixed Classes of Traffic Obeying Different Queueing Rules with Reference to Integrated Packet Switched Networks." *1978 IEEE Canadian Conf. on Comm. and Power, Record:* 1–4.

7. D. Minoli. "General Geometric Arrival, Discrete Server Queue." *NTC 1978 Conference Record:* 44.2.1–44.2.5.

8. D. Minoli. "Optimal Packet Length for Packet Voice Communication." *IEEE Trans. on Comm.* (concise paper) COMM-27 (March 1979): 607–611.

9. D. Minoli. "Satellite On-Board Processing of Packetized Voice." *ICC 1979 Conference Record:* 58.4.1–58.4.5.

10. D. Minoli. "Some Design Parameters for PCM Based Packet Voice Communication." *1979 International Electrical/Electronics Conference Record.*

11. D. Minoli and K. Schneider. "Computing Average Loss Probability in a Circuit Switched Network." *IEEE Trans. on Comm.* COMM-28 (January 1980): 27–33.

12. D. Minoli and K. Schneider. "An Algorithm for Computing Average Loss Probability in a Circuit Switched Network." *Telecommunications Journal* 29-1 (June 1979): 28–37.

13. D. Minoli. "Digital Techniques in Sound Reproduction. Part 1" *Audio* (April 1980): 54–61.

14. D. Minoli and W. Nakamine. "Mersenne Numbers Rooted on 3 for Number Theoretic Transforms." *1980 IEEE International Conf. on Acoust., Speech and Signal Processing.*

15. D. Minoli. "Cost Effective Design of Local Access Networks Using Common Carriers Bulk Service Offering." *Electrical Communication* 55 (2): 118–126.

16. D. Minoli. "Diseno mas economico de redes de acceso locales usando las ofertas de servicio masivo de las companias explotadoras." *Comunicaciones Electricas* 55 (2): 118–126.

17. D. Minoli. "Gestaltung Kostengunstinger Anschlussnetze für das FAXPAK-Netz." *Elektriches Nachrichtenwesen* 55 (2): 118–126.

18. D. Minoli. "Optimisation de cout des reseaux d'acces locaux utilisant les options de tarif forfaitaires pour communications publiques." *Revue des Telecommunicationes* 55 (2): 118–126.

19. D. Minoli. "Digital Voice Communication over Digital Radio Links." *SIGCOMM Computer Communications Review* 9 (4): 6–22.

20. D. Minoli. "Sizing Trunk Bundles Which Can Be Seized at Both Ends with Different Grade of Service." *IEEE Trans. on Comm.* COMM-28 (6): 794–801.

21. D. Minoli. "Getting the Most WATS for Every Communication Dollar." *Data Communications* (September 1980): 91–102.

22. D. Minoli. "Engineering Two-Way Foreign Exchange Trunk Bundle Systems." *Computer Communication* 3 (2): 69–76.

23. D. Minoli. "Digital Techniques in Sound Reproduction. Part 2." *Audio* (May 1980): 34–42.

24. D. Minoli. "Selection of Communications Facilities under a Multigraduated Tariff." *Computer Networks* 4 (6): 295–301.

25. D. Minoli. "Optimal Allocation in a Multi-Resources Graduate Tariff Communication Environment." *Computer Communications* 3 (4): 117–124.

26. D. Minoli. "Unmasking a Puzzling New Tariff: A Look at Some Hard Facts On WATS." *Telephony* 199 (21): 24–27.

27. D. Minoli. "A Case for Simpler Tariffs." *Telephony* 201 (7): 22–24.

28. D. Minoli. "Designing Large Scale Private Voice Networks." *Telephony* 201 (12): 130ff.

29. D. Minoli. "Strategy in Multigraduated Tariffs under Random Usage." *Computer Communications* 4 (6).

30. D. Minoli. "A New Design Criterion for Store-and-Forward Networks." *Computer Networks* 7 (1983): 9–15.

31. D. Minoli. "Designing Practical Voice and Data Communications Networks. Part 1." *Computer World* (May 6, 1985): 67, 73.

32. D. Minoli. "All About Channel Banks: Technology Briefing." *Datapro Report* CA-80-010-902 (October 1987).

33. D. Minoli. "Evaluating Communications Alternatives. Part 1: Cost Analysis Methods." *Datapro Report* CA03-010-401 (June 1986).

34. D. Minoli. "Evaluating Communications Alternatives. Part 2: Pragmatic Network Design Issues." *Datapro Report* CA09-010-451 (June 1986).

35. D. Minoli. "Phone Changes Benefit Users." *Computer World* (May 12, 1986): 19, 23.

36. D. Minoli. "Integrated Voice/Data PBX." *Teleconnect* (May 1986).

37. D. Minoli. "Engineering PBX Networks. Part 1: Design Modules." *Datapro Report* MT30-315-101 (September 1986).

38. D. Minoli. "Engineering PBX Networks. Part 2: Gathering Support Data." *Datapro Report* MT30-315-201 (September 1986).

39. D. Minoli. "ISDN: Good News for the Communications Manager. Part 2." *Computer World* (January 20, 1986).

40. D. Minoli. "ISDN: Good News for the Communications Manager. Part 1." *Computer World* (January 13, 1986).

41. D. Minoli. "An Overview of ADPCM Transcoders." *Datapro Report* CA80-010-604 (November 1986).

42. D. Minoli. "Designing Voice Networks." *Datapro Report* 5401MVN (May 1995).

43. D. Minoli. "Traffic Engineering Basics." *Datapro Report* 5410MVN (June 1995).

44. D. Minoli. "Designing End-to-End Networks for New Multimedia Applications. *Proceedings, ICA.* Portland, OR, 1995.

45. D. Minoli. "Common Channel Signaling System Number 7." *Datapro Report* 8420 (March 1996).

46. D. Minoli. "Designing Voice Networks." *Datapro Report* 5401 (April 1996).

47. D. Minoli. "Queueing Fundamentals for Telecommunications." *Datapro Report* 5430 (January 1996).

48. D. Minoli. "Signaling Concepts." *Datapro Report* 2912 (February 1996).

49. D. Minoli. "Advanced Intelligent Networks." *Datapro Report* 3070 (March 1996).

50. D. Minoli. "Installing and Maintaining a Premises-Based Voice Wiring System." *Datapro Report* 5701 (March 1997).

51. D. Minoli. "Private T1 Networks for Business." *Datapro Report* (May 1996).

52. D. Minoli. "The Telephone Room Environment." *Datapro Report* 5720 (May 1996).

53. D. Minoli. "Traffic Engineering Basics." *Datapro Report* 5420 (July 1996).

54. D. Minoli. "Interstate Private Line Facilities." *Datapro Report* 3501 (August 1996).

55. D. Minoli. "T-Carrier Network Planning and Design." *Datapro Report* 5240 (September 1996).

56. D. Minoli. "AT&T Tariff 12." *Datapro Report* 3010 (November 1996).

CHAPTER 4

Voice Technologies for Packet-Based Voice Applications

4.1 Introduction

This chapter provides a synopsis of voice digitization and compression methodologies. After the general discussion, it focuses on ADPCM techniques for packet networks (ITU-T G.727). Specific standardized vocoding methods are discussed in more detail in Chapter 5.

General Overview of Speech Technology

This section provides an overview of speech encoding methodologies that are relevant to voice over IP applications. In general, low-bit-rate voice (LBRV) methods are of interest for IP at this time. Two disciplines play a role:

- *Speech analysis* is that portion of voice processing that converts speech to digital forms suitable for storage on computer systems and transmission on digital (data or telecommunications) networks.

- *Speech synthesis* is that portion of voice processing that reconverts speech data from a digital form to a form suitable for human usage. These functions are essentially the inverse of speech analysis.

Speech analysis processes are also called *digital speech encoding* (or coding), and speech synthesis is also called *speech decoding.* The objective of any speech-coding scheme is to produce a string of voice codes of minimum datarate, so that a synthesizer can reconstruct an accurate facsimile of the original speech in an effective manner, while optimizing the transmission (or storage) medium.

Many of the LBRV methods make use of the features of human speech, in terms of the properties that can be derived from the vocal tract apparatus. The vocal tract is excited by air from the lungs. The excitation source is either voiced or unvoiced. In *voiced speech*, the vocal cords vibrate at a rate called the *fundamental frequency;* this frequency is what we experience as the pitch of a voice. *Unvoiced speech* is created when the vocal cords are held firm without vibration, and the air is either aspirated through the vocal tract or is expelled with turbulence through a constriction at the glottis, tongue, teeth, or lips.

Waveform Coding

Two major techniques are used in speech analysis, *waveform coding* and *vocoding.* Waveform coding, which is applicable to traditional voice networks and voice over ATM, is treated extensively in the Wiley companion book to this volume [1]. Therefore, only a summary treatment is included here.

Two processes are required to digitize an analog signal, as follows:

1. *Sampling.*   This discretizes the signal in time.
2. *Quantizing.*   This discretizes the signal in amplitude.

The devices that accomplish speech analysis (digitization) are called *codecs,* for coder/decoder. Coders include *analog to digital* (A/D) converters, which typically perform a digitization function, and *analysis modules,* which further process the speech to reduce its datarate and prepare it for transmission. The reverse process uses *synthesis modules* to decode the signal and *D/A converters* to reconvert the signal back to analog format.

Naturally, the goal of the entire digitizing process is to derive from an analog waveform a digital waveform that is a faithful facsimile (at the acoustical perception level) of the original speech. The *sampling theorem* indicates that if the digital waveform is to represent the analog waveform in useful form, then the sampling rate must be at least twice the highest frequency present in the analog signal. Waveform coding methods are driven by this theorem. Toward that end, analog telephonic speech is filtered before digitization to remove higher frequencies. The human speech spectrum contains frequencies beyond 12,000 Hz, but for telephony applications the higher frequencies can be safely filtered out. Specifically, the channel bank and digital loop carrier equipment in telephone networks is designed to eliminate frequencies above 3.3 kHz, although nominally the voice band is 4 kHz. Consequently, analog speech signals are sampled at 8000 Hz for pulse code modulation (PCM) applications. PCM is currently the most often used digitization in telephony. Today, nearly every telephone call in the United States is digitized at some point along the way using PCM.

As noted, sampling used in the waveform coding of voice makes an analog waveform discrete in time, and quantizing makes it discrete in amplitude. This discreteness is a direct consequence of the fact that computers are digital devices, wherein the values that are allowed for variables are discrete. The digitization process measures the analog signal at each sample time and produces a digital binary code value representing the instantaneous amplitude.

Optimizing speech quality means production of a digital waveform that can be reconverted to analog with as small an error as possible. Quantization is the process that maps a continuum of amplitudes into a finite number of discrete values. This results in a loss of information and the ensuing introduction of noise, called *quantization noise* or *quantization error.* In waveform coding this loss of information is small, and the results are called (*nearly*) *lossless;* vocoding methods discard much more information and are therefore called *lossy.* Signal-to-noise ratio (SNR), expressed in decibels, is a measure used to discuss voice quality. For telephony applications, speech coders are designed to have a signal-to-noise ratio above 30 dB over most of their range.

Uniform Quantization

In a basic PCM system, input to the quantizer hardware comes in the form of an analog voltage provided by the sampler circuit. The simplest approach would be to use a uniform quantization method. Here, the range of input voltages is divided into 2^n segments, and a unique codeword of n bits is associated with each segment. The width of each segment is known as the *step size*. The range R of an n-bit quantizer with step size s is clearly

$$R = s(2^n)$$

This implies that if the input voltage were to exceed R, clipping would result. To address this issue, logarithmic quantization is used.

Logarithmic Quantization

The goal of logarithmic quantization is to maintain a reasonably constant signal-to-noise ratio over a wide range of analog amplitudes; using this technique the signal-to-noise ratio will not vary with incoming signal amplitude. To accomplish this, one quantizes not the incoming signal but the log value of the signal; for example, for analog values w, the equation $y = h + k \log (w)$ with h and k constant provides such a logarithmic function.[1]

Logarithmic quantization is a compression process: It reduces the dynamic range of a signal according to a logarithmic function. After compression a reverse process, exponentiation, is required to recover a facsimile of the original; the entire cycle is often referred to as *companding*, for compressing/expanding [2].

Figure 4.1 depicts a logarithmic curve and a linear approximation to it. The x axis shows the input level; the y axis shows the companded value. The piecewise linear approximation defines, for illustrative purposes, eight regions, four on the positive side of the x axis and four on the negative side of the axis (in North America, a specific logarithmic scheme called μ-*law* is used; in Europe a similar but not identical approach called *A-law*; both methods employ 8-bit logarithmic quantization with 16 regions and 16 steps per region). For the illustrative example, 6 bits are used to encode the incoming signal: 3 bits for the region and 3 bits for eight quantization levels in each region, based on the piecewise linear approximation. For example, one can assign the binary region number to the leftmost 3 bits of the code as noted in the figure; each step in the region is uniquely identified, this assignment being the same in each region.

Adaptive Quantization

To achieve further reductions in voice bitrate, one can employ analysis algorithms that make use of the technique of dynamically adapting the quantizer step size in response to variations in input signal amplitude. The goal is to maintain a quantizer range that is matched to the input signal's dynamic range.

PCM techniques that adapt step size are referred to as *adaptive PCM* (APCM). The technique can be applied to both uniform and logarithmic (nonuniform) quantizers. There are several adaptation algorithms, but all aim to estimate the slowly varying amplitude of the input signal while balancing the need to increase step size to attain appropriate range against the worsening in signal-to-noise ratio that results from larger step sizes. For *syllabic companding*

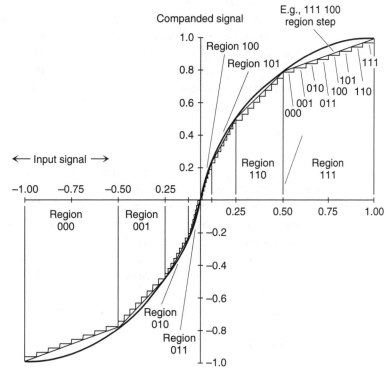

Figure 4.1
Example of discrete-step piece-wise linear approximation to logarithmic function.

techniques, the quantization characteristics change at about the same rate as syllables occur in speech. Other methods use *instantaneous companding*. Yet other methods calculate signal amplitude statistics over a relatively short group of samples and adjust the step size accordingly (e.g., *feed-forward adaptive PCM* and *feedback adaptive PCM*).

Waveform Coding Mechanisms

Speech signals contain a significant amount of redundant information. By making use of this fact and by removing some of these redundancies through processing, one is able to produce data parameters describing the waveform with a lower datarate than is otherwise possible and is still able to make a reasonably faithful reconstruction of the original. Speech samples generated at the Nyquist rate are correlated from sample to sample. (Actually, they remain moderately correlated over a number of consecutive samples.) This implies that values of adjacent samples do not differ significantly. Consequently, given some number of past samples, it is possible to predict with a degree of accuracy the value of the next sample. Some of these techniques are discussed next.

In the differential coding technique (also called *linear prediction[2]*), rather than coding the input waveform directly, one codes the difference between that waveform and one generated from linear predictions of past quantized samples. At sample time j, this encoder codes $e(j)$, the prediction errors at time j, where

$$e(j) = y(j) - [a_1 y(n-1) + a_2 y(n-2) + \ldots + a_p y(j-p)]$$

and where $y(j)$ is the input sample and the term in square brackets is a predicted value of the input based on previous values. The terms a_i are known as *prediction coefficients*. The output values $e(j)$ have a smaller dynamic range than the original signal; hence, they can be coded with fewer bits.[3]

This method entails *linear* predictions because, as the preceding equation shows, the error predictions involve only first-order (linear) functions of past samples. The prediction coefficients a_i are selected so as to minimize the total squared prediction error

$$E = e^2(0) + e^2(1) + \ldots + e^2(n)$$

where n is the number of samples. Once computed, the coefficients are used with all samples until they are recalculated. In differential coding, a trade-off can be made by adapting the coefficients less frequently in response to a slowly changing speech signal. In general, predictor coefficients are adapted every 10 to 25 ms.

As is the case with adaptive quantization, adaptive prediction is performed with either a feedback or feed-forward approach. In the case of feedback predictive adaptation, the adaptation is based on calculations involving the previous set of n samples; with feed-forward techniques, a buffer is needed to accumulate n samples before the coefficients can be computed (this, however, introduces a delay, because the sample values have to be accumulated) [2]. Values of $n = 4$ to $n = 10$ are used. For $n \geq 4$, adaptive predicators achieve signal-to-noise ratios of 3 or 4 dB better than the nonadaptive counterparts and more than 13 dB better than PCM.

A basic realization of linear prediction can be found in differential PCM (DPCM) coding, where, rather than quantizing samples directly, the difference between adjacent samples is quantized. This results in one less bit being needed per sample compared to PCM, while maintaining the signal-to-noise ratio. Here, if $y(j)$ is the value of a sample at a time j for a PCM waveform, then the DPCM sample at time j is given by $e(j)$, where

$$e(j) = y(j) - [a_1 y(n-1) + a_2 y(n-2) + \ldots + a_p y(j-p)]$$

and where a_1 is a scaling factor, while $a_2 = a_3 = \ldots = a_p = 0$; namely,

$$e(j) = y(j) - a_1 y(n-1)$$

Further gains over PCM and DPCM are obtained by including adaptation. This is done either by incorporating adaptive quantization or by adjusting the scale factor (at syllabic rate), or both. The adaptive differential PCM (ADPCM) method uses these techniques.

A simplified version of differential coding is found in a scheme called *delta modulation* (DM). DM is a first-order linear prediction where the codeword is limited to one bit. A *sign bit* representing the direction of the difference between the input waveform and the accumulated output is stored at sample time. The sign bits are used by the decoder to determine whether to increment or decrement the output waveform by one step size [2].

In a variant technique called *adaptive delta modulation* (ADM), the step size of the baseline DM is adapted according to a number of possible algorithms. The objective of these various algorithms is more accurate tracking of the input signal. This is accomplished by increasing the step size during periods of slope overload and decreasing it when slope overload is not occurring.

Vocoding (Analysis/Synthesis) in the Frequency Domain

The waveform methods previously discussed above relate to time-domain (signal amplitude versus time) representation of the speech signal. Another approach is to look at the signal in the frequency domain. A spectrum represents the frequency distribution of energy present in speech over a period of time. There are advantages at looking at the signal in this fashion. Frequency-domain coders attempt to produce code of minimum data rate by exploiting the resonant characteristics of the vocal tract. There is a lot of information that can be extracted and exploited in the speech spectrum.

Formats

Certain frequencies resonate within the vocal tract, depending on the tract's size and shape. Resonant frequencies appear in the spectrum as local maxima and are called *formant frequencies* or *formants*. The energy at these frequencies is reinforced when reflections of the wave coincide and additively build on each other; energy in other frequencies tends to dissipate. This results in the distinctive formants, as depicted in Figure 4.2.

Filters

Filters are utilized to derive the frequency spectrum from the speech waveform. Traditionally, filters have used analog circuitry.

The *discrete Fourier transform* (DFT) is a mathematical process for filtering waveforms digitally. Typically, DFTs are used to calculate correlation functions and to produce frequency spectra from discrete waveforms of finite length. The DFT divides the spectrum from 0 Hz through the sampling frequency (say, 4000 Hz) into n equal steps and provides an energy value for each [2].

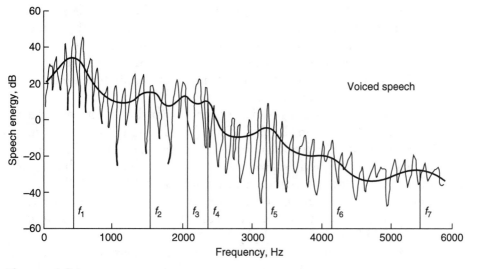

Figure 4.2
Example of formants.

Specifically, formant frequencies can be determined from the digital representation of a frequency spectrum. The result of DFT processing of the logarithm of a frequency spectrum is called a *cepstrum*, which is useful in the analysis process.

Parametric Vocoders

Parametric vocoders model speech production mechanisms rather than the resulting waveforms. They do so by taking advantage of the slow rate of change of the signals originating in the vocal tract, allowing one set of parameters to approximate the state over a period up to about 25 ms. Most vocoders aim to characterize the frequency spectrum and the vocal tract excitation source (lungs and vocal cords) with only a small set of parameters. These parameters, called a *data frame*, include the following:

- About a dozen coefficients that define vocal tract resonance characteristics
- A binary parameter specifying whether the excitation source is voiced or unvoiced
- A value for the excitation energy
- A value for pitch (during voicing only)

The vocal tract state is approximated by analyzing the speech waveform every 10 to 25 ms and calculating a new set of parameters at the end of the period. A sequence of data frames is used remotely (or on playback from storage) to control synthesis of a mirror waveform. Because only a handful of parameters are transmitted, the voice datarate is low.

One of the advantages of vocoders is that they often separate excitation parameters: Pitch, gain, and voiced and unvoiced indications are carried individually in the data frame, so each of these variables can be modified separately before or during synthesis (see Figure 4.3). Vocoder datarates run from about 1200 to 8000 bps; the rate is dependent upon the frame rate, the number of parameters in the frame, and upon the accuracy with which each parameter is coded (see Table 4.1) [3].

As seen in Figure 4.3, there are excitation sources (voice and unvoiced), loudness controls, and a vocal tract filter network. The excitation source for voiced speech consists of a periodic impulse generator and a pulse-shaping circuit. The impulse period adjusts to follow the original pitch according to the pitch frequency parameter being fed to it from the data frame. The vocal tract filter network emulates resonance characteristics of the original vocal tract.

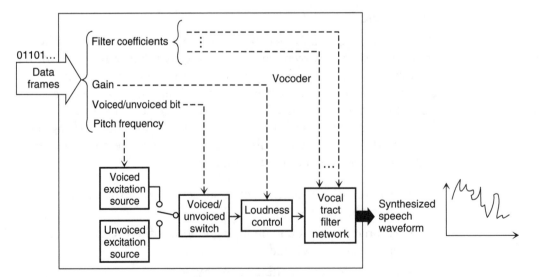

Figure 4.3
Block diagram of a typical decoder.

Table 4.1   Datarate Requirements of Various Encoders

Coder	Minimum datarate, kbps		
	Toll quality	*Communications quality*	*Synthetic quality*
log-PCM	56	36	
Adaptive delta modulation	40	24	
Adaptive DPCM	32	16	
Subband coder	24	9.6	
Adaptive predictive	16	7.2	
Channel vocoder			2.4
LPC			2.4
Formant vocoder			0.5

SOURCE: Reference [3].

The synthetic glottal waveform entering this section of the synthesizer is transformed to a speech waveform approximating the original [2]. Different vocoder technologies have different filter network designs, as shown in Table 4.2.

Linear Predictive Coding

Linear predictive coding (LPC) utilizes linear prediction methods. The term is applicable to those vocoding schemes that represent the excitation source parametrically and that use a higher-order linear predictor ($n > 1$). LPC analysis enjoys a number of desirable features in the estimation of such speech parameters as spectrum, formant frequencies, pitch, and other vocal tract measures. LPC analysis is conducted as a time-domain process.

LPC coding produces a data frame at a rate of about 40 to 100 frames per second (lower frame rates produce lower-quality speech). As should be clear, the size of the frame depends on the

Table 4.2   Vocal Tract Mechanism for Various Vocoders

Vocoder	*Vocal tract mechanism*
Formant vocoder	Reproduces the formants; a filter for each of the first few formants is included, then all higher formants are lumped into one final filter.
Channel vocoder	Network divides the spectrum into a number of bands.
Homomorphic vocoder	Uses calculation of a cepstrum every 10 or 20 ms for coding of both excitation and vocal tract parameters.
Phase vocoders	Considers the phase of a signal in addition to its magnitude in an attempt to achieve a lower datarate for the same voice quality.
LPC vocoders	Concatenated acoustic tubes (see text).

number of coefficients (e.g., the order of the predictor) and the accuracy to which each of the parameters is quantized. It should be noted that speech synthesized from LPC coders is most sensitive to the first few coefficients; this, in turn, implies that the coefficients need not necessarily all be quantized with the same accuracy.

The analog model that is solved by LPC is an approximation of the vocal tract (glottis and lips, but no nasal cavities) using concatenated acoustic tubes. If the number of cylinders is appropriately selected in the model, the frequency domain mathematics of the concatenated tubes problem approximately solves the vocal tract problem. LPC allows one to estimate frequency-domain acoustic tube parameters from the speech waveform, as follows.

The LPC prediction coefficients obtained from the time-domain signal can be converted to reflection coefficients representing the set of concatenated tubes. This implies that with this methodology frequency-domain estimations that approximately describe the vocal tract can be obtained from time-domain data, using linear algebra. Specifically, the n prediction coefficients of an nth order predictor can be calculated by solving a system of n linear equations in n unknowns; the n reflection coefficients that are present in equations describing resonances in a concatenated acoustic tube on $0.5 * (n - 1)$ sections can be calculated from the n prediction coefficients. Hence, LPC analysis generates a set of reflection coefficients, excitation energy, voice/unvoiced indication bit, and fundamental frequency (if signal is voiced). This functionality is very similar to what is implied in Figure 4.3.

Residual-Excited Linear Prediction

Residual-excited linear prediction (RELP) does not derive pitch, gain, and the voiced/unvoiced decision from the prediction residual, as is done in LPC. Instead, a filter network can be driven directly by the residual waveform. RELP is also referred to as *voice-excited linear prediction*. Reflection coefficients are used (as in LPC) instead of prediction coefficients [2].

Vector Quantization

Vector quantization (VQ) replaces a vector of information with a single value (or symbol) that represents a clustering of vectors that are close, based on some measure of distance. A vector may consist of a block of accumulated digital samples, a set of LPC reflection coefficients (with or without excitation parameters), or other frame or block of parameters.

Given a set of vectors, K clusters can be defined in such a manner that each vector is a member of some cluster.[4] Each cluster in its entirety can be represented in a codebook by one of its members or by some symbol or vector. The codebook contains K entries, one for each cluster. The clusters and codebook are chosen to best represent the original collections of vectors.

At coding time, each time a vector is presented to the vector quantizer decision entity. At that juncture, the vector quantizer entity decides which cluster the vector belongs to, according to the same specific distance measure, and substitutes the appropriate symbol or value for the incoming vector. Here, quantization noise is measured by the distance between the codebook entry and the input vector [2]. Vector quantization methods have not yet seen widescale deployment.

4.2 G.727: ADPCM for Packet Network Applications

The International Telecommunications Union (ITU) is a body within the United Nations Economic, Scientific and Cultural Organization (UNESCO). In the ITU-T (the sector dedicated to telecommunications), Study Group 15 (SG15) is charged with making recommendations related to speech and video processing. Study Group 14 (SG14) makes recommendations for modems, such as V.34 and V.32. This section discusses G.727. Although vocoder technology is expected to enter the scene for voice over IP, many carriers and suppliers of carrier equipment are still looking at ADPCM technologies—even for voice over ATM using AAL 2 techniques that, being a very recent development, could conceivably have leapfrogged the digitization techniques all the way to vocoder technology.

Introduction
ITU-T Recommendation G.727 contains the specification of an embedded adaptive differential pulse code modulation (ADPCM) algorithm with 5, 4, 3, and 2 bits per sample (i.e., at rates of 40, 32,

24, and 16 kbps).[5] The characteristics following are recommended for the conversion of 64-kbps *A*-law or µ-law PCM channels to or from variable rate-embedded ADPCM channels. The recommendation defines the transcoding law when the source signal is a pulse code modulation signal at a pulse rate of 64 kbps developed from voice frequency analog signals as specified in ITU-T G.711. Figure 4.4 [4] shows a simplified block diagram of the encoder and the decoder.

Applications where the encoder is aware and the decoder is not aware of the way in which the ADPCM codeword bits have been altered, or where both the encoder and decoder are aware of the

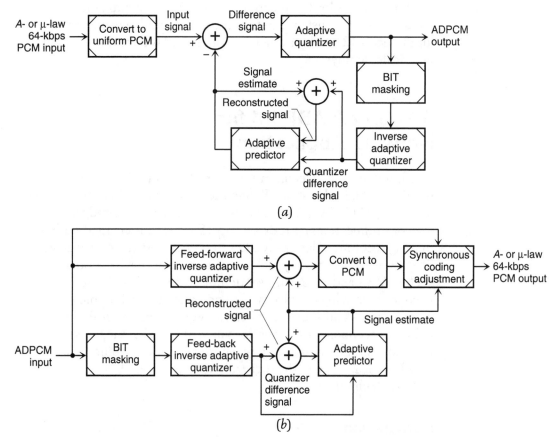

Figure 4.4
Simplified block diagrams of (a) the G.727 encoder and (b) the G.727 decoder.
(From Reference [4].)

ways the codewords are altered, or where neither the encoder nor the decoder are aware of the ways in which the bits have been altered, can benefit from other embedded ADPCM algorithms.

The embedded ADPCM algorithms specified in G.727 are extensions of the ADPCM algorithms defined in ITU-T G.726,[6] and are recommended for use in packetized speech systems operating according to the Packetized Voice Protocol (PVP) specified in Draft Recommendation G.764.

PVP is able to relieve congestion by modifying the size of a speech packet when the need arises. Utilizing the embedded property of the algorithm described here, the least significant bits of each codeword can be disregarded at packetization points and/or intermediate nodes to relieve congestion. This provides for significantly better performance than is achieved by dropping packets during congestion.

Embedded ADPCM Algorithms

Embedded ADPCM algorithms are variable-bit-rate coding algorithms with the capacity of bit-dropping outside the encoder and decoder blocks. They consist of a series of algorithms such that the decision levels of the lower rate quantizers are subsets of the quantizer at the highest rate. This allows bit reductions at any point in the network without the need for coordination between the transmitter and the receiver. In contrast, the decision levels of the conventional ADPCM algorithms, such as those in Recommendation G.726, are not subsets of one another; therefore, the transmitter must inform the receiver of the coding rate and the encoding algorithm.

Embedded algorithms can accommodate the unpredictable and bursty characteristics of traffic patterns that require congestion relief. This might be the case in IP-like networks, or in ATM networks with early packet discard. Because congestion relief may occur after the encoding is performed, embedded coding is different from the variable-rate coding where the encoder and decoder must use the same number of bits in each sample. In both cases, however, the *decoder* must be told the number of bits to use in each sample.

Embedded algorithms produce codewords that contain enhancement bits and core bits. The feed-forward (FF) path utilizes enhancement and core bits, while the feedback (FB) path uses core bits only. The inverse quantizer and the predictor of both the encoder and the decoder use the core bits. With this structure, enhancement bits can be discarded or dropped during network congestion.[7] However, the number of core bits in the FB paths of both the encoder and decoder must remain the same to avoid mistracking.

The four embedded ADPCM rates are 40, 32, 24, and 16 kbps, where the decision levels for the 32-, 24-, and 16-kbps quantizers are subsets of those for 40 kbits per quantizer. Embedded ADPCM algorithms are referred to by (x, y) pairs, where x refers to the FF (enhancement and core) ADPCM bits and y refers to the FB (core) ADPCM bits. For example, if y is set to 2 bits, (5, 2) represents the 24-kbps embedded algorithm and (2, 2) the 16-kbps algorithm. The bit rate is never less than 16 kbps because the minimum number of core bits is 2. Simplified block diagrams of both the embedded ADPCM encoder and decoder are shown in Figure 4.4.

The G.727 recommendation provides coding rates of 40, 32, 24, and 16 kbps and core rates of 32, 24, and 16 kbps. This corresponds to the following pairs: (5, 2), (4, 2), (2, 2); (5, 3), (4, 3), (3, 3); and (5, 4), (4, 4).

ADPCM Encoder

Subsequent to the conversation of the A-law or μ-law PCM input signal to uniform PCM, a difference signal is obtained by subtracting an estimate of the input signal from the input signal itself. An adaptive 4-, 8-, 16-, or 32-level quantizer is used to assign 2, 3, 4, or 5 binary digits to the value of the difference signal for transmission to the decoder. (Not all the bits necessarily arrive at the decoder since some of these bits can be dropped to relieve congestion in the packet network. For a given received sample, however, the core bits are assumed to be guaranteed arrival if there are no transmission errors and the packets arrive at their destination.) FB bits are fed to the inverse quantizer. The number of core bits depends on the embedded algorithm selected. For example, the (5, 2) algorithm will always contain 2 core bits. The inverse quantizer produces a quantized difference signal from these binary digits. The signal estimate is added to this quantized difference signal to produce the reconstructed version of the input signal. Both the reconstructed signal and the quantized difference signal are operated upon by an adaptive predictor that produces the estimate of the input signal, thereby completing the feedback loop.

ADPCM Decoder

The decoder includes a structure identical to the FB portion of the encoder. In addition, there is also an FF path that contains a uniform PCM to *A*-law or µ-law conversion. The core, as well as the enhancement bits, is used by the synchronous coding adjustment block to prevent cumulative distortion on synchronous tandem codings (ADPCM-PCM-ADPCM, etc., digital connections) under certain conditions. The synchronous coding adjustment is achieved by adjusting the PCM output codes to eliminate quantizing distortion in the next ADPCM encoding stage.

ADPCM Encoder Principles

Figure 4.5 shows a block schematic of the encoder. For each variable to be described, *k* is the sampling index and samples are taken at 125-µs intervals. A description of each block is given in the subsections that follow.

Input PCM Format Conversion

This block converts the input signal $s(k)$ from *A*-law or µ-law PCM to a uniform PCM signal $s_l(k)$.

Difference Signal Computation

This block calculates the difference signal $d(k)$ from the uniform PCM signal $s_l(k)$ and the signal estimate $s_e(k)$:

$$d(k) = s_l(k) - s_e(k)$$

Adaptive Quantizer

A 4-, 8-, 16-, or 32-level nonuniform midrise adaptive quantizer is used to quantize the difference signal $d(k)$. Prior to quantization, $d(k)$ is converted to a base-2 logarithmic representation and scaled by $y(k)$, which is computed by the scale factor adaptation block. The normalized input/output characteristic (infinite precision values) of the quantizer is given in tables in the standard for the 16-, 24-, 32-, and 40-kbps algorithms, respectively (Table 4.3 depicts the normalized input/output characteristics for 40 kbps, for illustrative purposes). Two, three, four, or five binary digits are used to specify the quantized level representing $d(k)$ (the most significant bit represents the sign bit and the remaining bits represent the

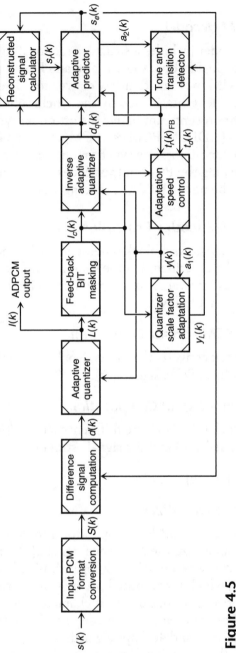

Figure 4.5
Encoder block schematic.

magnitude). The 2-, 3-, 4-, or 5-bit quantizer output $I(k)$ forms the 16-, 24-, 32-, or 40-kbps output signal and is also fed to the bit-masking block. $I(k)$ includes both the enhancement and core bits.

Bit Masking

This block produces the core bits $I_c(k)$ by logically right-shifting the input signal $I(k)$ so as to mask the maximum droppable (least-significant) bits. The number of bits to mask and the number of places to right-shift depend on the embedded algorithm selected. For example, this block will mask the two least-significant bits (LSBs) and shift the remaining bits two places to the right when the (4, 2) algorithm is selected. The output of the bit-masking block $I_c(k)$ is fed to the inverse adaptive quantizer, the quantizer scale factor adaptation, and the adaptation speed control blocks.

Inverse Adaptive Quantizer

The inverse quantizer uses the core bits to compute a quantized version $d_q(k)$ of the difference signal using the scale factor $y(k)$ and

Table 4.3 Quantizer Normalized Input/Output Characteristic for 40-kbps Embedded Operation

Normalized quantizer input range* $\log_2|d(k)| - y(k)$	$|I(k)|$	Normalized quantizer output $\log_2|d_q(k)| - y(k)$
$(-\infty, -1.05)$	0	−2.06
$[-1.05, -0.05)$	1	−0.48
$[-0.05, 0.54)$	2	0.27
$[0.54, 0.96)$	3	0.76
$[0.96, 1.30)$	4	1.13
$[1.30, 1.58)$	5	1.44
$[1.58, 1.82)$	6	1.70
$[1.82, 2.04)$	7	1.92
$[2.04, 2.23)$	8	2.13
$[2.23, 2.42)$	9	2.33
$[2.42, 2.60)$	10	2.51
$[2.60, 2.78)$	11	2.69
$[2.78, 2.97)$	12	2.87
$[2.97, 3.16)$	13	3.05
$[3.16, 3.43)$	14	3.27
$[3.43, \infty)$	15	3.56

*[indicates that the endpoint value is included in the range, and (or) indicates that the endpoint value is excluded from the range.

the tables alluded to previously (e.g., Table 4.3) and then taking the antilog to the base 2 of the result. The estimated difference $s_e(k)$ is added to $d_q(k)$ to reproduce the reconstructed version $s_l(k)$ of the input signal. The tables previously alluded to are applicable only when there are specific bits (e.g., 5 bits for Table 4.3) in the FF path.

Quantizer Scale Factor Adaptation

This block computes $y(k)$, the scaling factor for the quantizer and for the inverse quantizer. [The scaling factor $y(k)$ is also fed to the adaptation speed control block.] The inputs are the bit-masked output $I_c(k)$ and the adaptation speed control parameter $a_l(k)$.

The basic principle used in scaling the quantizer is bimodal adaptation: *fast* for signals (e.g., speech) that produce difference signals with large fluctuations, and *slow* for signals (e.g., voiceband data and tones) that produce difference signals with small fluctuations.

The speed of adaptation is controlled by a combination of fast and slow scale factors.

The fast (unlocked) scale factor $y_u(k)$ is recursively computed in the base-2 logarithmic domain from the resultant logarithmic scale factor $y(k)$:

$$y_u(k) = (1 - 2^{-5})\, y(k) + 2^{-5} W[I_c(k)]$$

where

$$1.06 \le y_u(k) \le 10.00$$

For 2-core-bit operation (1 sign bit), the discrete function $W[I_c(k)]$ is defined as in Table 4.4a. For 3-core-bit operation (1 sign bit), the discrete function $W[I_c(k)]$ is defined as in Table 4.4b. For 4-core-bit operation (1 sign bit), the discrete function $W[I_c(k)]$ is defined as in Table 4.4c.

The factor $(1 - 2^{-5})$ introduces finite memory into the adaptive process so that the states of the encoder and decoder converge following transmission errors.

The slow (locked) scale factor $y_l(k)$ is derived from $y_u(k)$ with a low-pass filter operation:

$$y_l(k) = (1 - 2^{-6})\, y_l(k - 1) + 2^{-6} y_u(k)$$

Table 4.4   Values of W[$I_c(k)$]

(a)

$|I_c(k)|$	1	0
$W[I_c(k)]$	27.44	−1.38

(b)

$|I_c(k)|$	3	2	1	0
$W[I_c(k)]$	36.38	8.56	1.88	−0.25

(c)

$|I_c(k)|$	7	6	5	4	3	2	1	0
$W[I_c(k)]$	69.25	21.25	11.50	6.13	3.13	1.69	0.25	−0.75

The fast- and slow-scale factors are then combined to form the resultant scale for

$$y(k) = a_1(k)\, y_u(k-1) + [1 - a_1(k)]\, y_1(k-1)$$

where

$$0 \le a_1(k) \le 1$$

Adaptation Speed Control

The controlling parameter $a_1(k)$ can assume values in the range [0, 1]. It tends toward unity for speech signals and toward zero for voiceband data signals. It is derived from a measure of the rate of change of the difference signal values.

Two measures of the average magnitude of $I_c(k)$ are computed:

$$d_{ms}(k) = (1 - 2^{-5})\, d_{ms}(k-1) + 2^{-5}\, F[I_c(k-1)]$$

and

$$d_{m1}(k) = (1 - 2^{-7})\, d_{m1}(k-1) + 2^{-7}\, F[I_c(k-1)]$$

where $F[(I_c(k)]$ is defined as

$[I_c(k)]$	1	0
$F[I_c(k)]$	7	0

for 2-core-bit (1 sign bit) operation; or

$[I_c(k)]$	3	2	1	0
$F[I_c(k)]$	7	2	1	0

for 3-core-bit (1 sign bit) operation; or

$[I_c(k)]$	3	6	5	4	3	2	1	0
$F[I_c(k)]$	7	3	1	1	1	0	0	0

for 4-core-bit (1 sign bit) operation.

Thus, $d_{ms}(k)$ is a relatively short-term average of $F[I_c(k)]$ and $d_{ml}(k)$ is a relatively long-term average of $F[I_c(k)]$.

Using these two averages, the variable $a_p(k)$ is defined:

$$a_p(k) = \begin{cases} (1 - 2^{-4})a_p(k-1) + 2^{-3} & \text{if } |d_{ms}(k) - d_{ml}(k)| \geq 2^{-3}d_{ml}(k) \\ (1 - 2^{-4})a_p(k-1) + 2^{-3} & \text{if } y(k) < 3 \\ (1 - 2^{-4})a_p(k-1) + 2^{-3} & \text{if } t_d(k) = 1 \\ 1 & \text{if } t_r(k) = 1 \\ (1 - 2^{-4})a_p(k-1) & \text{otherwise} \end{cases}$$

Thus, $a_p(k)$ tends toward the value 2 if the difference between $d_{ms}(k)$ and $d_{ml}(k)$ is large [average magnitude $I_c(k)$ changing], for an idle channel [indicated by $y(k) < 3$] or for partial band signals [indicated by $t_d(k) = 1$ as described following]. The value of $a_p(k)$ tends toward the value 0 if the difference is small [average magnitude of $I_c(k)$ relatively constant]. Note that $a_p(k)$ is set to 1 upon detection of a partial band signal transition [indicated by $t_r(k) = 1$].

$a_p(k-1)$ is then limited to yield the $a_1(k)$ used in the "Quantizer Scale Factor Adaptation" subsection.

$$a_1(k) = \begin{cases} 1 & \text{if } a_p(k-1) > 1 \\ a_p(k-1) & \text{if } a_p(k-1) \leq 1 \end{cases}$$

This asymmetrical limiting has the effect of delaying the start of a fast- to slow-state transition until the absolute value of $I_c(k)$ remains constant for some time. This tends to eliminate premature transitions for pulsed input signals, such as switched carrier voiceband data.

Adaptive Predictor and Feedback Reconstructed Signal Calculator

The primary function of the adaptive predictor is to compute the signal estimate $s_e(k)$ from the quantized difference signal $d_q(k)$. Two adaptive predictor structures are used, a sixth-order section that models zeroes and a second-order section that models poles in the input signal. This dual structure effectively caters to the variety of input signals that might be encountered.

The signal estimate is computed by

$$s_e(k) = a_1(k-1)s_r(k-1) + a_2(k-1)s_r(k-2) + s_{ez}(k)$$

where

$$\begin{aligned} s_{ez}(k) = &\, b_1(k-1)d_q(k-1) + b_2(k-1)d_q(k-2) \\ &+ b_3(k-1)d_q(k-3) + b_4(k-1)d_q(k-4) \\ &+ b_5(k-1)d_q(k-5) + b_6(k-1)d_q(k-6) \end{aligned}$$

and the reconstructed signal is defined as

$$s_r(k-i) = s_e(k-i) + d_q(k-i)$$

Both sets of predictor coefficients are updated using a simplified gradient algorithm, as shown in Figure 4.6.

Tone and Transition Detector

In order to improve performance for signals originating from frequency shift keying (FSK) modems operating in the character mode, a two-step detection process is defined. First, partial band signal (e.g., tone) detection is invoked so that the quantizer can be driven into the fast mode of adaptation:

$$t_d(k) = \begin{cases} 1 & \text{if } a_2(k) < -0.71875 \\ 0 & \text{otherwise} \end{cases}$$

In addition, a transition from a partial band is defined so that the predictor coefficients can be set to zero and the quantizer can be forced into the fast mode of adaptation:

Figure 4.6
Gradient algorithms for updating prediction coefficients.

For the second-order predictor:

$$a_1(k) = (1 - 2^{-8})a_1(k - 1) + (3 \cdot 2^{-8}) \operatorname{sgn} [p(k)] \operatorname{sgn} [p(k - 1)]$$
$$a_2(k) = (1 - 2^{-7})a_2(k - 1) + 2^{-7}\{ \operatorname{sgn} [p(k)] \operatorname{sgn} [p(k - 2)]$$
$$- f[a_1(k - 1)] \operatorname{sgn} [p(k)] \operatorname{sgn} [p(k - 1)]\}$$

where

$$p(k) = d_q(k) + s_{ez}(k)$$

$$f(a_1) = \begin{cases} 4a_1 & |a_1| \le 2^{-1} \\ 2 \operatorname{sgn} (a_1) & |a_1| > 2^{-1} \end{cases}$$

sgn $[0] = 1$, except sgn $[p(k - i)]$ is defined to be 0 only if $p(k - i) = 0$ and $i = 0$; with the stability constraints; $|a_2(k)| \le 0.75$ and $|a_1(k)| \le 1 - 2^{-4} - a_2(k)$

If $\quad t_r(k) = 1 \quad$ then $\quad a_1(k) = a_2(k) = 0$

For the sixth-order predictor:

$$b_i(k) = (1 - 2^{-8})b_i(k - 1) + 2^{-7} \operatorname{sgn} [d_q(k)] \operatorname{sgn} [d_q(k - i)]$$

for $i = 1, 2, \ldots, 6$.

If $\quad t_r(k) = 1 \quad$ then $\quad b_1(k) = b_2(k) = \cdots = b_6(k) = 0$

As above, sgn $[0] = 1$, except sgn $[d_q(k) - i)]$ is defined to be 0 only if $d_q(k - i) = 0$ and $i = 0$. Note that $b_i(k)$ is implicitly limited to ± 2.

$$t_r(k) = \begin{cases} 1 & \text{if } a_2(k) < -0.71875 \text{ and } |d_q(k)| > 24 * 2^{y_1(k)} \\ 0 & \text{otherwise} \end{cases}$$

ADPCM Decoder Principles

Figure 4.7 shows a block schematic of the decoder. There is an FB path and an FF path. The FB path uses the core bits to calculate the signal estimate. The FF path contains the core and enhanced bits and reconstructs the output PCM code word.

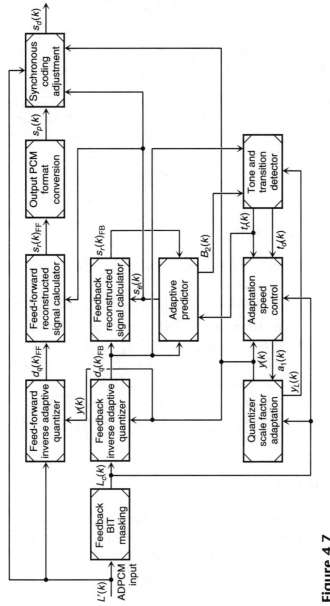

Figure 4.7
Decoder block schematic.

145

4.3 Example of Application

For intercontinental connections, the use of ADPCM at 32 or 40 kbps for improved voice transmission efficiency has become commonplace. ITU-T standards for ADPCM support about the same bandwidth as PCM but provide a reduced SNR: about 21 dB at 32 kbps (G.721), or about 28 dB at 40 kbps (G.726). Proprietary 32 kbps ADPCM encoders/decoders (codecs) that support a reduced bandwidth of less than 3200 Hz at an SNR of about 28 dB are also in common use [5]. Use of this technology over IP networks is also possible, although not all that common.

References

1. D. Minoli and E. Minoli. *Delivering Voice over Frame Relay and ATM*. New York: Wiley, 1998.
2. G. E. Pelton. *Voice Processing*. New York: McGraw-Hill, 1993.
3. John Bellamy. *Digital Telephony*. New York: Wiley, 1982.
4. ITU-T Recommendation G.727: *5-, 4-, 3-, and 2-bits Sample Embedded Adaptive Differential Pulse Code Modulation (ADPCM)*. Geneva, CH: ITU, 1990.
5. G. D. Forney, et al. "The V.34 High-Speed Modem Standard." *IEEE Communications Magazine*, (December 1996): 28 ff.

Notes

[1] This function is applicable when $w > 0$. A piecewise linear approximation to the function can be utilized that is valid both for the value zero and for negative values.

[2] Devices that use this technique are referred to as *adaptive predictive coders* (APCs).

[3] Alternatively, one can achieve a higher signal-to-noise ratio with the same number of bits.

[4] Membership in a cluster is specified by some rule, typically an n-dimensional distance measure in vector space.

[5]This section is based on the ITU-T Recommendation G.727. This material is for pedagogical purposes only. Developers, engineers, and readers requiring more information should acquire the recommendation directly from the ITU-T [4].

[6]The reader may wish to consult the companion Wiley text [1], for a description of ITU-T G.726

[7]In the anticipated application with G.764, the Coding Type (CT) field and the Block Dropping Indicator (BDI) fields in the packet header defined in G.764 will inform the coder of what algorithm to use. For all other applications, the information that PVP supplies must be made known to the decoder.

CHAPTER 5

Technology and Standards for Low-Bit-Rate Vocoding Methods

5.1 Introduction

As noted in the previous chapter, during the past quarter century there has been a significant level of research and development in the area of vocoder technology and compressed speech. During the early to mid-1990s, the ITU-T (specifically SG14 and SG15) standardized several vocoders that are applicable to low-bit-rate multimedia communications in general, and to voice over IP Internet and intranet applications in particular. Standardization is critical for interoperability and assurance of ubiquitous end-to-end connectivity. The recent standards are G.728, G.729, G.729A, and G.723.1. For some applications, the dominant factor is cost; for other applications, quality is paramount. This is part of the reason why several standards have evolved in the recent past. For completeness, Table 5.1 depicts the various standards that are available. However, to be ultimately successful, voice over IP will have to narrow down to one choice so that anyone can call anyone else (as is done today with modems and telephones) without worrying about what technology the destination party may be using. The winner will likely be the algorithms that will be bundled with an operating system, such as Windows 97, or a popular business application.

The vocoders discussed in this chapter require between 10 and 20 million instructions per second (MIPS). In contemplating running these on a desktop PC, it is worth noting that a 33 MHz 80486 ran at 27 MIPS; a 266 MHz Pentium II runs at 560 MIPS; and the successor to the Pentium Pro is expected to operate at 300 MHz and achieve 700 MIPS. There is also the expectation that by the year 2000, 500 MHz machines will deliver 1000 MIPS. Network capacity does not grow at the same rapid pace as Moore's law, which says, in effect, that the power of the microprocessor goes up by an order of magnitude every five years (in fact, it has been documented by the senior author that usable aggregate network speed has historically been going up by an order of magnitude every 20 years). Corporate enterprise networks and intranets are chronically congested. Hence, these observations seem to imply that the only way to really have voice over IP take off is to trade off high desktop computational power for compressing speech down to the lowest possible rates to keep congestion low, but to do this without compromising the delay budget. (This could even mean developing higher-complexity algorithms with less end-to-end delay; however, these would not be applicable to mobile and cellular applications).

This discussion focuses principally on G.729, G.729A, and G.723.1; G.728 is also covered, but its datarate (16 kbps) may be too high for IP applications. ITU-T G.729 is an 8-kbps conjugate-

Table 5.1   ITU-T Speech Coding Standards

Standard	*Description*
G.711	64 kbps pulse code modulation (PCM) (both *A*-law and μ-law)
G.722	Wideband vocoder operating at 64, 56, or 48 kbps
G.726	ADPCM vocoder recommendation that folds G.721 and G.723
G.727	Embedded ADPCM operating at 40, 32, 24, or 16 kbps (see Chapter 4)
G.728	16-kbps low-delay code-excited linear prediction vocoder (LD-CELP)
G.729	8-kbps conjugate-structure algebraic-code-excited linear prediction (CS-ACELP)
G.723.1	Low-bit-rate vocoder for multimedia communications operating at 6.3 and 5.3 kbps [this vocoder standard number has an extension (.1) because all the numbers in the G series have been used already]

structure algebraic-code-excited linear-prediction (CS-ACELP) speech algorithm providing good speech quality. The algorithm has a 15-ms algorithmic codec delay. G.729 was originally designed for wireless environments, but it is applicable to IP and multimedia communications as well. Annex A of Recommendation G.729 (also called G.729A) describes a reduced-complexity version of the algorithm that has been designed explicitly for integrated voice and data applications [called Digital Simultaneous Voice and Data (DSVD)] that are prevalent in small office and home office (SOHO) low-bit-rate multimedia communications. These vocoders use the same bitstream format and can interoperate with one another.[1]

The ITU Recommendation G.723.1 is a 6.3- and 5.3-kbps vocoder for multimedia communications that was originally designed for low-bit-rate videophones. The algorithm's frame size is 30 ms and the one-way codec delay is 37.5 ms. In applications where low delay is important, the delay in G.723.1 may not be tolerable; however, if the delay is tolerable, G.723.1 provides a lower-complexity lower-bandwidth alternative to G.729, at the expense of a small degradation in speech quality.

Each of these three ITU Recommendations has the potential to become a key commercial mechanism for voice over IP on the Internet and other networks, since all three are low-bandwidth and are simple enough in complexity to be executed on the host processor, such as a PC, or be implemented on a modem chip. Hence, this chapter examines these standards in some level of detail.

Overview

As noted in Chapter 4, the design goal of vocoders is to reduce the bit rate of speech for transmission or storage, while maintaining a quality level acceptable for the application at hand. On intranets and the Internet, voice applications may be standalone or multimedia-based. Since multimedia implies the presence of a number of media, speech coding for such applications implies that the speech bitstream shares the communication link with other signals. Some such applications include the following:

- Simultaneous voice and video, for example, a videophone, stored video presentation, and so forth
- Digital simultaneous voice and data (DSVD) whiteboarding applications where the data stream could be transmission of

shared files that the parties are developing, discussing, creating, updating, or synthesizing

- Simultaneous voice and fax, where a copy of a document is transmitted from one person to a group of one or more recipients

In principle, the use of a uniquely specified vocoder might be desirable. Unfortunately, short-term local optimization considerations have lead developers to the conclusion that it is more economical to tailor the vocoder to the application at hand. Consequently, a number of new vocoders were standardized during the mid-1990s. Specifically, three new international standards (ITU-G.729, G.729A, and G.723.1), and three new regional standards (enhanced full-rate vocoders for North American and European mobile systems) have emerged of late. As a consequence of this overabundance of standards, making an appropriate choice can be challenging. Vocoder attributes can be used to make trade-off analyses during the vocoder selection process that the developer of an intranet or Internet multimedia or telephony application (i.e., speech bandwidth of 200 to 3400 Hz sampled at 8 kHz) needs to undertake.

Vocoder Attributes

Vocoder speech quality is a function of bit rate, complexity, and processing delay. Developers of intranet and Internet telephony products must review all these attributes. There usually is a strong interdependence between all these attributes and they may have to be traded off against each other. For example, low-bit-rate vocoders tend to have more delay than higher-bit-rate vocoders. Low-bit-rate vocoders also require higher VLSI complexity to implement. As might be expected, low-bit-rate vocoders often have lower speech quality than the higher-bit-rate vocoders.[2]

Bit Rate

Since the vocoder is sharing the access communications channel or the likely overloaded enterprise network or Internet with other information streams, the peak bit rate should be as low as possible, particularly for SOHO applications. Today, most vocoders operate at a fixed bit rate regardless of the input signal characteristics; however, the goal is to make the vocoder variable-rate. For simultaneous voice and data applications, a compromise is to create a *silence compression algorithm* (see Table 5.2) as part of the coding standard. A common solution is to use a fixed rate for active speech and a low rate for background noise [1]. The performance of the silence compression mechanism is critical to speech quality: If speech is declared too often, the gains of silence compression are not realized. The challenge is that with loud background noises it may be difficult to distinguish between speech and noise. Another problem is that if the silence compression mechanism fails to recognize the onset of speech, the beginning of the speech will be cut off; this front-end clipping significantly impairs the intelligibility of the coded speech.

The comfort noise generation mechanism must be designed in such a way that the encoder and decoder remain synchronized, even when there are no bits transmitted during some intervals. This allows for smooth transitions between active and nonactive speech segments.

Delay

The delay in a speech coding system usually consists of three major components:

- Frame delay
- Speech processing delay
- Bridging delay

Typically, low-bit-rate vocoders process a frame of speech data at a time, so that the speech parameters can be updated and trans-

Table 5.2   Silence Compression Algorithms

Algorithm	Description
Voice activity detector (VAD)	Determines if the input signal is speech or background noise. If the signal is declared to be speech, it is coded at the full fixed bit rate; if the signal is declared to be noise, it is coded at a lower bit rate. As appropriate, no bits are transmitted.
Comfort noise generation (CNG)	Mechanism is invoked at the receiver end to reconstruct the main characteristic of the background noise.

mitted for every frame. Hence, before the speech can be analyzed it is necessary to buffer a frame's worth of speech samples. The resulting delay is called *algorithmic delay*. It is sometimes necessary to analyze the signal beyond the frame boundary (this is referred to as *look-ahead*); here, additional speech samples need to be buffered, with additional concomitant delay. Note that this is the only implementation-independent delay (other delay components depend on the specific implementation, e.g., how powerful the processor used to run the algorithm is, the kind of RAM used, etc.). Algorithmic delays are unavoidable; hence, they need to be considered as part of the delay budget by the planner.

The second major component of the delay originates from the processing time it takes the encoder to analyze the speech and the processing time required by the decoder to reconstruct the speech. This processing delay depends on the speed of the hardware used to implement the vocoder. The combined algorithmic and processing delay is called the *one-way system delay*. The maximum tolerable value for the one-way system delay is 400 ms, if there are no echoes, but for ease and efficiency of communication it is preferable to have the one-way delay below 200 ms. If there are echoes, the tolerable one-way delay is 20 to 25 ms; therefore, the use of echo cancellation is often necessary.

In applications such as teleconferencing, it may be necessary to bridge several callers with a *multipoint control unit* (MCU) in order to allow each person to communicate with the others. This requires decoding each bitstream, summing the decoded signals, and then reencoding the combined signal. This process doubles the delay and at the same time it reduces the speech quality because of the multiple (tandem) encodings. Given the previous observation, a bridged system can tolerate a maximum one-way delay of 100 ms, because the bridging will result in the doubling of the one-way system delay to 200 ms.

Algorithm's Complexity

Vocoders are often implemented on DSP hardware. Complexity can be measured in terms of computing speed in MIPS, of random access memory (RAM), and of read-only memory (ROM). Complexity determines cost; hence, in selecting a vocoder for an application, the developer must make an appropriate choice. When the vocoder shares a processor with other applications, the developer must decide how much of these resources to allocate to the vocoder. Vocoders utilizing less than 15 MIPS are considered to be low-complexity; those using 30 MIPS or more are considered to be high-complexity.

As noted, increased complexity results in higher costs and greater power usage. Power usage is an important consideration in portable applications, since greater power usage implies reduced time between battery recharges or the necessity of using larger batteries, which, in turn, means more expense and weight.

Quality

The measure used in comparisons is how good the speech sounds under ideal conditions—namely, clean speech, no transmission errors, and only one encoding (note, however, that in the real world these ideal conditions are often not met because there can be large amounts of such background noise as street noise, office noise, air conditioning noise, etc.). Table 5.3 shows the quality of the major coding schemes being utilized in voice over data networks.

How well the vocoder performs under adverse conditions (e.g., what happens when there are channel errors or the loss of entire frames; how good the vocoder sounds when the speech is encoded and decoded in tandem, as is the case in a bridging application; how good it sounds when transcoding with another standard vocoder; how it sounds for a variety of languages) is the question that the standards bodies try to answer during the testing phase of the standards drafting and generation process.

Linear Prediction Analysis-by-Synthesis (LPAS) Coding

The ITU-T Recommendations G.723.1, G.728, and G.729 belong to a class of linear prediction analysis-by-synthesis (LPAS) vocoders.

Table 5.3   Quality of Coding Schemes

Algorithm	G.723.1	G.729 G.729A	G.728	G.726 G.727	G.711
Rate, bps	5.3–6.3	8	16	32	64
Quality	Good	Good	Good	Good	Good
Complexity	Highest	High	Lower	Low	Lowest

Figure 5.1
Block diagram of an LPAS vocoder.

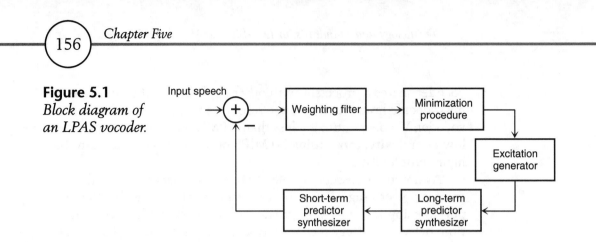

Code-excited linear predictive (CELP) vocoders are the most common realization of the LPAS technique. Figure 5.1 shows a block diagram of an LPAS vocoder.

Basic Mechanisms

Decoded speech is produced by filtering the signal produced by the excitation generator through both a long-term (LT) predictor synthesis filter and a short-term (ST) predictor synthesis filter. The excitation signal is found by minimizing the mean-squared-error signal (the difference between the original and the decoded signal) over a block of samples.[3] It is weighted by filtering it through an appropriate filter. Both ST and LT predictors are adapted over time. Since the encoder analysis procedure includes the decoder synthesis procedure, the description of the encoder also defines the decoder.

The ST synthesis filter models the short-term correlations in the speech signal. This is an all-pole filter with an order between 8 and 16. The predictor coefficients of the short-term predictor are adapted in time, with rates varying from 30 to as high as 400 times per second. The LT predictor filter models the long-term correlations in the speech signal. Its parameters are a delay and a gain coefficient. For periodic signals, the delay corresponds to the pitch period (or possibly to an integral number of pitch periods); for nonperiodic signals the delay is random. Typically, the long-term predictor coefficients are adapted at rates varying from 100 to 200 times per second [1].

A frequently used alternative for the pitch filter is the *adaptive codebook*. Here, the LT synthesis filter is replaced by a codebook that contains the previous excitation at different delays. These vectors are searched, and the one that provides the best match is selected. To simplify the determination of the excitation for delays smaller than the length of the excitation frames, an optimal scaling factor can be determined for the selected vector. To achieve a low bit rate, the average number of bits per sample for each frame of excitation samples must be kept small.

The *multipulse excitation vocoder* represents the excitation as a sequence of pulses located at nonuniformly spaced intervals. The excitation analysis procedure determines both amplitudes and positions of the pulses. Finding these parameters all at once is a difficult problem, and simpler procedures, such as determining locations and amplitudes one pulse at a time, are typically used. The number of pulses required for an acceptable speech quality varies from four to six pulses every 5 ms. For each pulse, both amplitude and location have to be transmitted, requiring about 7 or 8 bits per pulse [1].

Code-excited linear predictive vocoders approach the issue of reducing the number of bits per sample as follows: Both encoder and decoder store the same collection of C possible sequences of length L in a codebook, and the excitation for each frame is described by the index to an appropriate vector in the codebook. This index is typically found by conducting an exhaustive search of the codebook vectors and identifying the one that produces the smallest error between the original and decoded signals. To simplify the search procedure, many implementations use a gain-shape codebook where the gain is searched and quantized separately. The index requires $(\log_2 C)/L$ bits per sample, typically 0.2 to 2 bits per sample, and the gain requires 2 to 5 bits for each codebook vector.

The *algebraic codebook-excited linear prediction* (ACELP) introduces further simplification by populating the codebook vectors with a multipulse structure: By using only a few nonzero unit pulses in each codebook vector, the search procedure can be sped up. The partitioning of the excitation space is known as an *algebraic codebook*, hence the name of the vocoder.

Error-Weighting Filter

The approach described in the preceding of minimizing a mean squared error results in a quantization noise that has equal energy across the spectrum of the input signal. However, by making use of properties of the human auditory system, the vocoder designer can focus on reducing the *perceived* amount of noise. It has been found that greater amounts of quantization noise are undetectable in the frequency bands where the speech signal has high energy. Namely, the designer wants to shape the noise as a function of the spectral peaks in the speech signal. To put this masking effect to work in the vocoder design, the quantization noise has to be properly distributed among different frequency bands. This can be achieved by minimizing a *weighted error* from the short-term predictor filter.

Adaptive Postfilter

The noise in speech caused by the quantization of the excitation signal remains an area of vocoder design improvement (in the low-energy frequency regions in particular, the noise can dominate the speech signal). The perceived noise can be further reduced by using a postprocessing technique called *postfiltering* after reconstruction by the decoder. This operation trades off spectral distortion in the speech versus suppression of the quantization noise, by emphasizing the spectral peaks and attenuating the spectral valleys. The postfilter is generally implemented as a combination ST/LT filter. The ST postfilter modifies the spectral envelope, it being based on the transmitted ST predictor coefficients (it can also be derived from the reconstructed signal.) The parameters for the LT postfilter are either derived from the transmitted LT predictor coefficients or computed from the reconstructed speech [1].

5.2 Introduction to G.729 and G.723.1

The excitation signals (e.g., ACELP) and the partitioning of the excitation space (the algebraic codebook) represent a distinguishable vocoder design feature. For example, G.729 and G.732.1 can be differentiated in this manner, although both assume that all pulses have the same amplitudes and that the sign information will be transmitted. The two vocoders also show major differences in terms of delay.

Differentiations

G.729 has excitation frames of 5 ms and allows four pulses to be selected. The 40-sample frame is partitioned into four subsets. The

Figure 5.2
Parameters for new vocoders.

Vocoder parameter	G.729	G.729A	G.723.1
Bit rate, kbps	8	8	5.3–6.3
Frame size, ms	10	10	30
Subframe size, ms	5	5	7.5
Algorithmic delay, ms	15	15	37.5
MIPS	20	10	14–20
RAM, bytes	5.2K	4K	4.4K
Quality	Good	Good	Good

first three subsets have eight possible locations for pulses, the fourth has sixteen. One pulse must be chosen from each subset. This is a four-pulse ACELP excitation codebook method (see Figure 5.2).

G.723.1 has excitation frames of 7.5 ms, and also uses a four-pulse ACELP excitation codebook for the 5.3-kbps mode. For the 6.3-kbps rate a technique called *multipulse excitation with a maximum likelihood quantizer* (MP-MLQ) is employed. Here the frame positions are grouped into even-numbered and odd-numbered subsets. A sequential multipulse search is used for a fixed number of pulses from the even subset (either five or six, depending on whether the frame itself is odd- or even-numbered); a similar search is repeated for the odd-numbered subset. Then, the set resulting in the lowest total distortion is selected for the excitation [1].

At the decoder stage, the linear prediction coder (LPC) information and adaptive and fixed codebook information are demultiplexed and then used to reconstruct the output signal. An adaptive postfilter is used. In the case of the G.723.1 vocoder, the LT postfilter is applied to the excitation signal before it is passed through the LPC synthesis filter and the ST postfilter.

Standardization Process

As noted, standardization is a critical requirement if the technology is to proliferate. Standards should also be developed quickly and not be unduly complex or long. As part of the standardization process, a document called *terms of reference* (ToR) is generated that contains a schedule and the performance requirements and objectives—in this instance, in the areas of quality, bit rate, delay, and complexity.

In terms of bit rates, the ToR requirements for the ITU-T standards under discussion were derived from the amount of speech data that could be carried over a 14.4-kbps modem or over a digital cellular system. Specifically, for G.729, the ToR requirements were that the vocoder should operate at 8 kbps to support the range of first-generation digital cellular standards (about 7 kbps for Japanese systems, 8 kbps for U.S. systems, and 13 kbps in the European systems), as well as complete the vocoder bit rate sequence (that is, 64, 32, 16, and now 8 kbps). For G.723.1, the ToR requirement was that the vocoder should operate below 9.6 kbps. Participant contributions were based on 5.0- to 6.8-kbps technologies, hence, a 6.3-kbps rate was settled upon; in the later development of G.723.1, a rate of 5.3 kbps was added for flexibility. For the digital simultaneous voice and data (DSVD) vocoder (G.729A), modem throughput (specifically, that of the V.34 modem) was used as a peg, and the rate was selected at 8 kbps. Initially, none of the vocoders had a silence compression capability as part of the recommendation. More recent work has standardized silence compression schemes for both G.723.1 and G.729, now being included as annexes to the recommendations.

The ToR requirement for delay for G.729 was discussed for some time. The frame size settled on was 10 ms. The algorithm has a 5 ms look-ahead. Hence, assuming a 10-ms processing delay and a 10-ms transmission delay, the one-way system delay of G.729 is 35 ms. G.723.1 has a look-ahead of 7.5 ms and a frame size of 32 ms, making the one-way system delay 97.5 ms. This delay was back-engineered from the intended application, namely, low-bit-rate videophones. These videophones typically operate at 5 frames (or fewer), with a video frame period of 200 ms. The standard development group picked a one-way delay of 100 ms for the vocoder, keeping the delay in a bridging environment to 200 ms. Working backward from the 100-ms value, a maximum frame size of 32 ms was set. In selecting the delay requirements for a DSVD vocoder (G.729A), the delay inherent in V.34 modems was taken into account (one-way delays are greater than 35 ms); also, the issue of bridging was noted, with modem delay now greater than 70 ms. Therefore, SG14 and SG15 agreed on a one-way codec delay maximum of 40 ms (G.723.1 was rejected for DSVD applications because the combined one-way delay for a single encoding could be 135 ms or greater).

Delay and complexity are often traded off against each other. For G.729, the ITU-Radiocommunications Standard Sector (ITU-R) was concerned about complexity, but eventually accepted a delay target that allowed a reduction in complexity compared with the G.728 vocoder. The vocoder needs 17 MIPS; however, the amount of RAM required is 50 percent more than for G.728, with the additional memory being used to process larger frames. G.723.1 is of lower complexity than G.729 (14 to 16 MIPS). The DSVD vocoder has a 10-MIPS complexity.

Quality is a complex topic, as Table 5.4 illustrates for the G.729 vocoder. See Reference [1] for a discussion.

Standardization Interval

The standardization discussed in this chapter occurred from mid-1990 to late 1995. G.729 work started in July 1990 and was completed by November 1995 (total time 64 months). G.723.1 work started in November 1992 and was completed by November 1995 (36 months). G.729A work started in November 1994 and was completed by May 1995 (18 months). As noted, there is a desire to bring out standards as quickly as can be done (during the 1980s, standards used to take four to eight years to complete). One can partition the process into three main parts:

Table 5.4   Example of Quality Requirements (G.729)

Issue or parameter	*Example of requirement*
Quality without bit errors	No worse than G.726 (32 kbps)
Quality with errors	
Random bit errors < 10^{-3}	No worse than G.726
Detected frame erasures (random and bursty)	No more than 0.5 MOS degradation from 32-kbps ADPCM without errors
Undetected burst errors	None
Level dependency	No worse than G.726
Talker dependency	No worse than G.726
Music support	No artifacts generated
Tandeming	
General capability	Two codings with distortion <4 G.726 codings
With other ITU vocoders	Two codings with distortion <4 G.726 codings
With new regional standards	For further study
Idle channel noise	No worse than G.726
Capability to carry signaling tones	DTMF and others

(1) time spent determining the requirements and objectives (which is culminated by the completion of the ToR), (2) time spent on submissions and testing (which is culminated by the selection of the vocoder), and (3) time spent drafting the recommendation and following the procedures of the ITU required for ratification [1].

5.3 G.723.1

G.723.1 specifies a coded representation that can be used for compressing the speech or other audio signal component of multimedia services at a very low bit rate.[4] In the design of this coder, the principal application considered by the Study Group was very low bit rate visual telephony as part of the overall H.324 family of standards.

Introduction

This coder has two bit rates associated with it, 5.3 and 6.3 kbps. The higher bit rate gives greater quality. The lower bit rate gives good quality and provides system designers with additional flexibility. Both rates are a mandatory part of the encoder and decoder. It is possible to switch between the two rates at any 30-ms frame boundary. An option for variable rate operation using discontinuous transmission and noise fill during nonspeech intervals is also possible.

The G.723.1 coder was optimized to represent speech with a high quality at the stated rates, using a limited amount of complexity. Music and other audio signals are not represented as faithfully as speech, but can be compressed and decompressed using this coder.

The G.723.1 coder encodes speech or other audio signals in 30-ms frames. In addition, there is a look ahead of 7.5 ms, resulting in a total algorithmic delay of 37.5 ms. All additional delay in the implementation and operation of this coder is due to the following:

1. Actual time spent processing the data in the encoder and decoder
2. Transmission time on the communication link
3. Additional buffering delay for the multiplexing protocol

Encoder/Decoder

The G.723.1 coder is designed to operate with a digital signal by first performing telephone bandwidth filtering (Recommendation G.712) of the analog input, then sampling at 8000 Hz, and then converting to 16-bit linear PCM for the input to the encoder. The output of the decoder is converted back to analog by similar means. Other input/output characteristics, such as those specified by Recommendation G.711 for 64-kbps PCM data, should be converted to 16-bit linear PCM before encoding or from 16-bit linear PCM to the appropriate format after decoding.

The coder is based on the principles of linear prediction analysis-by-synthesis coding and attempts to minimize a perceptually weighted error signal. The encoder operates on blocks (frames) of 240 samples each. That is equal to 30 ms at an 8-kHz sampling rate. Each block is first high-pass filtered to remove the DC component and then is divided into four subframes of 60 samples each. For every subframe, a tenth-order linear prediction coder filter is computed using the unprocessed input signal. The LPC filter for the last subframe is quantized using a predictive split vector quantizer (PSVQ). The quantized LPC coefficients are used to construct the short-term perceptual weighting filter, which is used to filter the entire frame and to obtain the perceptually weighted speech signal [2].

For every two subframes (120 samples), the open-loop pitch period L_{LO} is computed using the weighted speech signal. This pitch estimation is performed on blocks of 120 samples. The pitch period is searched in the range from 18 to 142 samples.

From this point, the speech is processed on a basis of 60 samples per subframe.

Using the estimated pitch period computed previously, a harmonic noise shaping filter is constructed. The combination of the LPC synthesis filter, the format perceptual weighting filter, and the harmonic noise shaping filter is used to create an impulse response. The impulse response is then used for further computations.

Using the estimated pitch period estimation L_{LO} and the impulse response, a closed-loop pitch predictor is computed. A fifth-order pitch predictor is used. The pitch period is computed as a small differential value around the open-loop pitch estimate. The contribution of the pitch predictor is then subtracted from the initial target vector. Both the pitch period and the differential values are transmitted to the decoder.

Finally, the nonperiodic component of the excitation is approximated. For the high bit rate, multipulse maximum likelihood quantization (MP-MLQ) excitation is used, and for the low bit rate, an algebraic code excitation is used.

The block diagram of the encoder is shown in Figure 5.3. The mathematics of the following are beyond the scope of this text (the interested reader should consult G.723.1 directly [2]):

- Framer
- High-pass filter
- LPC analysis

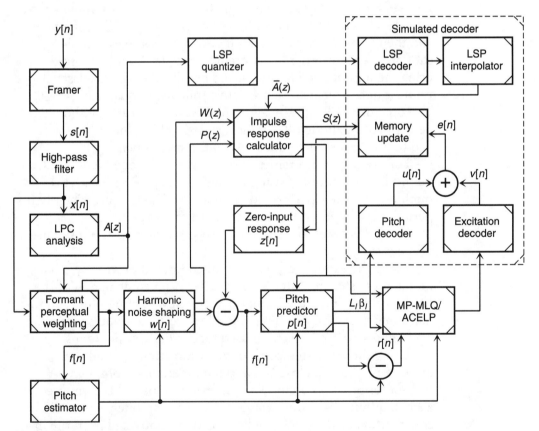

Figure 5.3
Block diagram of the speech coder.

- Line spectral pair (LSP) quantizer
- LSP decoder
- LSP interpolation
- Formant perceptual weighting filter
- Pitch estimation
- Subframe processing
- Harmonic noise shaping
- Impulse response calculator
- Zero-input response and ringing subtraction
- Pitch predictor
- High-rate excitation (MP-MLQ)
- Excitation decoder
- Pitch information decoding

5.4 G.728

ITU-T Recommendation G.728 contains the description of an algorithm for the coding of speech signals at 16 kbps using low-delay code-excited linear prediction (LD-CELP).[5] The LD-CELP algorithm consists of an encoder and a decoder, as illustrated in Figure 5.4 [3]. The essence of the CELP technique, which is an analysis-by-synthesis approach search, is retained in LD-CELP. However, LD-CELP uses backward adaptation of predictors and gain to achieve an algorithmic delay of 0.625 ms. Only the index to the excitation codebook is transmitted. The predictor coefficients are updated through LPC analysis of previously quantized speech. The excitation gain is updated by using the gain information embedded in the previously quantized excitation. The block size for the excitation vector and gain adaptation is five samples only. A perceptual weighting filter is updated using LPC analysis of the unquantized speech.

LD-CELP Encoder

After the conversion from A-law or μ-law PCM to uniform PCM, the input signal is partitioned into blocks of five consecutive input

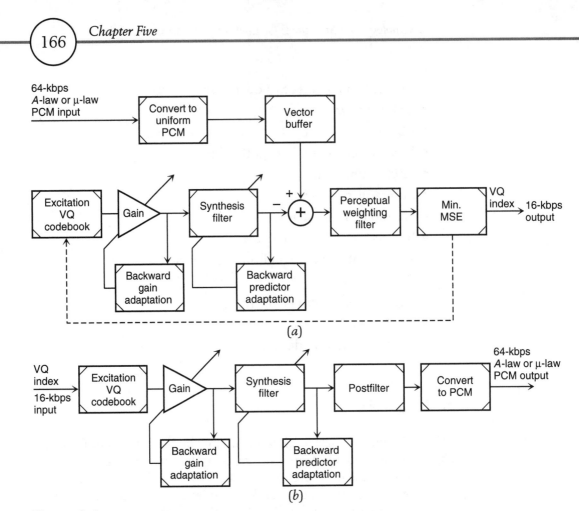

Figure 5.4
Simplified block diagram of the LD-CELP coder: (a) *coder and* (b) *decoder.*
(From Reference [3].)

signal samples. For each input block, the encoder passes each of 1024 candidate codebook vectors (stored in an excitation code-book) through a gain-scaling unit and a synthesis filter. From the resulting 1024 candidate quantized signal vectors, the encoder iden-tifies the one that minimizes a frequency-weighted mean squared error measured with respect to the input signal vector. The 10-bit codebook index of the corresponding best codebook vector (or *codevector*) that gives rise to that best candidate quantized signal vector is transmitted to the decoder. The best code vector is then passed through the gain-scaling unit and the synthesis filter to establish the correct filter memory in preparation for the encoding of the next signal vector. The synthesis filter coefficients and the gain are periodically updated on the previously quantized signal and gain-scaled excitation in a backward-adaptive manner.

LD-CELP Decoder

The decoding operation is also performed on a block-by-block basis. Upon receiving each 10-bit index, the decoder performs a table look-up to extract the corresponding codevector from the excitation codebook. The extracted codevector is then passed through a gain-scaling unit and a synthesis filter to produce the current decoded signal vector. The synthesis filter coefficients and the gain are then updated in the same way as in the encoder. The decoded signal vector is then passed through an adaptive postfilter to enhance the perceptual quality. The postfilter coefficients are periodically updated, using the information available at the perceptual quality. The postfilter coefficients are periodically updated using the information available at the decoder. The five samples of the postfilter signal vector are next converted to five A-law or μ-law PCM output samples.

5.5 G.729

ITU-T Recommendation G.729 contains the description of an algorithm for the coding of speech signals at 8 kbps using conjugate-structure algebraic code-excited Linear Prediction (CS-ACELP).[6]

This coder is designed to operate with a digital signal obtained by first performing telephone bandwidth filtering (Recommendation G.712) of the analog input signal, then sampling it at 8000 Hz, followed by conversion to 16-bit linear PCM for the input to the encoder. The output of the decoder should be converted back to an analog signal by similar means. Other input/output characteristics, such as those specified by Recommendation G.711 for 64-kbps PCM data, should be converted to 16-bit linear PCM before encoding, or from 16-bit linear PCM to the appropriate format after decoding.

The CS-ACELP coder is based on the code-excited linear prediction (CELP) coding model. The coder operates on speech frames of 10 ms, corresponding to 80 samples at a sampling rate of 8000 samples per second. For every 10-ms frame, the speech signal is

Table 5.5   Bit Allocation of the 8-kbps CS-ACELP Algorithm (10-ms Frame)

Parameter	Codeword	Subframe 1	Subframe 2	Total per frame
Line spectrum pairs	L0, L1, L2, L3			18
Adaptive-codebook delay	P1, P2	8	5	13
Pitch-delay parity	P0	1		1
Fixed-codebook index	C1, C2	13	13	26
Fixed-codebook sign	S1, S2	4	4	8
Codebook gains (stage 1)	GA1, GA2	3	3	6
Codebook gains (stage 2)	GB1, GB2	4	4	8
Total				80

analyzed to extract the parameters of the CELP model (linear-prediction filter coefficients and adaptive- and fixed-codebook indices and gains). These parameters are encoded and transmitted. The bit allocation of the coder parameters is shown in Table 5.5. At the decoder, those parameters are used to retrieve the excitation and synthesis filter parameters. The speech is reconstructed by filtering this excitation through the short-term synthesis filter, as is shown in Figure 5.5. The short-term synthesis filter is based on a tenth-order linear prediction (LP) filter. The long-term, or pitch synthesis, filter is implemented using the adaptive-codebook approach. After computing the reconstructed speech, it is further enhanced by a postfilter [4].

Encoder

The encoding principle is shown in Figure 5.6 [4]. The input signal is high-pass filtered and scaled in the preprocessing block. The pre-processed signal serves as the input signal for all subsequent analy-

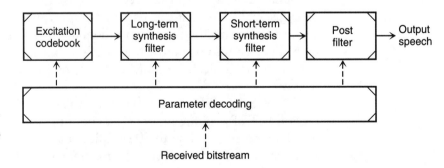

Figure 5.5
Block diagram of conceptual CELP synthesis model.

Figure 5.6
Encoding principle of the CS-ACELP encoder. (From Reference [4].)

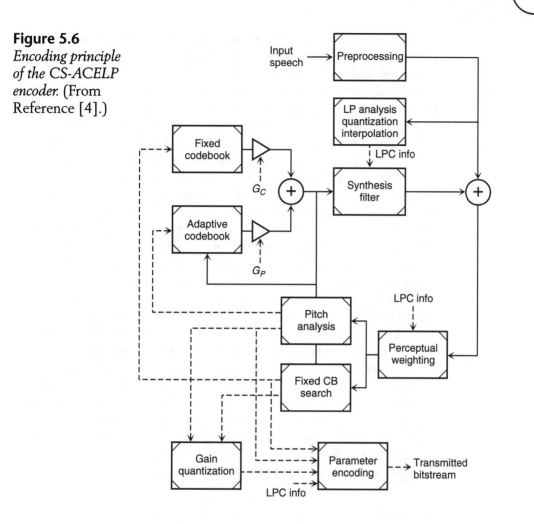

sis. LP analysis is done once per 10-ms frame to compute the LP filter coefficients. These coefficients are converted to line spectrum pairs (LSPs) and quantized using predictive two-stage vector quantization (VQ) with 18 bits. The excitation signal is chosen by using an analysis-by-synthesis search procedure in which the error between the original and reconstructed speech is minimized according to a perceptually weighted distortion measure. This is done by filtering the error signal with a perceptual weighting filter whose coefficients are derived from the unquantized LP filter. The amount of perceptual weighting is made adaptive to improve the performance for input signals with a flat frequency response.

The excitation parameters (fixed- and adaptive-codebook parameters) are determined per 5-ms subframe (40 samples). The quantized and unquantized LP filter coefficients are used for the second subframe, while in the first subframe interpolated LP filter coefficients are used (both quantized and unquantized). An open-loop pitch delay is estimated once per 10-ms frame, based on the perceptually weighted speech signal. Then the following operations are repeated for each subframe. The target signal $x(n)$ is computed by filtering the LP residual through the weighted synthesis filter $W(z)/\hat{A}(z)$. The initial states of these filters are updated by filtering the error between LP residual and excitation. This is equivalent to the common approach of subtracting the zero-input response of the weighted synthesis filter from the weighted speech signal. The impulse response $h(n)$ of the weighted synthesis filter is computed. Closed-loop pitch analysis is then done to find the adaptive-codebook delay and gain by searching around the value of the open-loop pitch delay, using the target $x(n)$ and the impulse response $h(n)$. A fractional pitch delay with 1/3 resolution is used. The pitch delay is encoded with 8 bits in the first subframe and is differently encoded with 5 bits in the second subframe. The target signal $x(n)$ is used in the fixed-codebook search to find the optimum excitation. An algebraic codebook with 17 bits is used for the fixed-codebook excitation. The gains of the adaptive- and fixed-codebook contributions are vector-quantized with 7 bits, with moving average prediction applied to the fixed-codebook gain. Finally, the filter memories are updated using the determined excitation signal.

Decoder

The decoder principle is shown in Figure 5.7. First, the parameter's indices are extracted from the received bitstream. These indices are decoded to obtain the coder parameters corresponding to a 10-ms speech frame. These parameters are the LSP coefficients, the two fractional pitch delays, the two fixed-codebook vectors, and the two sets of adaptive- and fixed-codebook gains. The LSP coefficients are interpolated and converted to LP filter coefficients for each subframe. Then, for each 5-ms subframe the following steps are done:

- The excitation is constructed by adding the adaptive- and fixed-codebook vectors scaled by their respective gains.

Figure 5.7
Principle of the CS-ACELP decoder.

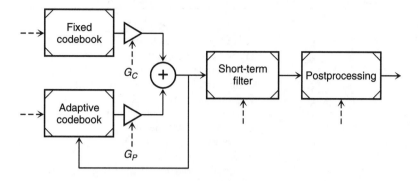

- The speech is reconstructed by filtering the excitation through the LP synthesis filter.
- The reconstructed speech signal is passed through a postprocessing stage, which includes an adaptive postfilter based on the long-term and short-term synthesis filters, followed by a high-pass filter and scaling operation.

As implied from this discussion, the coder encodes speech and other audio signals with 10-ms frames. In addition, there is a look-ahead of 5 ms, resulting in a total algorithmic delay of 15 ms. All additional delays in a practical implementation of this coder are due to the following:

- processing time needed for encoding and decoding operations
- transmission time on the communication link
- multiplexing delay when combining audio data with other data

The mathematics of the algorithm are beyond the scope of this text. Table 5.6 depicts the functions, signals, and variables required by the coder, giving a sense of the nontrivial nature of the computational and analytical machinery involved. The interested reader should consult G.729 directly [4].

5.6 Example of Applications

In this section, some applications of low-bit-rate vocoders are discussed.

Table 5.6 Functions, Signals, and Variables Required by the Coder

Name	Description
Variables	
g_p	Adaptive-codebook gain
g_c	Fixed-codebook gain
g_l	Gain term for long-term postfilter
g_f	Gain term for short-term postfilter
g_t	Gain term for tilt postfilter
G	Gain for gain normalization
T_{op}	Open-loop pitch delay
a_i	LP coefficients $(a_0 = 1.0)$
k_i	Reflection coefficients
k_1'	Reflection coefficient for tilt postfilter
o_i	LAR coefficients
ω_i	LSF normalized frequencies
$\hat{p}_{i,j}$	MA predictor for LSF quantization
q_i	LSP coefficients
$r(k)$	Autocorrelation coefficients
$r'(k)$	Modified autocorrelation coefficients
w_i	LSP weighting coefficients
$\hat{l}_i$	LSP quantizer output
Symbols	
$1/\hat{A}(z)$	LP synthesis filter
$H_{h1}(z)$	Input high-pass filter
$H_p(z)$	Long-term postfilter
$H_f(z)$	Short-term postfilter
$H_t(z)$	Tilt-compensation filter
$H_{h2}(z)$	Output high-pass filter
$P(z)$	Prefilter for fixed codebook
$W(z)$	Weighting filter
Signals	
$c(n)$	Fixed-codebook contribution
$d(n)$	Correlation between target signal and $h(n)$
$ew(n)$	Error signal
$h(n)$	Impulse response of weighting and synthesis filters
$r(n)$	Residual signal
$s(n)$	Preprocessed speech signal
$\hat{s}(n)$	Reconstructed speech signal
$s'(n)$	Windowed speech signal
$sf(n)$	Postfiltered output
$sf'(n)$	Gain-scaled postfiltered output
$sw(n)$	Weighted speech signal
$x(n)$	Target signal
$x'(n)$	Second target signal
$u(n)$	Excitation to LP synthesis filter
$v(n)$	Adaptive-codebook contribution
$y(n)$	Convolution $v(n) * h(n)$
$z(n)$	Convolution $c(n) * h(n)$

H.263 Video Coding for Low-Bit-Rate Communication

There is a growing interest in video coding technology and its applications over both circuit-switched and packet-switched (e.g., IP) networks. Applications include video telephony and videoconferencing, computer-supported cooperative work, whiteboarding, and other value-added services. The limited transmission rate available on the public switched telephone network (PSTN), on wireless networks, and on intranets and the Internet presents a significant challenge to digital video communications. With V.34 modem technology the bit rate achievable on the PSTN has increased, but it currently is still limited to 33.6 kbps, which is a stretch for video applications. Digital wireless communication, which has gained acceptance recently, is also limited to a few kilobits per second in available transmission rate. Therefore, there is an increasing interest in video coding at such low bit rates [5]. Although there may be more bandwidth in the backbone of a network, the access speed, particularly for telecommuters, SOHO workers, and residential users, remains a key gating factor. Implicit in these video applications is the use of compressed speech, as shown in Figure 5.8 (modeled after Reference [6]).

ITU-T recommendations for very low bit rate multimedia terminals include the following two algorithms [5]:

- *H.263.* Based on existing technology, developed by late 1995 (same time schedule as for the recommendations for the H.324 terminal description, multiplexing, control, and speech). The objective for H.263 is to provide significantly better picture quality than the existing ITU-T algorithm for video compression (H.261), while operating at 28.8 to 33.6 kbps.
- *H.263/L.* The long-term algorithm, including technology with more advanced performance, to be developed by 1998. The objective for H.263/L is to provide considerably better picture quality than H.263, with improved resiliency.

In this context, it should be noted that V.34 is a relatively new standard (1994) for full-duplex data transmission over the PSTN at bit rates up to 28.8 kbps (recently extended to 33.6 kbps). V.34 modems are low-priced and are now displacing 14.4-kbps V.32bis modems (1990) in such applications as remote access to corporate

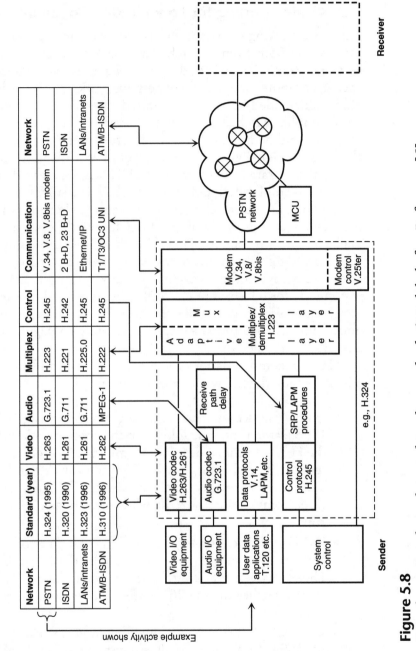

Figure 5.8
Use of compressed speech in multimedia standards. (Modeled after Reference [6]).

174

networks, online services, and the Internet. The increased bit rates of V.34 modems, combined with the recent advances in digital voice codings previously described that provide near-toll quality for certain applications at rates below 8 or 16 kbps, allow the simultaneous transmission of voice, data, and video over ordinary voice-grade PTSN lines. These advances have recently led to the development of new multimedia modem standards, such as H.324 [7].

H.324 Multimedia Communication

ITU-T Recommendation H.324, *Terminal for Low Bitrate Multimedia Communication* (1995), is the new international standard for multimedia conferencing on circuit-switched networks (e.g., PSTN); however, many of the elements of H.324 can be adapted to run on IP networks, as inspection of Figure 5.8 shows.

Focusing on the audio component, H.324 specifies the G.723.1 speech codec, which (although it runs at 5.3 or 6.3 kbps, as previously noted) provides near-toll-quality speech, using a 30-ms frame size and 7.5-ms look-ahead. A G.723.1 implementation is estimated to require 14 to 20 fixed-point MIPS in a general-purpose DSP. Terminals may use either rate and can change rates for each transmitted frame, since the vocoder rate is sent as part of the syntax for each frame (receivers can use an H.245 message to signal their preference for low- or high-rate audio) [6]. The average audio bit rate can be lowered further by using silence suppression. In such implementations, silence frames are not transmitted or are replaced with smaller frames carrying background noise. Generally, both end users rarely speak at the same time, so this can save significant bandwidth for use by video or data channels.

The G.723.1 codec imposes about 97.5 ms of end-to-end audio delay, which, together with modem, jitter buffer, transmission time, multiplexer, and other system delays, results in about 150-ms total end-to-end audio delay (propagation delay incremental) [6]. Interestingly, this audio delay is often less than the delay of the video codec; hence, additional delay at the receiver (see Figure 5.8) has to be added in the audio path to achieve lip synchronization (here H.245 is employed to send a message indicating the time differential between the transmitted video and audio signals).[7] A number of H.324 applications may not require lip synchronization, or not require video at all. For these applications, optional H.324 audio codecs (e.g., 8-kbps speech codec G.729) can be used—which, as noted earlier, can reduce the total end-to-end audio delay to about 85 ms.

H.323 Multimedia Communications Standard for LANs and Enterprise Networks

ITU-T Recommendation H.323, *Visual Telephone Systems and Equipment for Local Area Networks which Provide a Non-Guaranteed Quality of Service* (1996), is a recommendation that defines the components, procedures, and protocols necessary to provide audio-visual communication LANs. H.323 can be used in any packet-switched network, regardless of the ultimate physical layer. At the upper layers, IP can be utilized in conjunction with a reliable transport mechanism via Transmission Control Protocol (TCP), as well as in conjunction with an "unreliable" transport mechanism [e.g., User Datagram Protocol (UDP)]. As noted in Chapter 2, reliable transport mechanisms use acknowledgment and retransmission to guarantee delivery of PDUs, while unreliable transport mechanisms make a best effort to deliver PDUs without the overhead and delay incurred by retransmission. H.323 also uses the Real-time Transfer Protocol/Real-Time Control Protocol (RTP/RTCP) of the Internet Engineering Task Force (IETF), with extensions for call signaling and additional audio and video coding algorithms.

H.323 is independent of network topology per se,[8] and H.323 terminals (see Figure 5.9, which is a particularization of Figure 5.8), can communicate over LANs (via hubs, LAN switches, etc.), over local or remote internets (via routers, bridges, etc.), and over dial-up connections. Proponents see the "most exciting application" of this recommendation as video telephony over the Internet [8].

The H.323 recommendation provides various service levels of multimedia communication over a data network: for example, voice only; voice and video; voice and data; or voice, video, and data communications. All of these provide collaborative tools in support of the virtual corporation paradigm, via intranets, extranets or the Internet. For example, with H.323-ready devices, on-demand interactive multipoint multimedia conferences can be established without the need for reservations.

H.323 recommendations govern the operation of H.323 equipment and the communications between H.323 endpoints. The rec-

Figure 5.9
Logical and proto-col views of H.323.

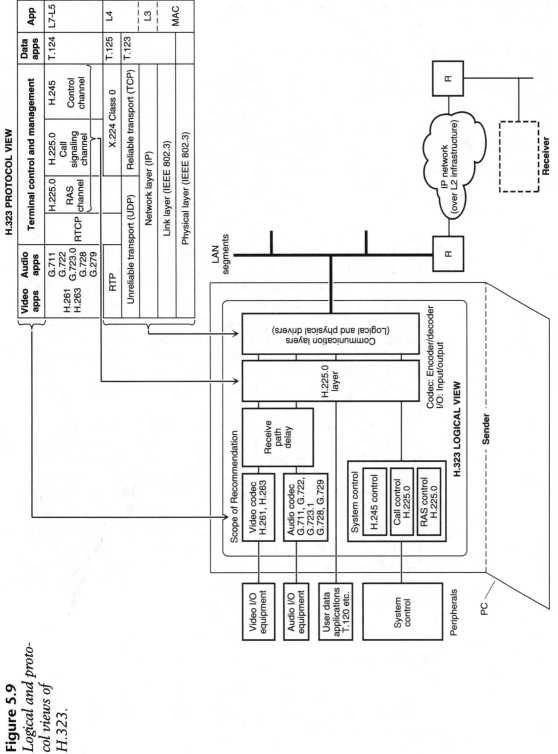

The H.323 protocol view table:

Video apps	Audio apps	Terminal control and management			Data apps	App
H.261 H.263	G.711 G.722 G.723.0 G.728 G.279	H.225.0 RAS channel	H.225.0 Call signaling channel	H.245 Control channel	T.124	L7-L5
	RTP	RTCP	X.224 Class 0		T.125	L4
	Unreliable transport (UDP)		Reliable transport (TCP)		T.123	L3
	Network layer (IP)					
	Link layer (IEEE 802.3)					L3
	Physical layer (IEEE 802.3)					MAC

H.323 PROTOCOL VIEW

Scope of Recommendation

Receive path delay

Video codec H.261, H.263

Audio codec G.711, G.722, G.723.1 G.728, G.729

System control H.245 control

Call control H.225.0

RAS control H.225.0

H.225.0 layer

Communication layers (Logical and physical drivers)

Codec: Encoder/decoder
I/O: Input/output

H.323 LOGICAL VIEW

Sender

Video I/O equipment

Audio I/O equipment

User data applications T.120 etc.

System control

Peripherals

PC

LAN segments

R

IP network (over L2 infrastructure)

R

Receiver

177

Table 5.7 **Umbrella of H.323 Standards**

Standard	*Description*
H.323	Provides system and component descriptions, call model descriptions, call signaling procedures, control messages, multiplexing, audio codecs, video codecs, and data protocols. Baseline standard that references other ITU-T documents.
H.255.0	Describes the media (audio and video) stream packetization, media stream synchronization, control stream packetization, and control message formats.
H.245	Describes the messages and procedures used for opening and closing logical channels for audio, video, and data; capability exchange; mode requests; control; and indications.

ommendation is a baseline standard that references many other ITU-T documents. H.323 provides the system and component descriptions, call model descriptions, and call signaling procedures. Table 5.7 provides a synopsis of the related recommendations. Other recommendations are listed in H.323 for audio and video coding. For audio coding, G.711 is mandatory, while G.722, G.728, G.723.1, and G.729 are optional; for video coding, H.261 QCIF mode is mandatory, while H.261 CIF and all H.263 modes are optional. The T.120 series of recommendations is used for data applications [8].

A design goal in the development of the H.323 recommendation was interoperability with other multimedia terminal types, including H.320 terminals on N-ISDN, H.321 terminals on ATM, H.322 terminals on IsoEthernet, H.324 terminals on the public switched telephone network, and H.310 terminals over ATM. The H.323 terminal provides real-time bidirectional audio, video, and data communications. Figure 5.9 depicts an H.323 terminal from both a logical and a protocol point of view. (Note, however, that H.323 does not specify audio or video equipment, data applications, or the network interface, these being outside the scope of the specification.)

References

1. R. V. Cox and P. Kroon. "Low Bit-Rate Speech Coders for Multimedia Communication." *IEEE Communications Magazine* (December 1996): 34 ff.

2. ITU-T Recommendation G.723.1: *Dual Rate Speech Coder for Multimedia Communications Transmitting at 5.3 and 6.3 kbps.* Geneva, CH: ITU, March 1996.

3. ITU-T Recommendation G.728: *Cooding of Speech at 16 kbps Using Low-Delay Code Excited Linear Prediction.* Geneva, CH: ITU, September 1992.

4. ITU-T Recommendation G.729: *Coding of Speech at 8 kbps Using Conjugate-Structure Algebraic-Code-Excited Linear-Predication (CS-ACELP).* Geneva, CH: ITU, March 1996.

5. K. Rijkse. "H.263: Video Coding for Low-Bit-Rate Communication." *IEEE Communications Magazine* (December 1996): 42 ff.

6. D. Lindbergh. "The H.324 Multimedia Communication Standard." *IEEE Communications Magazine* (December 1996): 47 ff.

7. G. D. Forney, et al. "The V.34 High-Speed Modem Standard." *IEEE Communications Magazine* (December 1996): 28 ff.

8. G. A. Thom. "H.323: The Multimedia Communications Standard for Local Area Networks." *IEEE Communications Magazine* (December 1996): 52 ff.

Notes

[1] A signal analyzed with the G.729A coder can be reconstructed with the G.729 decoder, and vice versa. The major complexity reduction in G.729A is obtained by simplifying the codebook search for both the fixed and adaptive codebooks; by doing this the complexity is reduced by nearly 50 percent, at the expense of a small degradation in performance.

[2] Additional factors that influence the selection of a speech vocoder are availability, licensing conditions, or the way the standard is specified (some standards are only described as an algorithmic description, while others are defined by bit-exact code) [1].

[3] That is, the vocoder parameters are selected in such a manner that the error energy between the reference and the reconstructed signal is minimized.

[4] This section is based on ITU-T Recommendation G.723.1. This material is for pedagogical purposes only. Developers, engineers,

and readers requiring more information should acquire the recommendation directly from the ITU-T [2].

[5]This section is based on ITU-T Recommendation G.728. This material is for pedagogical purposes only. Developers, engineers, and readers requiring more information should acquire the recommendation directly from the ITU-T [3].

[6]This section is based on ITU-T Recommendation G.729. This material is for pedagogical purposes only. Developers, engineers, and readers requiring more information should acquire the recommendation directly from the ITU-T [4].

[7]Since the receiver knows its local decoding delay for the video and audio stream, the time-skew message allows the receiver to insert the appropriate audio delay. Alternatively, the receiver can bypass lip synchronization and present the audio with minimal delay.

[8]Specifically, the protocol architecture up to Layer 3.

CHAPTER 6

Voice over IP
and the Internet

6.1 Introduction

This chapter provides an overview of the issues that impact voice over IP (VOIP) deployment and some of the product categories now emerging.[1] There will be several potential uses of this technology, including traditional carriers looking for new revenues, Internet service providers (ISPs) looking to offer more on the Internet, and corporate planners looking to save money for domestic and international calls. As an example of the new entrants, America Online recently announced an IP voice service; the service is targeted at consumers, the quality being far from business-standard. Given the potential, proponents of VOIP make the statement that "computer telephony holds such service and price promise that corporate America soon will not stand for less" [1].

As noted elsewhere, ATM is a multimedia, multiservice, multipoint technology; hence, support of voice is technically more practical, at the theoretical level, than is the case over IP. Several specifications have emerged recently to support voice using either Constant Bit Rate methods (via ATM Adaptation Layer 1) or Variable Bit Rate methods (via ATM Adaptation Layer 2). The issue, however, is that ATM is not widely deployed, particularly in SOHO and branch locations, and is still relatively expensive. On the other hand, IP-based networks are ubiquitous in the corporate landscape. Hence, there is keen interest in applying IP technology to voice.

The Internet now has several million hosts connecting millions of people worldwide. Many individuals use the Internet for a variety of applications: business people, educators, telecommuters, researchers, government officials, and hobbyists, to list just a few. However, use of the Internet for multimedia applications, including voice, is a relatively new development, at least for business applications.

The evolving ability to carry voice and fax across an IP enterprise network or the Internet will afford a cost-effective way of managing intracorporate communications. Very soon, a corporate user will be able to dial a long-distance number or an office extension, and not be aware that the call is making the journey over the Internet or the intranet. And this will happen (at least initially) for the price of a call to the local ISP. VOIP can support intercorporate communications by bringing down the cost of the equipment and facilities necessary to build an integrated communication infrastructure and by greatly simplifying call center management and troubleshooting. For businesses customers, Internet-based telephony promises many new features, including, but not limited to, Internet-only call transport, fax over the Internet, conference calling, respond-now customer service, and voicemail that broadcasts calendar scheduling to groupware programs, electronic organizers, or even one's smart watch. There are also new service and revenue opportunities for such service providers as LECs, CLECs, IXCs, and cable TV operators.

Table 6.1 depicts a classification of product categories now becoming available. Figure 6.1 depicts a server for Internet and intranet support. Figure 6.2 depicts a hybrid server/desktop example for intranet or PSTN access.

6.2 IP/Internet Background

Network communications can be categorized into two basic types, as implied in Chapter 2: *circuit-switched* (sometimes called connection-oriented) and *packet-* or *fastpacket-switched* (these can be connectionless or connection-oriented). Circuit-switched networks operate by forming a dedicated connection (circuit) between two points. In packet-switched networks, data to be transferred across a network is segmented into small blocks called *packets* [also called datagrams or

Table 6.1 Classification of VOIP Equipment

	Internet only	Intranet only	Internet and intranet	Internet and PSTN	Intranet and PSTN	Internet, intranet, and PSTN
Desktop only (dedicated or shared PC hardware/ software)	IP phones	IP phones	IP phones and routing support	IP phones and legacy support	IP phones and legacy support	IP phones and legacy/routing support
Server only	Regular phones, but PBX/key system connections	Regular phones, but PBX/key system connections	Regular phones, but PBX/key system connections (e.g, Figure 6.1)	Regular phones, but PBX/key system connections	Regular phones, but PBX/key system connections	Regular phones, but PBX/key system connections
Hybrid desktop/ server	Hardware for IP-phone-like function in PC and PBX/key system connections	Hardware for IP-phone-like function in PC and PBX/key system connections	Hardware for IP-phone-like function in PC and PBX/key system connections	Hardware for IP-phone-like function in PC and PBX/key system connections	Hardware for IP-phone-like function in PC and PBX/key system connections (e.g., Figure 6.2)	Hardware for IP-phone-like function in PC and PBX/key connections system

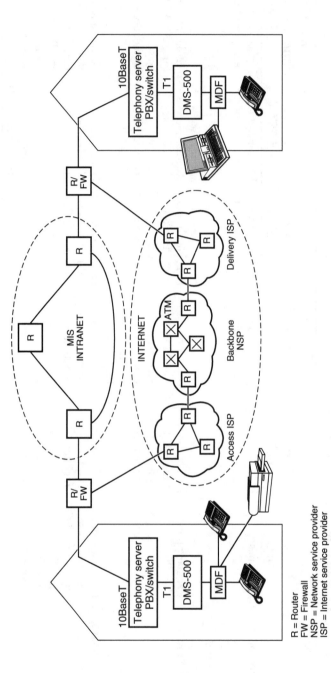

R = Router
FW = Firewall
NSP = Network service provider
ISP = Internet service provider

Figure 6.1
Voice over the Internet and intranets: server-based.

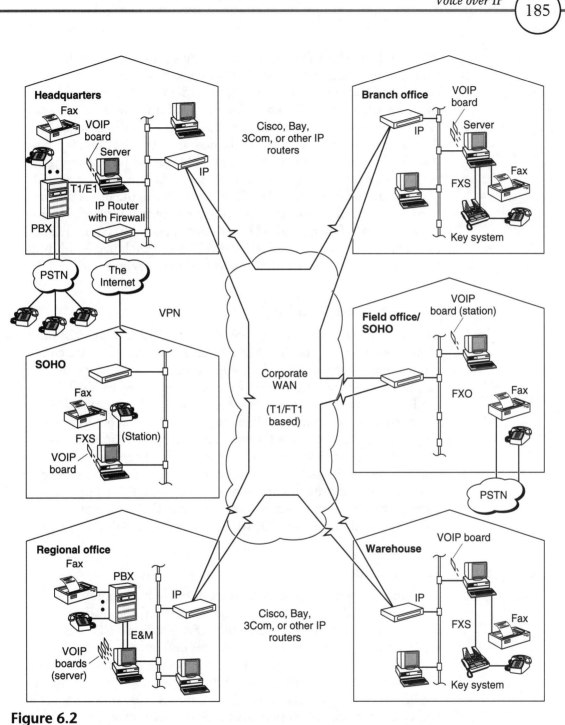

Figure 6.2
Voice over an intranet: hybrid server/station-based. (Courtesy of Microsoft Corp.)

Protocol Data Units (PDUs)] that are multiplexed onto high-capacity intermachine connections. A packet, which usually contains few hundred bytes of data, carries identification that enables the network hardware to know how to send it forward to the specified destination. In frame relay, the basic transfer unit is the data link layer *frame;* in cell relay, this basic unit is the data link layer *cell.* Services such as frame relay and ATM use circuit-switching principles; namely, they use a call setup mechanism similar to that of a circuit-switched (ISDN) call. IP has become the de facto standard connectionless packet network layer protocol for both local area networks (LANs) and wide area networks (WANs). In a connectionless environment there is no call setup. Each packet finds its way across the network independently of the previous one.

Internet Protocol Suite

Chapter 2 provides a basic review of the TCP/IP and UDP/IP suite of networking protocols. TCP/IP is a family of over 100 data communications protocols used in the Internet and in intranets. In addition to the communication functions supported by TCP (end-to-end reliability over a connection-oriented session) and IP (subnetwork-level routing and forwarding in a connectionless manner), the other protocols in the suite support specific application-oriented tasks, for example, transferring files between computers, sending mail, or logging into a remote host. TCP/IP protocols support layered communication, with each layer responsible for a different facet of the communications (as seen in Table 6.2). Some of the VOIP applications utilize TCP, while others utilize RTCP and UDP.

The Internet

The same IP technology now used extensively in corporate internets is also used in (and, in fact, originated from) the Internet. The Internet is an international collection of interconnected government, education, and business computer networks—in effect, a network of networks. Recently there has been a near-total commercialization of the Internet, allowing it to be used for pure business applications (the original roots of the Internet were in the research and education arenas). A person at a computer terminal or personal

Table 6.2   Functionality of the TCP/IP Suite Layers

Network interface layer	This layer is responsible for accepting and transmitting IP datagrams. This layer may consist of a device driver (e.g., when the network is a local network to which the machine attaches directly) or of a complex subsystem that uses its own data link protocol.
Network layer (Internet layer)	This layer handles communication from one machine to the other. It accepts a request to send data from the transport layer, along with the identification of the destination. It encapsulates the transport layer data unit in an IP datagram and uses the datagram routing algorithm to determine whether to send the datagram directly onto a router. The internet layer also handles the incoming datagrams and uses the routing algorithm to determine whether the datagram is to be processed locally or be forwarded.
Transport layer	In this layer the software segments the stream of data being transmitted into small data units and passes each packet, along with a destination address, to the next layer for transmission. The software adds information to the packets, including codes that identify which application program sent it, as well as a checksum. This layer also regulates the flow of information and provides reliable transport, ensuring that data arrives in sequence and with no errors.
Application layer	At this level, users invoke application programs to access available services across the TCP/IP internet. The application program chooses the kind of transport needed, which can be either messages or stream of bytes, and passes it to the transport level.

computer equipped with the proper software communicates across the Internet by having the driver place the data in an IP packet and addressing the packet to a particular destination on the Internet. Communications software in routers in the intervening networks between the source and destination networks reads the addresses on packets moving through the Internet and forwards the packets toward their destinations. TCP guarantees end-to-end integrity.

From a thousand or so networks in the mid-1980s, the Internet has grown to an estimated 1 million connected networks with about 100 million people having access to it (as of 1997). The majority of these Internet users currently live in the United States or Europe, but the Internet is expected to have ubiquitous global reach over the next few years.

In 1973, ARPA initiated a research program to investigate techniques and technologies for interlinking packet networks of various kinds. The objective was to develop communication protocols that would allow networked computers to communicate transparently across multiple packet networks. The project became very successful and there was increasing demand to use the network, so the government separated military traffic from civilian research traffic, bridging the two by using common protocols to form an internetwork or *internet*. The term *internet* is defined as "a mechanism for connecting or bridging different networks so that two communities can mutually interconnect." So, in the mid-1970s ARPA became interested in establishing a packet-switched network to provide communications between research institutions in the United States. With the goal of heterogeneous connectivity in mind, ARPA funded research by Stanford University and Bolt, Beranek, and Newman to create an explicit series of communication protocols. The ARPA-developed technology included a set of network standards that specified the details of the computers that would be able to communicate, as well as a set of conventions for interconnecting networks and routing traffic. The result of this development effort, completed in the late-1970s, was the *Internet suite of protocols.* Soon thereafter, there were a large number of computers and thousands of networks using TCP/IP, and it is from their interconnections that the modern Internet has emerged. As noted in Chapters 1 and 3, ARPA was also interested in integrated voice and data.

While the ARPAnet was growing into a national network, researchers at Xerox Corporation's Palo Alto Research Center were developing one of the technologies that would be used in local area networking, namely, Ethernet. Ethernet became one of the important standards for implementing LANs. At about the same time, ARPA funded the integration of TCP/IP support into the version of the UNIX operating system that the University of California at Berkeley was developing. It followed that when companies began marketing non-host-dependent workstations that ran UNIX, TCP/IP was already built into the operating system software, and vendors such as Sun Microsystems included an Ethernet port on their devices. Consequently, TCP/IP over Ethernet became a common way for workstations to interconnect.

The same technology that made PCs and workstations possible made it possible for vendors to offer relatively inexpensive add-on cards to allow a variety of PCs to connect to Ethernet LANs. Software vendors took the TCP/IP software from Berkeley UNIX and ported it to the PC, making it possible for PCs and UNIX machines to use the same protocol on the same network.

In 1986, the U.S. National Science Foundation (NSF) initiated the development of the NSFnet. NSFnet has provided a backbone communication service for the Internet in the United States. It should be noted that the NSFnet operated utilizing a service acceptable user policy (AUP). The policy stated that the NSFnet was to support open research and education in and among U.S. research and intellectual institutions, plus support a research arm of for-profit firms when engaged in open scholarly communication and research. Use for other purposes was not acceptable. The commercialization of the Internet that is now being experienced is not based on the AUP. By the end of 1991, the Internet had grown to include some 5000 networks in over three dozen countries, serving more than half a million host computers. These numbers have continued to grow at geometric rates throughout the 1990s. There are now several thousand Internet service providers (ISPs), although the number is expected to decrease greatly over the next five years. Table 6.3 depicts highlights of the history of the Internet over a 30-year span.

TCP and IP were developed for basic control of information delivery across the Internet. Application layer protocols, such as TELNET (Network Terminal), file transfer protocol (FTP), simple mail transfer protocol (SMTP), and hypertext transfer protocol (HTTP) have been added to the TCP/IP suite of protocols to provide specific network services. Access and backbone speeds have increased from 56 kbps, to 1.5 Mbps (most common now), to 45 Mbps and beyond, for most of the backbones. Voice applications over IP have to ride over the Internet systems developed for traditional data services. Most problematic is the lack of QoS support; this, however, is expected to slowly change. Nonetheless, in spite of the emergence of new technologies, such as RSVP and RTP, a retarding factor to true QoS support is the Internet's own success: The numbers of people using it are increasing a such a rapid rate that it is difficult to add enough resource and protocol improvements to keep up with the demand.

Table 6.3   Snapshot of Internet-Related Activities over the Years

- Late 1960s: ARPA (DoD think tank) introduces the ARPAnet.
- 1970s: ARPAnet expands geographically and functionally to allow non-military traffic (e.g., universities and defense contractors).
- Late 1970s: The realization takes hold that the ARPAnet cannot scale.
- TCP/IP is developed for heterogeneous networking and interenterprise connectivity. Protocols to support global addressing and scalability are developed.
- Early 1980s (1983): TCP/IP is a standard operating environment for all attached systems.
- Network splits into a military component (MILNET) and a civilian component (ARPAnet).
- 1986: Six supercomputer centers are established by NSF.
- Interagency dynamics and funding considerations lead to the creation of the NSFnet by the NSF. IP protocol and newer equipment are utilized in the NSFnet. NSFnet and ARPAnet intersect at Carnegie Mellon University.
- Late 1980s: ARPAnet is absorbed into NSFnet.
- *Phase 1.*   Three-tiered architecture developed:
    1. NSF to undertake overall management and fund the backbone operationally and in terms of technology upgrades
    2. Regional and state network providers to supply Internet services between universities and the backbone and become self-supportive through service fees
    3. Campus networks and organizations, colleges, and universities to use TCP/IP-based systems to provide widespread access to researchers and students
- 1987: Six supercomputer sites interconnected using DEC routers and 56-kbps links.
- Traffic congestion begins to be experienced.
- *Phase 2.*   Merit partnership formed with IBM and MCI to upgrade network.
- Mid-1988: A DS1-line (1.544-Mbps) network connects more than a dozen sites, using IBM-based switches.
- 1989: Reengineering due to fast growth (15 percent per month); new routers and additional T1 links (MCI) are installed.
- *Phase 3.*   Third redesign of NSFnet, using an outsourcing approach—NSFnet is overlaid upon a public Internet (NSF is relieved from the responsibility of upgrading the network on an ongoing basis). Lines are upgraded to DS-3 rates (45 Mbps).
- Merit, IBM, and MCI form Advanced Network Services Inc. (ANS); the not-for-profit organization is to build and manage a commercial Internet.

- DS3 lines are provided by MCI; routers by IBM (RS/6000-based). Network is also called ANSnet. NSFnet is now a virtual network in the ANSnet (migration accomplished in two years).
- 1992: Original NSFnet is dismantled.
- ANS launches a for-profit subsidiary (ANS CORE) to face costs.
- Debates are sparked by commercial Internet providers:

  PSINet, CERFNet, and AlterNet form the Commercial Internet Exchange (CIX) as a backbone and bypass to the NSFnet. 155 other members join, including NEARnet, JvNCnet, SprintLink, and InfoLAN.

  (Based on the CIX approach, CICnet, NEARnet, BARRnet, North WestNet, NYSERnet WestNet, and MIDnet form the Corporation for Regional and Enterprise Networking (CoREN).

  Regional commercial providers (not in CoREN) compete against CoREN.

- *Phase 4.* Rapid increase requires NSF to redesign the backbone.
- Two years of bidding and planning leads to two awards to replace current NSFNet:
  1. MCI to deploy very high speed backbone network service (vBNS), based on 155-Mbps SONET/ATM, to connect NFS supercomputing centers
  2. Merit and USC Information Sciences Institute to do routing coordination
- Network access providers (NAPs) are to provide access to the vBNS; NAP functions go to Ameritech, Sprint, MFS, and PacTel.
- NFS institutes the Routing Arbiter for fair treatment among various Internet service providers with regards to routing administration; provision of a database of route information, network topology, routing path preferences, and interconnection information; and deployment of routing that supports type of service, precedence routing, bandwidth on demand, and multicasting (accomplished by route servers using Border Gateway Protocol and Interdomain Routing Protocol).
- Fund established to support a Network Information Center (NIC):

  Registration Services (by Network Solutions Inc.) include IP, Domain Names, whois, and whitepages.

  Directory Services (by AT&T) include a directory of directories and white and yellow pages.

  Information Services (by General Atomics) include coordination services, a clearinghouse for information, training, workshops, a reference desk, education (General Atomics then operated CERFnet—now owned by TCG/AT&T—and the San Diego Supercomputer Center).

- Shakeout of ISPs is predicted by 2002: of more than 1400 ISPs in 1995, about 100 are expected to survive by the turn of the century.

Intranets use the same WWW/HTML/HTTP and TCP/IP technology that is used for the Internet. When the Internet caught on in the early to mid-1990s, planners were not looking at it as a way to run their businesses. But just as the action of putting millions of computers around the world on the same protocol suite fomented the Internet revolution, so connecting islands of information in a corporation via intranets is now sparking a corporate-based information revolution. Thousands of corporations now have intranets. Across the business world, employees from engineers to office workers are creating their own home pages and sharing details of their projects with the rest of their companies.

6.3 Voice Transmission and Approaches in ATM, Frame Relay, and IP

In principle, the emerging technologies for transmitting voice over data networks present opportunities for organizations to reduce costs and enable new applications. In particular, traditional router vendors see the opportunity to cannibalize the existing voice traffic by adding appropriate features to their routers. Clearly, if a company uses separate facilities to carry on-net voice from company location to company location, there could be additional costs in terms of communication channels, equipment, and carrier charges.

In looking to carry voice over IP, one must keep in mind that voice transmissions can tolerate relatively low round-trip delay and jitter; in fact, for traditional commercial toll applications, that delay has been on the order of 10 to 30 ms. For voice over data networks, occasionally dropping packets, frames, or cells is not an issue, since the human ear can tolerate small glitches without loss of intelligibility. Also, for practical design considerations, delay ranges are allowed to be higher (up to 200 ms). Many of the algorithms utilized in voice over data networks are not transparent (being lossy), but preserve reasonable to good voice quality while greatly reducing data rates.

A synopsis of evolving voice over data protocols follows.

ATM

Current approaches for voice over ATM assume a PCM model where voice encoding and transmission takes place in real time. In effect, an entire DS1, comprised of up to 24 voice channels, is transported end-to-end over ATM using *network-interworking* techniques (structured $n \times 64$ kbps is also supported by newer equipment). This model imposes a need to preserve timing in speech delivery and playback. This can be accomplished with a kind of timestamping in the ATM Adaptation Layer 1 (AAL 1) header or via adaptive clocking. But there has been interest in using other kinds of AALs. The ATM Forum started work on voice transport in 1993, and it was not until April 1995 that the Voice and Telephony Services over ATM (VTOA) working group published its first document, which contained the structured and unstructured circuit emulation specifications. More specifications were approved in 1997. Other documents that utilize other AALs (AAL 2 or 5) for voice followed (see Figure 6.3).[2]

Frame Relay

A compressed and packetized model of voice transmission has emerged that separates the time scales for encoding, transmission, and playback. Hence, the need to preserve synchronous timing is no longer necessary: Improvements in encoding algorithms and faster and cheaper DSP hardware have changed the paradigm. At this juncture, most voice systems in this context use some kind of prediction technique (vocoding). In addition to proprietary methods, typical compression schemes being used include G.729 CS-ACELP, G.728 LD CELP, and G.723.1 MP-MLQ; also supported are G.726/G727 (ADPCM) and G.711 (PCM). Predictions are based on the most recently received information. Therefore, if a frame is lost, the newly arriving frame will show that the receiver's prediction is not current, since the missing frame did not update the receiver. It follows that the output is not correct, and the result is somewhat distorted speech. Hence, the performance is related to both delay and loss in the frame relay network. One of the issues is how much time is needed for the receiver to catch up with the arriving frames and get current, so that the voice output will be as intended. State of the art voice compression algorithms of the early 1990s could require several seconds to synchronize after a loss of bits; newer algorithms are able to self-synchronize within the length of a single vocoder frame, as implied by the discussions in Chapters 4 and 5. This makes each frame effectively independent. Since

Figure 6.3

Documents on server-based voice over the Internet and intranets.

ATM Forum Voice over ATM Documents

VTOA Phase 1 (September 1997)	Now "ATM Trunking Using AAL 1 for Narrowband Services" af-vtoa-0089.000—Approved July 1997 without MIB Yes: 36 No: 1 Abstain: 2 Total votes: 39 16.7% (215 principal members)
VTOA Phase 2 (late 1998)	Now "ATM Trunking Using AAL 2 for Narrowband Services" Draft—Coordinated with ITU-T
DBCES	Dynamic Bandwidth Utilization in 64-kbps Time Slot Trunking over ATM—Using CES af-vtoa-0085.000—Approved July 1997 Yes: 31 No: 0 Abstain: 6 Total votes: 37 14.4% (215 principal members)

Timetable for AAL 1 and AAL 2 Specifications

CES-V2 (SCE)	January 1997
I.363.1 (AAL 1 Rev)	September 1996
VTOA Phase 1	September 1997
I.363.2 AAL 2	September 1997
AAL 2 SSCS	Late 1998
VTOA Phase 2	Late 1998

ITU-T Recommendations

AAL 2 Structure			*AAL-SAP*
Service Specific Conversion	I.SEG	Frozen September 1997	Approval June 1998
Sublayer (SSCS)	I.TRUNK	Frozen June 1998	
Common Part Sublayer (CPS)	I.363.2 AAL 2	Frozen February 1997	Approval September 1997

I.SEG

- Segmentation and reassembly for data
- Three sublayers (assured mode and error protection optional)
    Assured mode (Q.921 or SSCOP)
    Error protection
    Basic SAR with AAL 5 trailer

I.Trunk

Application (SSCS user) support: The LLT SSCS will specify the support of the following traffic types:

- Compressed voice
- PCM voice
- Silence indication

Figure 6.3
(Continued)

- Status and alarm
- Control
- CAS
- Dialed digits
- Fax/modem demod/remod
- Circuit-mode data
- Frame-mode data

Companies Actively Involved with	
ITU-T AAL 2/SSCS Recommendations at presstime	
Alcatel	Nippon Ericsson K.K.
AT&T	NIST
Cable and Wireless	Nokia
Deutsche Telekom AG	Nortel
Ericsson Radio Systems AB	NTT
France Telecom	Oki
GDC	Sprint
Lucent	Swiss PTT
MOC-ISRAEL	Telefonica I+D
NEC	

human ears can compensate for the loss of 20 ms of sound, an occasional lost frame does not disrupt communications. (However, if every other frame were lost, then there would be a serious problem.) In 1997 the Frame Relay Forum adopted the FRF.11 Voice over Frame Relay specification to encourage interoperability. Until then the same frame relay access device (FRAD) was needed at both ends. There are many FRADs that support voice on the market. A number of FRADs now support voice switching, fax demodulation, echo cancellation, silence suppression, and dynamic bit rate adaption technologies, with support for both the FRF.11 and the ITU-T's G.729 standard voice algorithms.

IP

This model uses Web telephones that can be used in conjunction with Internet services to bypass the public telephone network. This approach envelopes frames of compressed speech into IP packets (IP encapsulation). Typically, voice is compressed to 8 kbps (or less) using proprietary or, preferably, standard methods. The IP overhead increases the datarate to 14.8 kbps. Some devices use silence compression technology, so that bandwidth is required only when someone is actually talking. (During periods of silence, bandwidth for voice is automatically freed up for other traffic on the enterprise network.) This typically reduces the bandwidth utilization to about 6 kbps (assuming 60 percent silence compression). Some devices also use forward error correction methods to minimize loss, and jitter-buffer techniques to reduce latency variations. Based on current technology at this writing, the quality of the speech generally needs improvement. Quality is impacted by both the compression algorithms (relatively less important) and by the lack of guaranteed QoS in the IP network (relatively more important).

In addition to the current quality issue, Web/IP phones suffer from the fact that they are proprietary—hence, the need for standards. Fortunately, as described in previous chapters, in 1995 the ITU-T standardized the ACELP voice algorithms for the coding of speech signals in wide area networks; ACELP is used for compression rates at or below 16 kbps. ITU-T G.729 (CS-ACELP) is an international standard that compresses the standard 64-kbps PCM streams as used in typical voice transmission to as low as 8 kbps. ITU-T G.728 (LD-CELP) is an international standard that compresses to 16 kbps. ITU-T G.723.1 compresses voice to rates as low as 5.3 kbps (it also operates at 6.3 kbps). Early supporters of G.723.1 include Microsoft, Intel, PictureTel, and the major video-conferencing vendors. This standard is used in the H.323 recommendation for conferencing over LANs. G.723.1 is considered to be a good first step and is best suited for intranets and controlled point-to-point IP-based connections. G.729A, a simplified version of G.729, operates at 7.9 kbps and is therefore slightly better in quality than G.723.1. Supporters include Netspeak, AT&T, Lucent, NTT, and France Telecom. A group has been formed to advance the technology. The Voice over IP (VOIP) Group is a consortium of vendors backed by Intel and Microsoft to recommend standards for telephony and audioconferencing over the Internet. Its goal is to ensure interworking among vendors of Web-based telephony. At a 1997 meeting, the VOIP agreed to recommend the ITU-T G.723.1 specification. An alternative is ITU-T G.729A.

ITU-T H.323 Group of Standards

If VOIP is going to be successful, standardization will be critical. As alluded to in Chapters 1 and 5, H.323 describes terminals, equipment, and services for multimedia communication over LAN and IP networks that do not provide a guaranteed quality of service (see Figure 6.4). H.323 terminals and equipment may carry real-time voice, data, and video, or any combination, including videotelephony. The LAN over which H.323 terminals communicate may be a single segment, or it may be multiple segments with complex intranet topologies. It should be noted that operation of H.323 terminals over multiple LAN segments (including the Internet) may actually result in poor performance, since the possible means by which quality of service might be assured on such types of LANs and internets is beyond the scope of the recommendation. H.323 terminals may be integrated into personal computers or implemented in standalone devices, such as videotelephones. Support for voice is mandatory in the standard, while data and video are optional; but, if supported, the ability to use a specified common mode of operation is required, so that all terminals supporting that media type can interwork. Other components in the H.323 series include H.225.0 packet and synchronization, H.245 control, H.261 and H.263 video codex, G.711, G.722, G.728, G.729, and G.723 audio and speech codex, and the T.120 series of multimedia communications protocols. H.323 terminals may be used in multipoint configurations and may interwork with H.310 terminals on B-ISDN, H.320 terminals on N-ISDN, H.321 terminals on B-ISDN, H.322 terminals on guaranteed QoS LANs (e.g., IEEE 802.9), H.324 terminals on PSTN and wireless networks, and V.70 terminals on PSTN.

Streaming Audio

Compression is also applicable to streaming audio and video that may also be delivered over IP and/or the Internet (e.g., Internet radio). *Streaming* is a technique of breaking up a file into pieces and sending those to the user in a sequence. The receiver is able to use or play the multimedia data as it arrives. User software can begin to process the pieces as soon as it receives them. For example, a streaming system would break compressed audio data into many packets, sized appropriately for the bandwidth available between

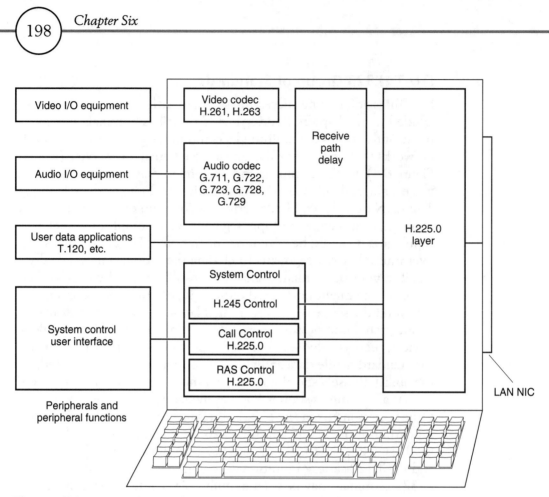

Figure 6.4
Terminal and terminal equipment.

the client and the server. When the client has received enough packets, the user software can be playing one packet, decompressing another, and receiving a third. This approach contrasts with the more traditional (and less user-friendly) method of delaying the playing until the entire file has been downloaded [2]. These systems use an encoding process for compressing and packetizing the data-stream and a decoding process for managing buffers according to available bandwidth, decompressing the packets and rendering its contents. Real-Time Streaming Protocol (RTSP) and Microsoft's Active Streaming Format may be employed.

Most products available today are based on proprietary methods, limiting interoperability. Because coder/decoder systems usually aim at reducing the contents' datarate, they are lossy. This implies that the quality of the contents will be degraded to various degrees. Lossy compression is one of the reasons these systems are proprietary. Some examples of audio streaming products are Internet Wave (VocalTec, vocaltec.com), RealAudio (Progressive Networks, realaudio.com), StreamWorks (Xing Technology, xingtech.com), ToolVox (Voxware, voxware.com), and TrueSpeech Internet (DSP Group, dspg.com).

6.4 QoS Problems and Solutions

Voice over IP is impacted by network congestion. QoS encompasses various levels of bandwidth reservation and traffic prioritization for multimedia and other bandwidth-intensive applications. The topic is discussed at the protocol level in Chapter 2.

The specific QoS solution depends on the applications and circumstances at hand. QoS is generally not required for batch applications; it is needed for most, if not all, real-time applications (see Table 6.4 [3]). For nonmultimedia applications, QoS in enterprise networks is useful for allocating and prioritizing bandwidth to specific users. For example, accounting departments may need more bandwidth when they are closing the books each month and CEOs need more bandwidth during extensive videoconferencing sessions. QoS is also important to supply the streams of data that continuously move across users' computer screens, such as stock tickers, real-time news, or viable data.

Various QoS solutions are available, beginning at the low end with more bandwidth to the LAN desktop via Layer 2 switching. New protocols and standards offer the next level of QoS for enterprise network environments, including 802.1p, 802.1q, and RSVP [3]. Using ATM as a backbone improves bandwidth between subnetworks, and Layer 3 switching adds performance improvements in environments where IP dominates. Finally, end-to-end ATM provides many levels of built-in QoS.

Besides the capability for bandwidth reservation, QoS is affected by the abilities of switches to perform real-time IP routing. Advances in silicon integration are being brought to bear to optimize the performance of third-wave switches and pave the way for

Table 6.4   Applications and QoS

	QoS required	*Applications*
Non-real-time data	Little or none	Data file transfer
		Imaging
		Simulation and modeling
Non-real-time multimedia	Little or none	Exchange text e-mail
		Exchange audio/video e-mail
		Internet browsing with voice and video
		Intranet browsing with voice and video
Real-time one-way	Various QoS levels	Multimedia playback from server
		Broadcast video
		Distance learning
		Surveillance video
		Animation playback
Real-time interactive	Various medium or high QoS levels	Videoconferencing
		Audioconferencing
		Process control

SOURCE: From Reference [3].

wire-speed IP routing capabilities.[3] Third-generation switches are optimized for switching at gigabit per second speeds. This is a possible thanks to advancements in high-performance custom ASICs that can process packets simultaneously and in real-time across multiple ports in a switch. Furthermore, the design of ultrawide data paths and multigigabit switching backplanes enable third-wave switches to perform at gigabit speeds through full-duplex connections on all ports without blocking.[4]

In VOIP, the need for QoS is driven by the plethora of performance-related requirements for speech. The Alliance for Telecommunication Solutions (ATIS) recently looked into requirements for voice over data networks. The following list enumerates some of the requirements for voice support in data networks, including IP [4]:

- Attenuation distortion goals
- Crosstalk goals
- Delay (steady-state) goals
- Delay (variation) goals
- Dropout goals
- Echo return loss

- Group delay
- Gain hits
- Listener echo
- Loss (single frequency)
- Noise (impulse)
- Noise (quantization, including total distortion)
- Noise (steady-state)
- Phase hit
- Phase jitter
- Relative level—output
- Return loss
- Signal clipping (power)
- Singing return loss
- Talker echo path loss

Some of these do not necessarily apply for PC-to-PC communication, but could apply when the voice over data network is interconnected with the PSTN.

6.5 Protocols for QoS Support for Audio and Video Applications

This section considers a number of the Resource Reservation Protocol (RSVP) streaming, and multicast applications.

RSVP Applications

RSVP, along with available network bandwidth, is required to ameliorate QoS support in IP networks. New applications are now emerging that require such capabilities. For example, some call centers are adding Web telephone access, letting customers reach the carrier's customer service agent by clicking a "speak to the agent" icon at the Web site (e.g., see Chapter 7). But in order to scale this on a broad scale, standards are required so that QoS can be supported and be made available as a network service.

RSVP is based on receiver-controlled reservation requests for unicast or multicast communication. RSVP carries a specific QoS through the network, visiting each node the network uses to carry the stream. At each node, RSVP attempts to make a resource reservation for the stream. To make a resource reservation at a node, the RSVP daemon communicates with two local decision modules, admission control and policy control. *Admission control* determines whether the node has sufficient available resources to supply the requested QoS. *Policy control* determines whether the user has administrative permission to make the reservation. If either check fails, the RSVP program returns an error notification to the application process that originated the request. If both checks succeed, the RSVP daemon sets parameters in a packet classifier and packet scheduler to obtain the desired QoS. The packet classifier determines the QoS class for each packet and the scheduler orders packet transmission to achieve the promised QoS for each stream (see Figure 6.5).

A receiver-controlled reservation allows scaling of RSVP for large multicast groups. This support is based on RSVP's ability to merge reservation requests as they progress up the multicast tree. The reservation for a single receiver does not need to travel to the

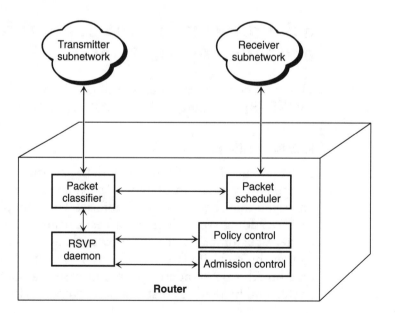

Figure 6.5
RSVP routing.

source of a multicast tree; rather, it travels only until it reaches a reserved branch of the tree.

RSVP does not perform its own routing; instead, it uses underlying routing protocols. Reportedly, there is vendor interest in delivering RSVP on routers. A draft version of RSVP was approved by the IETF in 1996, and by 1997 vendors such as Cisco and Bay Networks were expressing interest, although they were being quoted as stating that "there is little demand for RSVP from applications at the moment."

To ensure delivery through the network, RSVP allows listeners to request a specific quality of service for a particular data flow. Listeners can specify how much bandwidth they will need and what maximum delay they can tolerate; internetworking devices then set aside the bandwidth for that flow. Users are either granted the channel they have requested or are given a busy signal. RSVP hosts and networks interact to achieve a guaranteed end-to-end QoS transmission. All the hosts, routers, and other network infrastructure elements between the receiver and the sender must support RSVP. They each reserve such system resources as bandwidth, CPU, and memory buffers to satisfy a request.

RSVP operates on top of IP (either IPv4 or IPv6), occupying the place of a transport protocol in the protocol stack, but it provides session-layer services (it does not transport any data). The RSVP protocol is used by routers to deliver control requests to all nodes along the paths of the flows. Vendors have implemented RSVP both above and below Winsock. RSVP-aware applications can be developed with Winsock 2, which has a QoS-sensitive API. Another approach is to use an RSVP proxy that runs independently of the real application, making RSVP reservations.

RSVP raises questions about billing for Internet bandwidth. In the current model, ISPs oversell their available capacity, and customers accept slowdowns. Since resource reservation puts a specified demand on bandwidth, overselling would result in unacceptable performance by the admission control module. ISPs will probably offer different service levels, and premiums will be charged for RSVP reservations. Billing across multiple carriers will also have to be resolved, as will the allocation of computational resources to routers to inspect and handle packets on a prioritized basis. It is unclear whether existing routers would be able to handle widescale implementation of RSVP across the whole Internet.

Real-Time Streaming Protocol (RTSP) Applications and Active Streaming Format (ASF)

The Internet provided the impetus for the development of streaming technologies. The growth of real-time media on the Internet has stretched HTTP's capabilities for downloading files to their maximum. The IETF is now attempting to standardize such functions as starting and stopping data streams, synchronizing multiple media elements, and implementing other controls. To this end the main work is embodied in RTSP, which was jointly proposed by Progressive Networks, Netscape, and Columbia University in 1996.

RTSP essentially provides HTTP-level services to real-time streaming data types. However, RTSP differs from HTTP in that data delivery takes place out-of-band, utilizing a distinct protocol. RTSP establishes and controls single or several time-synchronized streams of continuous media. RTSP is expected to use TCP as the transport layer (for control only), but UDP may optionally be supported. Although in draft specification, RTSP implementations are available today.

In parallel with RTSP development, Microsoft has implemented a proprietary protocol called *Active Streaming Format* (ASF) in its new Netshow server platform. While it offers capabilities similar to those of RTSP, Microsoft's documents refer to ASF as a file format and describe it as a component of Microsoft's overall ActiveX strategy. It is a kind of metafile that packages multiple *media objects* into a unified framework. Like RTSP, it may be used to synchronize a number of multimedia objects, including audio, video, still images, events, URLs, HTML pages, script commands, and executable programs. Unlike RTSP, an ASF stream includes both control and content elements.

ASF content may either be constructed offline or captured in real time. This multimedia content is stored into ASF as objects. These elements may be combined into a single ASF file. ASF retains all forms of media (e.g., audio and video compression) and (optionally) synchronization information so that when the file is played over a network, the user sees and hears the file exactly as the file's creator intended [2].

ASF data objects are stored within an ASF file as *packets*. Each packet is designed to be directly inserted as is into the data field of a data communication transport protocol. These packets are designed to be streamed across a network at a specific bandwidth or bit rate. The packet structure contains one or more payloads (i.e., distinct media streams) of data. Each packet may contain the data from a single media stream or interleaved data from several media streams. A packet is a collection of multimedia data that is ready to be streamed over the Internet or an intranet. Ideally, the packet has been correctly sized so that all that needs to be done to ship it over the wire is to append the appropriate data communication protocol headers. ASF does not impose a packet size limitation; however, in practice, the packet sizes generally run from 512 bytes to the data communication's maximum transmission unit (MTU) size. Each packet may contain interleaved data (i.e., composed of data from multiple multimedia streams). The format of the packet data is fairly complex in order to ensure that the packet data is as dense as possible for efficient transmission over a network [2].

ASF data can be tailored to satisfy a variety of network requirements. For example, the data in each ASF file has been designed to stream at a distinct bit rate. The actual streaming bit rate is determined by the file's creator. The file's content creator has a wide range of streaming bit rates to choose between (e.g., 14.4 kbps to 6 Mbps). ASF content can thus be flexibly targeted for specific network environments with distinct capacity requirements. Similarly, there are no data communications dependencies within ASF: ASF data can be carried over a wide variety of differing transport protocols. ASF multimedia streams can be stored on traditional file servers, HTTP servers, or specialized media servers and can be transmitted efficiently over a variety of different network transports. These transports include TCP/IP, UDP/IP, RTP, and IPX/SPX. This data may be sent as either unicast (point-to-point) or multicast streams [2,5].

Internet Stream Protocol Version 2 (ST2)

The first version of the Stream Protocol (ST) was published in the late 1970s and was used throughout the 1980s for experimental transmission of voice, video, and distributed simulation. The experience gained in these applications led to the development of the revised protocol version ST2. The revision extends the original protocol to make it more complete and more applicable to emerging multimedia environments. The original specification of this protocol version is contained in RFC 1190, published in October 1990. Version 2 is described in RFC 1819, published in August 1995.

With more and more developments of commercial distributed multimedia applications underway and with a growing dissatisfaction at the network-secured QoS for audio and video over IP (particularly in the MBONE context), interest in ST2 has grown over the last few years. Companies have products available that incorporate the protocol. Implementations of ST2 for Digital Equipment, IBM, NeXT, Macintosh, PC, Silicon Graphics, and Sun platforms are available [6].

ST2 is an experimental resource reservation protocol intended to provide end-to-end real-time guarantees over the Internet or intranet. It allows applications to build multidestination simplex data streams with a desired quality of service. The ST2 is a connection-oriented internetworking protocol that operates at the same layer as connectionless IP. It has been developed to support the efficient delivery of data streams to single or multiple destinations in applications that require guaranteed quality of service. ST2 is part of the IP protocol family and serves as an adjunct to, not a replacement for, IP. The main application areas of the protocol are the real-time transport of multimedia data, for example, digital audio and video packet streams.

ST2 can be used to reserve bandwidth for real-time streams. This reservation, together with appropriate network access and packet scheduling mechanisms in all nodes running the protocol, guarantees a well-defined QoS to ST2 applications. It ensures that real-time packets are delivered within their performance targets, that is, at the time when they need to be presented. This facilitates a smooth delivery of data that is essential for time-critical applications, but that typically cannot be provided by best-effort IP communication [6].

ST2 consists of two protocols: Stream Transport (ST) for the data transport and Stream Control Message Protocol (SCMP) for all control functions. ST is simple and contains only a single PDU format that is designed for fast and efficient data forwarding in order to achieve low communication delays. SCMP, however, is more complex than IP's ICMP. As with ICMP and IP, SCMP packets are transferred within ST packets.

ST2 is designed to coexist with IP on each node. A typical distributed multimedia application would use both protocols: IP for the transfer of traditional data and control information, and ST2 for the transfer of real-time data. Whereas IP typically will be accessed from TCP or UDP, ST2 will be accessed via new end-to-end real-time protocols. The position of ST2 with respect to the other protocols of the Internet family is represented in Figure 6.6 [6].

Both ST2 and IP apply the same addressing schemes to identify different hosts. ST2 and IP packets differ in the first 4 bits, which contain the internetwork protocol version number: Number 5 is

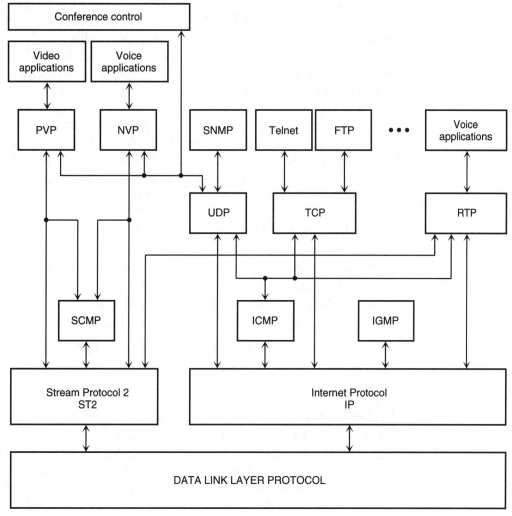

Figure 6.6
Hierarchy of protocols. (From Reference [6].)

reserved for ST2 (IP itself has version number 4). As a network layer protocol, like IP, ST2 operates independently of its underlying subnets.

As a special function, ST2 messages can be encapsulated in IP packets. This link allows ST2 messages to pass through routers, which do not run ST2. Resource management is typically not available for these IP route segments. IP encapsulation is, therefore, suggested only for portions of the network that do not constitute a system bottleneck [6]. In Figure 6.6, the RTP protocol is shown as an example of transport layer on top of ST2. Others include the Packet Video Protocol (PVP),[5] and the Network Voice Protocol (NVP).

ST2 proposes a two-step communication model. In the first step, the real-time channels for the subsequent data transfer are built. This is called *stream setup*. It includes selecting the routes to the destinations and reserving the correspondent resources. In the second step, the data is transmitted over the previously established streams. This is called *data transfer*. While stream setup does not have to be completed in real time, data transfer has stringent real-time requirements. The architecture used to describe the ST2 communication model includes the following [6]:

- A data transfer protocol for the transmission of real-time data over the established streams
- A setup protocol to establish real-time streams based on the flow specification
- A flow specification to express user real-time requirements
- A routing function to select routes in the Internet
- A local resource manager to appropriately handle resources involved in the communication

IP Multicast

For the Internet to be a viable real-time audio medium, it needs a method for serving a community of users. IP Multicast is a suite of tools that addresses the bandwidth cost, availability, and service-quality problems facing real-time, large-scale Webcasting.

Rather than duplicating data, multicast sends the same information just once to multiple users. When a listener requests a stream, the Internet routers find the closest node that has the signal and replicate it, making the model scaleable. IP multicast can run over just about any network that can carry IP, including ATM, frame relay, dial-up, and even satellite links. Originally developed in the late 1980s, it is now supported by all major internetworking vendors, and its implementation and usage is picking up speed.

Reliability is a problem with multicast because there is not necessarily a bidirectional path from the server to the user to support retransmission of lost packets. A string of lost packets could create enough return traffic to negate multicast's bandwidth savings. For this reason, TCP/IP cannot be used. Among the transport protocols developed for IP Multicast, RTP and RTCP are the main ones for real-time multimedia delivery. RTP adds to each packet header the timing information necessary for data sequencing and synchronization. It does not provide mechanisms to ensure timely delivery or provide QoS guarantees; it does not guarantee delivery, nor does it assume that the underlying network is reliable. RTP and RTCP are currently in draft status; both are expected to be finalized in early 1998.

Uninterrupted audio requires a reliable transport layer; nevertheless, existing basic concealment techniques, such as frequency domain repetition combined with packet interleaving, work reasonably well if packet loss is minimal and occasional departures from perfection can be tolerated.

One approach is to use forward error correction (FEC). Adding some redundant data improves performance considerably; combined with interleaving, this can be a good strategy, but it requires more bandwidth for a given quality level. This can be a challenge on a 28.8-kbps modem connection.

On the business side, reliable multicast can be used to increase the performance of many applications that deliver information or live events to large numbers of users, such as financial data or video streaming. Reliable multicast creates higher value application services for today's IP-based networks. According to a study recently conducted by the IP Multicast Initiative (IPMI), 54 percent of information systems managers stated that IP Multicast had created new business opportunities for their companies, and these numbers are likely to grow from year to year [5].

6.6 Internet Telephony Servers (ITSs)

Enterprises used to justify the cost of a private WAN by the cost savings these networks achieved for the on-net voice traffic. Now, bandwidth requirements for data networks are so great that organizations can add voice capabilities to these networks for relatively limited incremental costs.

A number of vendors offer voice over IP gateways that integrate hardware and software designed and developed to provide seamless voice and fax transmission over an IP network. For example, Micom (now a Nortel subsidiary) offers the V/IP Phone/Fax IP gateway, as shown in Figure 6.7. A system that is seeing significant deployment, Lucent's ITS, is covered in the appendix.

The gateway approach has the design advantage of installing directly in an organization's IP network and interoperating with existing PBX and key systems and, so, with existing telephones and fax machines. On the enterprise side of the network, the gateway interoperates with LANs, routers, switches, and WANs. The issue with this and other approaches is that they are proprietary solu-

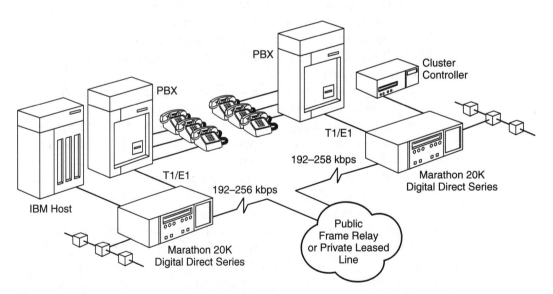

Figure 6.7
Companywide V/IP deployment. (Courtesy of Micom Communications Corp., copyright 1997.)

tions, and, hence, the same exact equipment must be employed at every site.

Gateways generally use both PC-bus compatible (e.g., ISA) interface cards, which terminate the PBX, compress the voice, and pack it into the IP datagram, and a suite of call management software. Each gateway typically receives a telephone number and an IP address, which are entered into the gateway's database. The database provides the mapping of the gateway telephone number to the appropriate IP address (see Figure 6.8).

In general, the planner needs to take into account the operating system, such as Novell NetWare, MS-DOS, or Microsoft Windows 95. Some gateways support multiple operating systems. The gateway must handle all aspects of the call setup: digitization and compression, IP encapsulation, IP address mapping, and datagram delivery to and from the closest router.

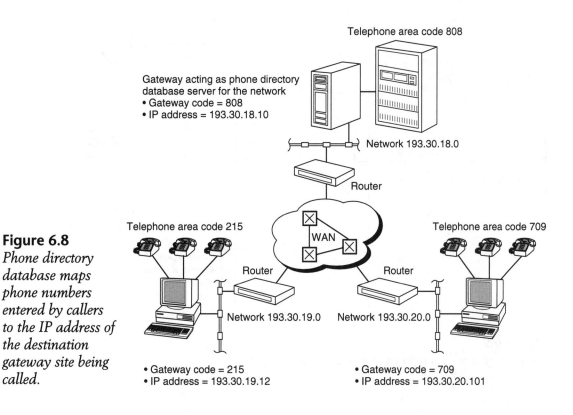

Figure 6.8
Phone directory database maps phone numbers entered by callers to the IP address of the destination gateway site being called.

The interface cards interface with the PBX and take the voice or fax signals from the existing system and convert them into a digital format that can be processed by a PC. These cards must be available for analog voice (e.g., older PBXs) and for digital voice (e.g., newer PBXs). Also, the cards must be available in single channel or multiple channel applications (say four-port T1/E1) and must support traditional termination modes (e.g., FXS/FXO) and signaling (e.g., E&M). Table 6.5 defines some of these terms (also see Figure 6.9). Digital signal processing capabilities are built into the cards to

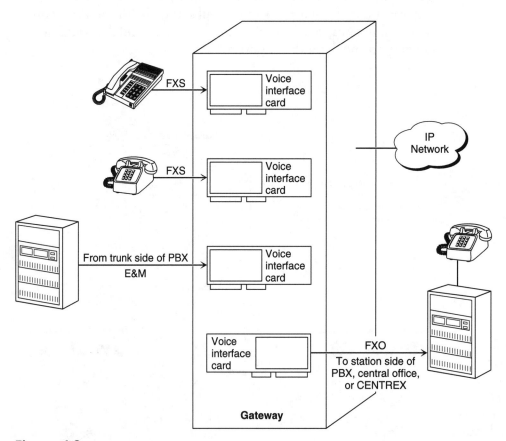

Figure 6.9
VF interfaces to be supported by IP gateways.

Table 6.5   Basic PBX Nomenclature

FXS	*Foreign exchange station.* An interface for connecting a standard telephone set, facsimile machine, key system, or PBX.
FXO	*Foreign exchange office.* An interface that emulates a telephone and connects to the station side of a PBX or directly to a central office.
E&M	*Ear & mouth.* A trunking arrangement used for two-way switch-to-switch or switch-to-network connections. An E&M tie line connects PBXs in different locations. The *E* lead receives signals, while the *M* lead transmits signals.

digitize and compress voice using some proprietary or, preferably, standard compression scheme, such as the ITU-T G. 729.

An enterprise-network-based call would proceed as follows:

1. The caller picks up a standard desk telephone, which is supported by a PBX. The PBX is physically connected to the gateway over one of the access cards.

2. The caller then dials an access code (e.g., 8) that tells the PBX to route this call over the PBX trunk connected to the gateway. Next, the caller types in the branch or extension number (e.g., 392-2345).

3. The gateway routes call setup messages over the enterprise network to the remote gateway. The gateway sets up the call via the PBX, and if the called party is available, voice bits will be encapsulated within the IP payload. More precisely,

   - The access number to the gateway, the destination office number, and the remote extension number trigger a calling-out signal that travels from the telephone through the PBX.

   - The calling-out signal goes into either an analog or a digital origination gateway interface card.

   - The origination gateway undertakes call setup based on the digits entered. The gateway's telephone database maps the destination office number to the remote gateway's IP address.

   - The gateway establishes the availability of an open channel on the remote gateway. If a priority queuing protocol such as RSVP is available, the gateway can use it to request allocation of bandwidth on the network. Otherwise, a standard best-effort IP service is utilized.

- During the course of a conversation, the voice signal is digitized and compressed into datagrams. The datagrams are encapsulated into IP protocol data units (PDUs). The PDUs are transmitted from the gateway's voice interface card through the PC's (Ethernet) network interface card over the LAN medium and over to the router. The router forwards these PDU across the network on a priority/RSVP basis or on a best-effort basis.
- The destination gateway handles comparable functions.

Desirable features of a voice over IP gateway include the following:

- Optimal use of bandwidth.
- Support of speech quality.
- Capability for flexible integration into a voice environment (e.g., PBX).
- Enterprise-network ready (e.g., must support LAN/WAN protocols for direct attachment).
- System-level scalability: must be easy to add PBX-side interfaces to support growth in requirements. This also means supporting the appropriate links (such as FXO, FXS, and E&M).
- Network-level scalability: must be able to support the mapping of a sufficient number of extensions (perhaps several thousands) to the respective IP addresses of the destination gateway. A master database with distributed upgrade may be desirable.
- Capability for attachment to the Internet, if desired, as illustrated in Figure 6.10.
- Support of fax.

There is interest in IP-voice technology from an Internet-enabled call center perspective. With the development of Web-based commerce, there is interest in providing an integrated contact

Figure 6.10
Internet-supported IP gateway for voice.

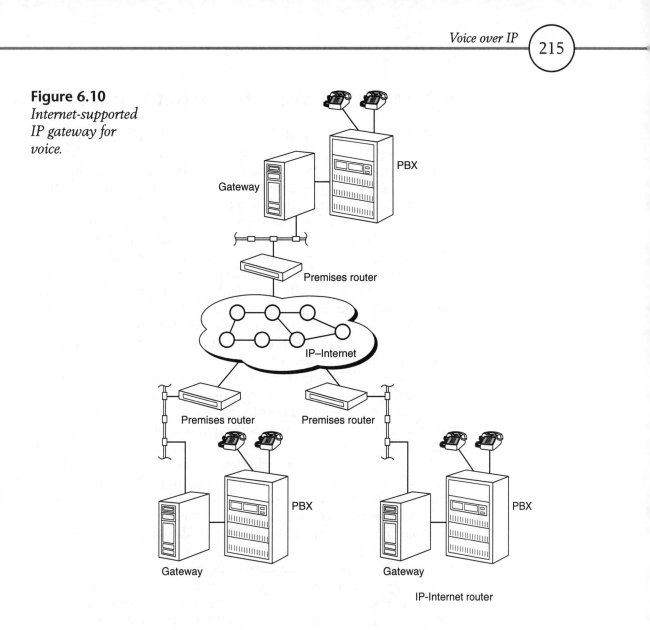

for online voice and data communications, while at the same time delivering convenient, quick, and high-quality service no matter where the transaction originates. Microsoft's Telephony Application Program Interface (TAPI), among other interfaces, can be used in conjunction with web browsers, Java, and voice over IP to provide a realization of computer telephony integration (CTI) and interactive voice response (IVR).

6.7 The Voice over IP/Internet Market

Most observers predict that the market for VOIP will grow rapidly. A recent report from Britain predicted that 15 percent of all voice calls will be made via the IP/Internet by 2000. Some have valued 1997 sales of Internet telephony products at $80 million. It is estimated that the market's worth will reach $500 million in 1999. According to figures from Forrester Research, the U.S. market is expected to be $30 million for Internet telephony in 1998, but by 2004 that figure will rocket to $2 billion. That is estimated to be more than 4 percent of U.S. long-distance revenues. Frost & Sullivan is even more bullish on Internet telephony: The firm estimates that spending will approach $2 billion as early as 2001 [7, 8].

Voice over the IP/Internet is developing in three directions: (1) PC-to-PC, where individuals online talk through their PCs, (2) PC-to-phone, where individuals make and receive voice calls and messages while on the Internet, and (3) phone-to-phone, where calls are made and received using normal phone handsets.

While a number of vendors tout products that support voice over the Internet, performance issues, particularly transmission delays and communications-quality audio signals (e.g., MOS around 3.0), have created what some characterize as "a lackluster response, especially among corporate IS managers seeking a business-quality voice over IP solution."[6] Corporate and other IP networks need to be better managed to handle real-time network traffic needs—for example, prioritization and bandwidth allocation. Evolving standards (per the previous section) promise to solve some of these problems, but support is limited. In addition, nearly all the CPE technology currently available at this writing is proprietary.

Up to now, vendors have been of the small upstart category, rather than the mainstay. This is because the initial interest came from nonbusiness Internet users looking for free telephone service over the Internet. Of late, high-tech leaders such as Cisco, Lucent, and Nortel have shown interest in entering the market. This equipment is generally inexpensive (e.g., less than $10,000 in some cases) and can pay for itself in a few months.

In the meantime, ISPs are developing technologies to start charging more for voice, video, and fax. For example, in early 1997, NetCentric and Compaq Computer announced a protocol called Metered Services Information Exchange (MSIX), which allows an

ISP to charge more not only for specific services, but also for access to specific sites. Developers agree that usage-based pricing could have a negative impact on user's willingness to use the Internet, because the perception continues to exist that it is free.

6.8 VOIP Regulatory Issues

Some claim that several key regulatory and economic issues need to be resolved before VOIP will see a major deployment, even by new entrants, such as the Regional Bell Operating Companies now tackling the long-distance telephony market. The attitude of some carriers may be similar to the following one appearing in the current trade press at this writing: "Yes, we want to eventually deliver voice-over-IP services, but everyone [regulators and carriers] wants to buy some time right now. There is so much involved when it comes to large-scale services, and this IXC just can't jump in and end up in a position where delivery is costing a fortune" [9].

The issue related to tariffs impacts local and international considerations. According to some, these tariffs will play a major role in determining the cost of offering such services and the prices that long-distance carriers can change.

Related to domestic communications, long-distance carriers have to determine how local access charges will affect Internet telephony. Local access charges are the fixed per-call rates that a long-distance carrier must pay to a LEC to complete a long-distance call to the final leg of its journey. In recent years, the long-haul carriers have taken the position that the access charge is too high and the current scheme is not fair. A reduction in local access charges will help IXCs finance the cost of developing and delivering Internet telephony services. In fact, Internet service providers do not pay access charges at all.

On the international front, the tariff in question, known as the *accounting rate*, is the same one that has been in the news lately because the FCC has announced that it will fight to lower the fees that U.S. carriers pay their overseas counterparts to deliver international calls in other countries. The ultimate resolution of the accounting rate issue will play a major role in determining the development of VOIP, because in some countries regulators have decided that the Internet is different than the telephone network, so the accounting rate does not apply to Internet long-distance calls. U.S. carriers want all foreign governments to decide that Internet telephony is a new service. Worldwide regulators, on the other hand, lean toward the position that they cannot allow the Internet to be tariff-free because that would cause established carriers and their public networks to lose lots of traffic and revenue [9].

Proponents make the case that a tariff-free market would be the best, because the products and services would come to market faster and costs would drop. This would aid the general proliferation of videoconferencing and whiteboarding services that packet networks enable.

Another issue is that carriers will still have to decide how to package and price Internet telephone services, in order to make them appealing to consumers. Some analysts estimate that packetized voice services would be lower than regular long-distance prices by about 20 percent, while others believe that not to be the case—that is, that consumers will see only a little discount, but in return will get more functionality for about the same cost as today's long-distance charges [9].

When the Internet infrastructure that must be built up to provide truly reliable phone service on a large scale is taken into account, one is talking about a significant expense. Almost everyone has heard of or used the Web, whether for personal or corporate use. But the Internet remains a mystical land for many, almost an unconquerable space of mythical scope, an uncircumscribable domain of nebulous consistency, an ephemeral cyberspace of fantastic dimensionality. Planners need to understand how the Internet is built: What the components are, and who the players are. How it can be expanded and improved. How a new company can offer the Internet. How new services can be developed. Such an angle is not necessarily as creative at it appears prima facie. Just make the mental association, for argument's sake, of the Internet with the PSTN we now have in the United States. The PSTN allows any properly equipped and connected user to reach any ear, brain, person that is suitably connected and equipped with a handset, in the United States or abroad. The Internet allows any properly equipped and connected user to reach any server or host that is suitably connected and equipped with appropriate hardware and software, in the United States or abroad. The PSTN is a collection of regional and backbone networks. The Internet is a collection of regional and backbone networks. The PSTN is an overlay of many regional and many backbone networks, and the user can pick a regional and a backbone network of choice; all these networks are interconnected so that any user can call any user. The Internet is an overlay of many regional and many backbone networks, and the user can pick a regional and a backbone network of choice; all these networks are interconnected so that any user can reach any host or server. The PSTN is comprised of switching gear belonging to a provider and interconnecting links owned or leased by the same provider. The Internet is comprised of routing gear belonging to a provider and interconnecting links owned or leased by the same provider.

Given this demystification of the PSTN, somebody wants to plan, design, deploy, own, extend, and interconnect (with existing players) some or all portions of the PSTN, including local or backbone components. Similarly, somebody should be able and want to plan, design, deploy, own, extend, and interconnect (with existing players) some or all portions of the Internet, including local or backbone components. At the macroeconomic scale (not from the casual surfer's point of view), the point remains: If we already have an optimized nationwide PSNT network, why do we need to develop another one of the same scale, reliability, and robustness?

There are a number of ways to charge for the Internet phone services. What users may be offered in the next couple of years is a menu of à la carte line items that will appear on the phone bill. It would include a basic charge for packetized service and extra charges for such additional services as whiteboarding, videoconferencing, operator assistance, tech-support packages, and equipment integration [9].

6.9 Examples of Recent Voice over IP Technologies

Voice over IP and Internet telephony have been attracting the attention of corporate customers and the manufacturers of communication products since 1996. Vendors such as Lucent Technologies, NetSpeak, NetPhone, VocalTec, Vienna Systems, and Northern Telecom's Micom have introduced products for VOIP. Solutions that companies can relay on today are mostly gateway servers that are used to connect PBX at each site where they want long-distance calls to travel over the intranet.

Lucent

Lucent has taken an early lead with its top-of-the-line Internet Telephony server for carrier-based applications. A detailed description of its product is found in the Appendix.

Micom Communications Corporation

Micom Communications Corporation's V/IP (Voice over IP) phone/fax IP gateway creates an overlay voice and fax network on top of an enterprise IP data network. V/IP allows any user, from any telephone or fax machine in the company, to make free, G.729 toll-quality intracompany calls over the company's IP network. The V/IP product family consists of analog and digital voice interface cards (VICs), featuring one and two voice/fax channels. The VIC card plugs into a PC at each enterprise location, operating NetWare, MS-DOS, Windows 95 or NT. The V/IP interface card is compatible with any telephone, fax machine, PBX, key system, Centrex, or CO trunk. V/IP's QoS technologies support both existing router priority protocols and the new RSVP (see Figure 6.11). The vendor claims that companies can typically save thousands of dollars per remote site annually with V/IP. A 50-site network could save half a million dollars in five years with payback in six to twelve months.[5]

To place a call using V/IP, a company employee dials a short extension number on a desktop phone or department fax machine for another phone or fax machine at another location in the enterprise. The phone or fax communicates automatically through the PBX key telephone system (KTS) to the V/IP card, through the PC's LAN Network Interface Card (NIC) onto the LAN, through the router over the WAN, and similarly to another phone or fax. V/IP is independent of the LAN and WAN technology: Any mix of technology for LANs (ATM, Ethernet, FDDI, and Token Ring), and for WANs (frame relay, leased lines, ISDN, satellite, ATM, and the Internet) can be used. However, these networks provide differing QoS and propagation delay.

V/IP is installed in a shared PC at each remote site on the corporate IP network and in a dedicated PC at headquarters. Any user

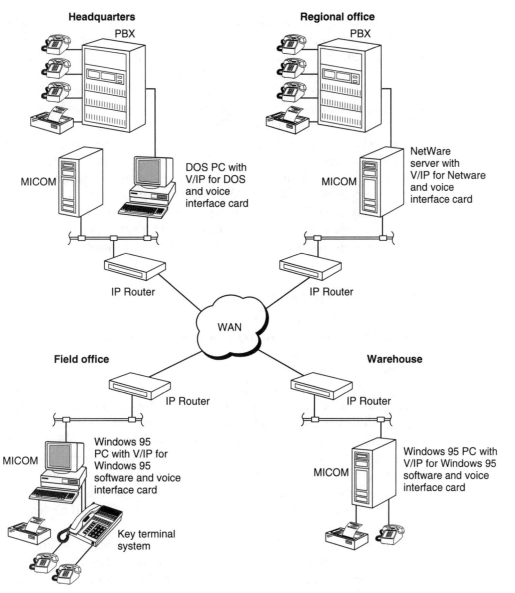

Figure 6.11
Micom V/IP phone/fax IP gateway integrates with data and phone equipment to create a voice/fax overlay on an IP network. (Courtesy of Micom Communications Corp., copyright 1997.)

can make a long-distance intracompany call for free. The new functionality appears as an off-premise extension, tie line, or a special phone extension. A typical branch office requires an average of two voice/fax channels, occupying one PC slot.

V/IP uses Micom's standards-based ClearVoice technology to deliver toll-quality voice over 8 kbps of WAN bandwidth. V/IP with ClearVoice combines ITU's G.729 voice compression standard, fax demodulation, silence suppression, forward error correction, and 40 MIPS digital signal processors (DSPs) to compress and convert voice and fax signals into IP packets. A voice channel consumes only 3 percent of a 56- or 64-kbps WAN connection during a typical workday. SNMP network management is also part of the V/IP package, providing full configuration, status, alarm, and events reporting, plus diagnostics and call-accounting capabilities.[7]

Microsoft Corporation

The leader of the software market, Microsoft Corporation, recently released commercial versions of two mostly software products addressing delivery of streaming data over the Internet: NetMeeting 2.0 and NetShow 2.0.

With NetMeeting, an individual using a PC and the Internet can hold face-to-face conversations with colleagues, friends, and family around the world. NetMeeting works with any video capture card or camera that supports Video for Windows. Black-and-white video cameras for the PC start at just $99, and color video cameras start at around $199. NetMeeting's data conferencing features let individuals collaborate with a group of people from within any Windows application—drawing on a shared whiteboard, sending text messages, and transferring files.

NetMeeting's real-time audio lets users talk to other people over the Internet, even with a 14.4-kbps modem. One can share ideas and information face-to-face and use the camera to view items displayed in front of the lens. Combined with the audio and data capabilities of NetMeeting, one can both see and hear the other person, as well as share information and applications. NetMeeting video conferencing includes the following features [2]:

- Ability to change the size of the video window.
- Compatibility with existing video capture hardware.

- Quality video, even over low-bandwidth connections. Net-Meeting produces quality, real-time video images using a standard 28.8-kbps modem Internet connection, IP over ISDN connection, or LAN connection.
- Ability to receive images without video hardware.
- Switchable audio and video. This allows one to participate in a meeting with many people and to switch the person one is seeing and talking to.
- Ability to copy video images to the clipboard.
- Ability to adjust video quality.
- Interoperability with other H.323 products and services. Net-Meeting supports the H.323 standard for audio and video conferencing, which includes the H.263 video codec. H.323 allows NetMeeting to interoperate with other compatible videophone clients, such as the Intel Internet Video Phone. Also, several leading industry vendors are currently developing H.323 conference servers and gateways that will enable NetMeeting users to participate in a call with multiple audio and video connections.
- Support for Intel MMX Technology.

One can make voice calls using NetMeeting and talk to people running NetMeeting and other compatible Internet phone products. NetMeeting audioconferencing offers such features as half-duplex and full-duplex audio support for real-time conversations, automatic microphone sensitivity level setting to ensure that people hear each other clearly, and microphone muting, which lets the user control the audio signal sent during a call. This audio conferencing supports network TCP/IP connections. NetMeeting 2.0 audio continues to operate with NetMeeting 1.0. One will notice better audio quality on PCs with a Pentium processor. Support for the H.323 protocol enables interoperability between NetMeeting and other H.323-compatible audio clients. The H.323 protocol supports the ITU G.711 and G.723 audio standards and IETF RTP and RTCP specifications for controlling audio flow to improve voice quality. On MMX-enabled computers, NetMeeting uses the MMX-enabled audio codecs to improve performance for audio compression and decompression algorithms. This will result in lower CPU use and improved audio quality during a call.

Support for multipoint data conferencing allows the user to communicate and collaborate with other people in real time over the Internet or a corporate intranet. NetMeeting enables users to share applications, exchange information between shared applications through a shared clipboard, transfer files, collaborate on a shared whiteboard, and communicate with a text-based chat feature. Also, support for the T.120 data conferencing standard enables Net-Meeting to interoperate with other T.120-based products and services. Multipoint data conferencing contains the following features:

- Application sharing
- Shared clipboard
- File transfer
- Whiteboard
- Chat

The other product is Microsoft NetShow 2.0. It provides an easy way to stream multimedia content across intranets and the Internet, giving content providers, corporations, developers, and Web professionals the ability to integrate audio and video into any Web application or site. Streaming allows content to be delivered to the client as a continuous flow of data with little wait time before playback begins. NetShow gives users the benefit of instant play and eliminates waiting for content to download. It uses ASF, discussed earlier (see Figure 6.12).

Microsoft NetShow supports both unicast and multicast delivery techniques. Unicast means that the server sends a stream each time it is requested. Unicast allows the user to control playback, much like having a program recorded on a VCR. The user can fast-forward, rewind, stop, and restart at will. Sending out unicast streams can quickly take up a lot of bandwidth, since it means one stream for each request. Multicast allows the server to send a single copy of the requested data over the network for many computers to receive. However, as with tuning into a live television program, the user loses the ability to fast-forward and rewind.

IDT Corporation

IDT Corporation Net2Phone enables any Internet user with a sound-equipped PC to initiate calls from a computer and transmit

Figure 6.12
NetMeeting/Net-Show environment.

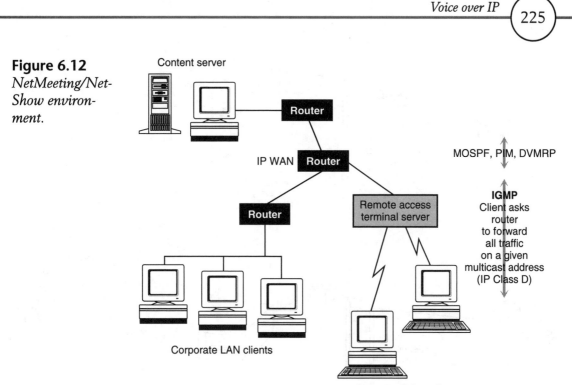

them over the Internet to IDT's central telephone switch. The switch automatically relays the call to its final destination—any telephone on the PSTN. The result is real-time, uninterrupted, full-duplex voice communication between two parties.

Figures 6.13 to 6.16 show four different scenarios for the utilization of features of Net2Phone products and services.

PictureTel

PictureTel Desktop Videoconferencing Systems offer a comprehensive solution for standards-based desktop videoconferencing and application sharing. With the Live family of products, users of PCs running Microsoft Windows can conduct real-time video meetings with users of any H.320- and T.120-compliant videoconferencing system anywhere in the world [10]. It offers the following features:

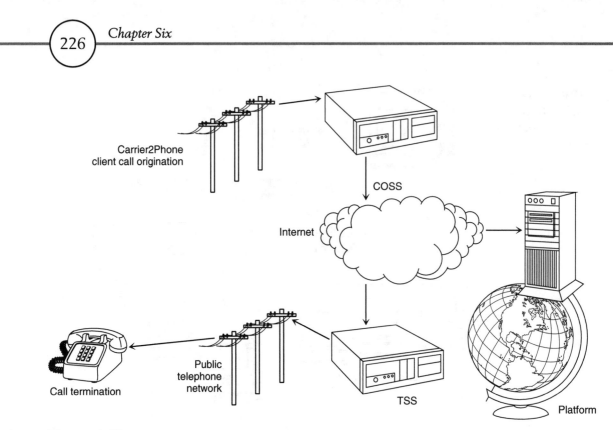

Figure 6.13
Carrier2Phone architecture. (Courtesy of IDT Corporation, copyright 1997.)

- Provides an easy-to-use videoconferencing solution, including videoconferencing boards, adjustable FlipCam camera, speakerphone, and PictureTel LiveShare Plus data collaboration software.
- Enables users of Windows-based PCs to conduct spontaneous video meetings and collaborate on projects to speed decision making.
- Supports the H.320 international videoconferencing standard, ensuring interoperability with other standards-based desktop and room systems.
- Works in a variety of network and telecommunications environments, including ISDN, Switched 56, and V.35/RS-449.
- T.120 data collaboration enables users to share applications and data with multiple far-end sites during a videomeeting, speeding the exchange of information and ideas.

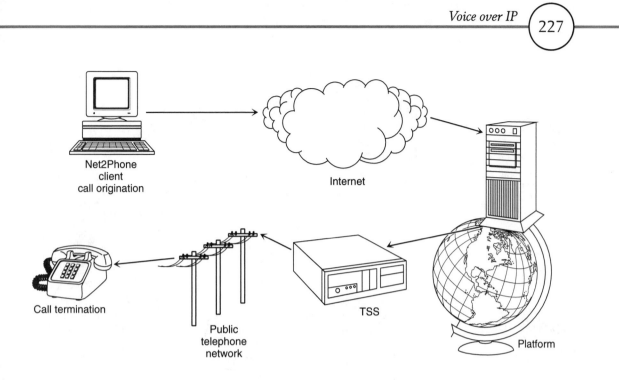

Figure 6.14
Net2Phone architecture. (Courtesy of IDT Corporation, copyright 1997.)

VocalTec

VocalTec Inc. (Northvale, NJ) offers an IP-based system called Internet Telephony Gateway, which has been sold to Telecom Finland, Dacom in Korea, and New Zealand Telecom. Motorola resells the product. Motorola uses the technology between its Austin, Chicago, and Phoenix offices. VocalTec is a founding member of the VOIP Forum.

VocalTec already ships its new Internet Phone product Release 5 with an enhanced client component. Release 5 has many new and improved features, including enhanced audio and video, support for international standards, PC-to-standard phone calling, and a new Community Browser. In addition to being a standalone product, Internet Phone is a key component of VocalTec's corporate and carrier Internet telephony client/server solutions. VocalTec's strategy focuses on aggressively pursuing OEM deals. Among those on the list of OEM relationships are IBM, Motorola, U.S. Robotics, America Online, CompuServe, Earthlink, Netcom, Prodigy, and Acer.

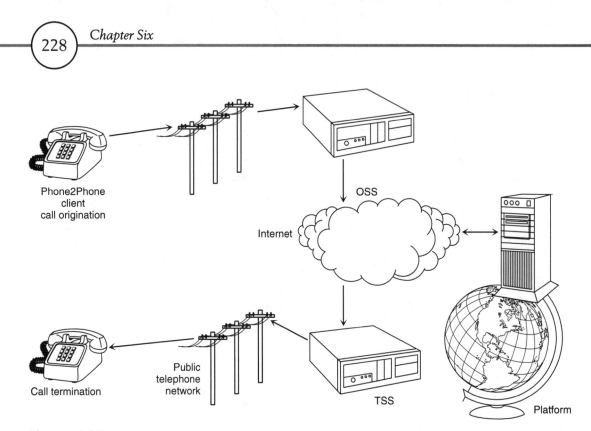

Figure 6.15
Phone2Phone architecture. (Courtesy of IDT Corporation, copyright 1997.)

Internet Phone Release 5 is priced at $49.95 at this writing. The Internet Phone Release 5 requires a computer with a 75-Mhz Pentium processor or faster and 16 MB of RAM, running Windows 95 or Windows NT 4.0 with a 32-bit Winsock-compatible TCP/IP Internet or direct network connection (14.4-kbps, SLIP or PPP minimum; 28.8 kbps recommended.) A Windows-compatible sound card, microphone, and speaker also are required. A full-duplex sound card is required for full-duplex operation. To send video, a parallel port video camera or a video camera with a standard Windows-compatible video capture card is required, plus a 28.8 modem. No special equipment is needed to receive video.

Internet Phone Release 5 is being launched with VocalTec's NextGen Telephony Co-Marketing Program, the first virtual worldwide calling network providing PC-to-phone service to consumers and businesses. Users can link directly to participating NextGen Internet Telephony Service Providers (ITSPs) from multiple screens

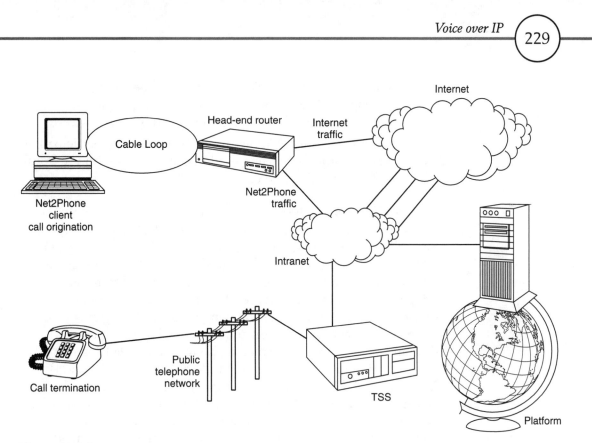

Figure 6.16
Net2Phone for cable architecture. (Courtesy of IDT Corporation, copyright 1997.)

within Internet Phone. Some new features of Internet Phone Release 5 include the following [11]:

- *Enhanced audio and video quality.* Provides faster frame delivery and a larger video picture; includes new packet loss reconstruction algorithms and better delay handling for improved audio.

- *ITU H.323 support.* Supports the international standard in audio and video communications over networks.

- *PC-to-phone calling.* Direct online links to Internet Telephony Service Providers (ITSPs) from the software allow users to sign up for phone service. Thereafter, users simply enter standard phone numbers to call regular phones from their PCs.

- *Community Browser.*   Serves as a virtual neighborhood in Cyberspace. The Community Browser lets people meet and speak with others around the world with similar interests.
- *Audioconferencing.*   Allows up to 100 people to participate in an audioconference when used in conjunction with the Vocal-Tec Conferencing Server.

VocalTec created the network in conjunction with qualified ITSPs and with industry support from Motorola, Dialogic Corporation, ITXC Corporation, Compaq Computer Corporation, and Digital Equipment Corporation. Through the network, users with dial-up Internet connections anywhere in the world can dial from their PCs using the market leading Internet Phone to regular telephones all over the world. Special calling rates are available to Australia (Melbourne, Perth, and Sydney), Brazil (Rio de Janeiro), Canada (Toronto), China (Beijing and Hong Kong), Colombia (Bogotá), France (Paris and Toulouse), Israel (Tel Aviv), Indonesia (Jakarta), Japan (Tokyo), Malaysia (Kuala Lumpur), Lebanon (Beirut), Paraguay (Asunción), Philippines (Manila), Russia (Moscow and St. Petersburg), Singapore, Taiwan (Hsinchu and Taipei), United Kingdom (London), and there is broad-based coverage in the United States (Boston, Los Angeles, Miami, New York City, Salt Lake City, San Diego, San Francisco, and Sunnyvale CA) [11].

According to the latest Frost & Sullivan report on the Internet telephony industry, both Internet Phone and the VocalTec Telephony Gateway server dominate the consumer and carrier segments of the Internet telephony market in 1996[8]; the market-share dynamics are, however, shifting in favor of other technology providers.

Other Companies

Table 6.6 compares existing offerings from different vendors on a price and feature basis.

6.10 Conclusion

The integration of several media is desirable due to the potential economic advantages. However, voice over IP remains somewhat of

Table 6.6 Partial List of VOIP Products on the Market

Company	Contact	Product	Application sharing	Audio	Video	T.120, H.320, H.323, and ASF support	Price per user	Platforms
Creative Labs Inc.	http://www .creaf.com	ShareVision PC3000	Point-to-point	Full-duplex	Yes	None	$450	Windows 3.1 Windows 95
Creative Software Technologies	http://www .cst.com.au	CollabOrator System 2000 Plus	Point-to-point	Full-duplex	Yes	None	$360	Windows 3.1 Windows 95
Microsoft Corporation	http://www .microsoft .com	Microsoft NetMeeting	Multipoint	Full-duplex	Yes	H.232 and H.263	Client is free	Windows 95 Windows NT 4
Farallon Communications Inc.	http://www .netopia.com	Netopia Virtual Office	Point-to-point	Half-duplex	No	T.120, H.320, and H.323	$50	Windows 3.1 Windows 95 Windows NT 4
PictureTel Corporation	http://www .picturetel .com	Live200	Multipoint	Full-duplex	Yes	H.320	$1495	Windows 95
Smart Technologies Inc.	http://www .smarttech .com	Smart 2000 Conferencing, Version 3.4	Multipoint	None	No	None	$299	Windows 3.1 Windows 95 Windows NT 3.5, 4.0
RSI Systems Inc.	http://www .rsisystems. com	Eris Visual Communications System	Point-to-point	Full-duplex	Yes	H.320	$3995	Windows 3.1 Windows 95 Mac System 7.0 and later
VocalTec Inc.	http://www .vocaltec .com	Internet Conference Professional 2.0	Multipoint (OLE only)	Full-duplex	No	None	$150	Windows 95 Windows 4.0

SOURCE: Courtesy of InfoWorld Publishing Company.

a technical novelty today. The likely prognosis over the next few years is that the advent of RSVP and increased enterprise network bandwidth (say, achieved with ATM WAN services) could give a boost to voice over IP.

References

1. Rivka Tadjer. "Web Commerce—Voice Over IP." *CMP Media Inc.* Issue 670 (June 30, 1997).
2. Microsoft ASF White Paper. www.microsoft.com.
3. Infonetics Research, Inc. Quality of Service White Paper. www.atminc.com.
4. ATIS Letter Ballot LB 526: "Transmission Performance Standards Issues." March, 1996.
5. Skip Pizzi and Steve Church. "Audio Webcasting Demystified." *Web Techniques Magazine* 2 (8).
6. L. Delgrossi and L. Berger. ST2 Working Group, Category: Experimental. August 1995.
7. News lead, *Sidney Morning Herald.* August 19, 1997.
8. *Yahoo! Technology News.* August 18, 1997.
9. R. Tadjer. "Tariffs Put Snarl in Carrier IP Plans." *Telepath* (September 1, 1997): 1 ff.
10. PictureTel. www.picturetel.com.
11. VocalTec Ltd. press release. www.vocaltec.com. November 12, 1996.

Notes

[1] Some portions of this chapter were contributed by G. Barisov, Senior Software Engineer, Wave Systems Corporation, Princeton, NJ.

[2] Based on personal communication with M. McLoughlin of GDC, September 1997.

[3]Extreme Networks, Inc., promotional material.

[4]Ibid.

[5]PVP is listed in RFC 1819, Internet Stream Protocol Version 2 (August 1995), and is based on a 1981 paper by R. Cole at the University of California, Los Angeles. Do not confuse this PVP (Packet Video Protocol) with the PVP (Packetized Voice Protocol) in Chapter 4 which is a voice protocol published by the ITV-T.

[6]Micom Communications Corp. promotional material.

[7]Micom Communications Corp. press release. September 3, 1996.

[8]In 1996, Internet Phone had nearly 79 percent, by revenue, of the consumer segment of the VOIP client market and the Telephony Gateway server had nearly 79 percent, by revenue, of the carrier market.

CHAPTER 7

Voice over the Internet Case Study: Benefits-Management Outsourcing

7.1 Introduction

This chapter provides both a description of how voice over the Internet can be utilized to open up new commercial opportunities in the areas of self-service, customer service, and other service-oriented functions, and a particular case study of the potential applicability of this technology to benefits-management outsourcing. The entire area of web commerce is exploding [1]. However, static Web sites are already becoming yesterday's news [2]. With the introduction of ITU-T H.320/323 PC multimedia and video-conferencing, dynamic Web-site access with voice and/or video and multimedia is expected to become rampant in the next few years [3]. Companies that understand these opportunities will prosper; other companies with a naive view of the technology may find themselves undone by agile, Internet-savvy cyberpreneurs.

With the inroads being made in corporate America by intranet and Internet technology, with workers' increased familiarity and ease with computer-based interfaces and applications, with consumers' desire for convenience and speed, payroll processing companies find themselves in an ideal position to capture what is expected to become a widely encompassing and likely lucrative market for human resources (HR) benefits outsourcing with online access capabilities. In addition, this strategy allows a payroll processing company to retain its competitive hold on employee's financial and related data in large and medium-sized firms, thereby thwarting the possibility that a dilution can occur over time with the gradual appearance of new niche providers who, upon rendering sideline benefits-management services at first, may later threaten a larger base of financially related functions, thereby developing the opportunity to erode a payroll processing company's traditional core business. On the flip side, however, it has been said that Web commerce is the great equalizer: With this technology, newer and smaller companies can compete effectively against larger and well-established companies and, possibly, take a nontrivial portion of their market share [1]. Also, there is a lot of interest on the part of many companies to outsource their noncore functions to specialty support organizations [4].

At the same time, some companies are not only looking at Internet-based services, but are using voice response over the Internet to support electronic commerce. As implied in the rest of this book, the use of IP/Internet audio is now poised to become prevalent in many industries. This chapter is simply one case study example of automatic data processing over the Internet, with which one of the authors was recently involved.[1]

The noteworthy fact in the synthesis of a such a digital product, supporting what is called *self-service*, is that a payroll processing company not only has the possibility of *creating* an entire new market, a new industry with new revenue and new employee-services opportunities—it has the potential of *owning* that nascent market. A payroll processing company can leverage its market presence in payroll services (specifically, generating paychecks for employees and handling the record-keeping and taxation responsibilities on behalf of the organization) into the broader HR functions (e.g., benefits management, record keeping, administration, etc.). This is done via intranet and Internet technology in general and via voice over the Internet in particular.

The payroll processing company product or service under development will here be branded TRACKER, for total records access/computer-kept repository. In order to successfully launch the program and to achieve targeted penetration levels for self-service capabilities via TRACKER, a payroll processing company needs to develop business strategies to leverage the existing relationships, the customer base, and the deployed systems and networking infrastructure. Clearly, computerized systems, running the informatics gamut (client software, access, networking, security, server, database management system, voice over IP, etc.), will be required to support this service. These will span both a payroll processing company and the target client organization.

Beyond technology, a payroll processing company will have to focus on marketing strategies and processes to execute the introduction of TRACKER in a synergistic, effective, and seamless manner. Target-audience-specific plans directed at employees, HR management, and payroll processing company telemarketers and salespeople have to be defined, documented, and socialized. In particular, an effective advertising campaign directed at the HR print media, coupled with telemarketing activities focused on prospective corporate segments, will be required.

Motivation for Voice-Enabled Web Commerce

This case study describes the opportunities and approaches for the introduction of a companion digital product to a payroll processing company's long-established core payroll processing service. This introduction supporting HR benefits self-service is made possible by the following:

1. The increased familiarity with, and availability of, graphical user interface–based computers, particularly PCs with Internet or intranet-originated browsers such as Netscape Navigator and Microsoft Explorer, along with the ease of use of a voice over Internet–based interface.
2. The consumers' desire for convenience, particularly 365×24 access to financial information.
3. The evolution toward employee-managed benefits, such as 401k, pension plan contributions and flexible reimbursement accounts (FRAs).
4. The corporate desire to streamline operations, to outsource noncore functions, and to increase the service scope to

employees by pooling resources and achieving economies of scale that are doable with multicompany aggregation facilitated by outsourcing.

5. The simplicity of concept and execution, possible with a turnkey system that does not require the target company to develop software, establish servers, and maintain rapidly obsolescing computer technology.

6. The ability of payroll processing companies to rely on Web-hosting organizations (such as TCG CERFnet), which package the establishment of cached nationwide Web servers in a rapid and cost-effective manner, thereby building the distributed Internet-based infrastructure needed for the rollout of the product. This same method can be utilized to support intranets of national reach, by letting the hosting carrier host the intranet server and establishing a virtual private network (VPN) over the Internet, thereby effectively extending the corporate intranet.

TRACKER could be deployed as a packaged product targeted to midsize companies that have neither the resources nor the desire to develop intranetlike technology for HR purposes and maintain the underlying data with a high level of integrity, security, and accessibility. The company's information will be centrally kept by the payroll processing company and will be accessible over access telecommunication facilities (e.g., the Internet) that extend an organization's enterprise network on a dedicated or on-demand (dial-up) basis. The same level of integrity and security that is the identifying mark of a payroll processing company in its payroll business is provided for the outsourced benefits data.

TRACKER supports the concept of ASAP: any service, any place—any second, any person. It lets employees be in touch with all of their benefits and company services, from any location, with one integrated and easy-to-follow interface.

After presenting additional background information, this case study addresses the three key components of a benefits-management outsourcing undertaking (Section 7.2). The chapter then addresses the leverageable resources that play in favor of a payroll processing company in entering this market and that must be capitalized upon in order to achieve rapid time-to-market deployment (Section 7.3).

Section 7.4 addresses the system synthesis, including interfaces, platforms, networking, server, and database technology. Section 7.5 addresses the marketing issues associated with launching TRACKER, which must not be underemphasized if there is to be a successful and financially rewarding deployment. Finally, Section 7.6 addresses rollout issues, including launch teams, telemarketing initiatives, and so forth.

Additional Background

It has long been recognized that offering a broad range of benefits that support both the employee and the worker's family enlarges the employee's pool, boosts morale, improves attendance, positively impacts productivity, better disposes the employee's outlook toward the ultimate customer, and enhances talent retention. Employee benefits cost corporations a considerable amount of actual money. Benefits for the average employee cost $14,659 in 1995, according to the U.S. Chamber of Commerce. Vacation, holidays, and rest periods covered 30 percent; health-related benefits covered 25 percent; legal mandates (FICA, unemployment, etc.) covered 21 percent; retirement and saving plans covered 18 percent; miscellaneous other covered 5 percent; and life insurance covered 1 percent. Of the health-benefit portion, 68 percent went for employee medical, 16 percent for retiree medical, 4 percent for short-term disability, 2 percent for long-term disability, 5 percent for dental insurance, and 5 percent for other (e.g., vision care) [5]. Therefore, it is well worth it to the company to make this information as visible to the employee as possible. Hence, a self-service system enjoys a range of advantages, including increased employee awareness of the worth of such company-provided benefits.

Areas that can be additionally supported by TRACKER's Web-based data/voice service include the following:

- Personal HR records, such as home address, telephone number, dependents, beneficiaries, and so forth (for example, addresses often change, and various departments in the corporation could have old addresses)
- Training and continuing education courses taken by the employee

- Vacation plan, sick days, and so forth (with management countersignature)
- 401k investment options, plans, contributions, vested amounts, withdrawals, pension plans, and actual compensation afforded the employee (including employer's share of FICA)
- Value of incentive plans, such as company stock options, stock grants, and related portfolio
- Elected benefits options, costs, available but unelected services, and so forth
- Dependent care reimbursement, health maintenance organization (HMO) network participants or services, fee-for-services reimbursements, and so forth
- Status of FRA and other flexible care accounts
- Paper or electronic forms to download to affect benefits and parameter changes, and so forth
- Keyword-indexed benefits manual

Company-provided benefits have become more difficult to understand as the number of features and options grows. One example is the FRA. Experts now recommend the use of a *virtual HR department* that employees can call up from any desktop or from any home PC. Voice support over the intranet or Internet will be particularly useful. In general, it is difficult to have ready access to this information, as it often either is available only in paper form across multiple subdepartments, or has been outsourced to various providers in a piecemeal fashion.

An online system, particularly one that is easy to use, install, and maintain, provides optimum access to this vital information. In turn, this can be viewed as another worthwhile benefit that the company provides to its workforce, in that it relieves the employee from having to address benefits issues directly to the HR department face-to-face—often at headquarters—and from being able to do so only during business hours. Rather than having to put off a decision while waiting to pick up a form at work or to have it mailed, the employee can get control of the benefits package and act on a lifestyle decision in real time. Some companies have outsourced some of these services to specialty houses, with limited employee access—if anything, access is provided over interactive voice response (IVR); traditional IVR, however, is slow, inefficient, and limited. The use of interactive computer-based voice response (ICVR) will greatly enhance the user's experience and ease of use. To support these functions, the voice over data network technologies described in this book will be required.

Specific to the situation of this case study, technology-enabled self-service capabilities are now viewed as critical to the future success of the HR department. Voice-enabled Web service will go a long way toward making self-services commercially successful. However, companies require a turnkey system that enables them to focus on core competencies instead of having to become system, application, and network integrators and technologists in order to launch these capabilities. Furthermore, all who have developed intranets or Web sites recognize that the largest portion of the overall project effort is in maintaining the data on site in an up-to-date fashion after it has been launched. A host of niche providers is expected to enter the market within a year of this publication. A payroll processing company must act now to secure this market.

Intranet or Internet based systems have the capability to revolutionize HR. Web access (text-based and/or voice/multimedia-based) gives employees more control, while enabling HR analysts to minimize or eliminate clerical and administrative tasks and step into more strategic roles. The intranet or Internet has the greatest potential to fundamentally alter the way HR services are provided to employees, particularly in conjunction with voice (ICVR) and multimedia. Usually, dozens of forms need to be filled out and kept up to date in conjunction with employment. Online forms management increases convenience and all-around productivity. Collection, updating, and viewing of the data is facilitated, while the user-friendly interfaces (data- and voice-based) eliminate the overhead of accessing a variety of distinct databases (each with its own touch and feel), while improving dissemination and analysis of the data. Mobile, remote, and virtual employees, in particular, gain immediate benefits.

There are now hundreds of thousands of Web sites—25,000 in health-related fields alone [6]. Many of these are offered by medical institutions. But there are also burgeoning offerings from insurers, managed care companies, consulting firms, HR professionals, trade associations, think tanks, and policy agencies. This supply of sites is simply a testament to the appetite for online access to information (e.g., www.benefitslink.com is an online benefits resource linked to numerous newsletters and magazines; www.eease.com describes the advantages of Internet and intranet technology geared to benefits outsourcing).

Clients are looking to systems such as TRACKER to remove barriers to information flow and establish a self-service environment where the HR staff, as well as the employees, can easily access and share information. The principle that satisfied employees in turn satisfy customers applies. TRACKER is one novel component of an overall employee-benefits package. It builds on the partnership idea and aims to improve employee satisfaction. There are a lot of HR software and online decision support tools out there that aim to automate various aspects of record and benefits management. However, TRACKER is more than just discrete software: It is a complete end-to-end turnkey service that supports input; local and remote access, data storage, maintenance, and integrity; and systematic linkage across various company applications.

Voice-based TRACKER empowers employees, as well as managers, to make better financial decisions with regard to benefits-related matters. It allows the HR department to engineer what information is needed to be available where and to decide how it can be effectively delivered across the enterprise (which is increasingly becoming more distributed).

Today, HR organizations often have duplicate data: the payroll data and the general administrative data. This results in duplication, extra effort, and inconsistencies. Another typical problem is retrieving the data from distinct and heterogeneous systems and then trying to consolidate it in a cohesive fashion, often with the help of external software tools. The wish-list sought by HR management is for automation that can streamline administrative functions by: (1) moving employee information management and use to employees and appropriate managers via self-service intranet or Internet technology, kiosks, or ICVR; (2) decreasing the benefits administration burden; and (3) speeding up communication and process dissemination and implementation through online technology that supports workflow, enterprisewide connectivity, and data exchange across multiple legacy systems. As a state-of-the-art HR system, TRACKER not only eliminates redundancies, but also provides a consistent and linked view of the corporate repository of HR-related data; it also provides for import/export capabilities using standardized mechanisms and a way to move that information across the intranet and/or enterprise network, including to virtual-corporation employees and telecommuters. The need for human interaction is thereby minimized.

7.2 Key Components of Benefits-Management Outsourcing

Industry analysts say that the keys to better business are automating wherever possible, outsourcing whenever appropriate, and enabling employees and managers to access (even manipulate) information as defined by their needs. At least in the context of benefits management, the scope of the user's transaction is generally well understood, it being a query against a set of benefits or employee record data, and perhaps an update. TRACKER utilizes WWW technologies, including voice over the Internet, to streamline HR administrative tasks by providing self-service applications (employees update their own records). However, instead of being just a shift of administrative responsibilities, it can be seen as opening up whole new conveniences for employees. Capabilities also include online consulting (again, with voice over the Internet or voice over IP).

Possible players in this market need to understand three key components of the digital service supported by TRACKER: the *market*, the *services*, and the *systems*.

Although HR tools have seen a constantly evolving suite of technologies in recent years—e-mail, client/servers, and workflow systems—only the intranet and Internet combination offers the opportunity for truly paperless transactions and interactivity, especially with voice and multimedia. Analysts see synergistic advantages in integrated benefit and payroll systems. In streamlining HR's administrative functions and placing many of them in the hands of employees (and/or line managers), where they naturally belong, the HR department (freed from data collection and record keeping) can focus on corporate trends analysis and strategic decision making. In effect, the HR department can do more with less. Hence, analysts see the rapid adoption of self-service client/server systems, including workflow-, groupware-, and intranet/Internet-based HRMSs.[2]

A payroll processing company must capture this market opportunity at this time, before niche entrants saturate the space.

The discussion provided in Section 7.1, along with secondary research conducted by McKensey and, most important, primary market research in the form of focus groups, shows that there is interest on both the employer and employee side. The market is sizable, including medium-sized companies with 75 to 999 associates. Employers quote the advantages of streamlining, focusing on core competencies, and freeing the HR department to pursue more strategic initiatives (e.g., ways of retaining, retraining, compensating, incentivizing, and recognizing employees, while at the same time offering competitive salaries—neither too high nor too low). Employees cite convenience, single point of contact, ability to address employee-specific questions, hassle-free and data-rich interactions, and ease of interaction via voice-enabled Web browsers. A payroll processing company must specifically recognize the existence of these two components to the market and direct attention to each individually, but within the same context of self-service support.

Beyond the basic concept of outsourced online access to records synergistically linked to the existing payroll data, a payroll processing company must address the specific services to be provided by TRACKER. These include the following:

For employers and HR departments:

- Outsourcing to a payroll processing company—stored, secure, and reliable benefits data, linked to payroll data. The data is kept up to date by a payroll processing company at the functional level, but with input from the firm's HR department and from the employees.
- Fully integrated solution by a payroll processing company: turnkey platforms, applications, networking, access, and user software.
- Specific applications subsets (from a menu, including, e.g., employee records, elected benefits, 401k status, etc.).
- Service features (e.g., fully outsourced, partially outsourced, service center support for employees, geographic scope, redundancy options, etc.).
- Service access mechanisms for both employees and the HR department (e.g., on-LAN intranet only, Internet-

accessible intranet, dedicated line, dial-up, update privileges, reporting capabilities, etc.).

- Pricing options, bundling, one-time versus recurring, size/activity dependencies, and so forth. This will be tied to a menu of service level agreements (SLAs) that can be selected by the employer.

For employees:

- What information is available online.
- What ancillary assistance is available online (e.g., voice over the Internet or intranet and access to the centralized assistance center).
- How information can be accessed, including software for home-PC loading, toll-free dial-in, Internet access numbers, and so forth.

To deliver self-services, a variety of front-end and back-end systems are required. At the most fundamental level, a payroll processing company must understand, develop, commercialize, and shrink-wrap the technology needed. This includes all the basic and employer cross-application software, the database management system, the presentation server software, the network access system on a payroll processing company site or Web-hosting company (this includes LAN extension technologies for companies wanting to physically extend their intranets, including firewalling, and Internet access technologies for companies relying on the Internet), and the company's and the company employee's software. In this context, a payroll processing company must make a *build-versus-buy* decision. The recommendation of many industry observers is to rely on as much off-the-shelf, standards-based software as possible.

As noted, the target company also needs to install TRACKER software on its designated servers and employee PCs, laptops, and home computers.

On the TRACKER-marketing level, a payroll processing company needs to be able to articulate the complexity and issues associated with developing an in-house solution to the prospective company, thereby extolling the advantages of outsourcing that service. Payroll processing company salespeople and telemarketers may have to be prepared to discuss the build-versus-buy case with the prospective user, emphasizing the advantages of contracting for the service in a complete end-to-end fashion, along with SLA choices.

7.3 Example: ADP Inc.

A company such as ADP Inc. can enter such a market by leveraging its existing relationships and infrastructure. ADP is the nation's largest provider of fully integrated human resource, benefit, and payroll solutions. Founded in 1949, ADP is one of the world's largest independent computing services firms, with 29,000 associates and more than $3.9 billion in revenue.

ADP already has a quasi-captive customer base, built over its core payroll processing services. Specifically, ADP Employer Services Division business solutions are already used to manage HR and benefits by more than 6000 employers, to pay 22 million wage earners worldwide, and to issue 35 million W-2 and earnings summaries every year to U.S. employers. ADP has been a leading HRMS vendor since the mid-1980s. ADP's offerings already serve the diverse needs of more than 6000 companies having 75 to 75,000 employees.

Several recent acquisitions have strengthened ADP's position in providing end-to-end HR, benefit, and payroll services. For example, benefits outsourcing was the focus of the Health Benefits America (HBA) acquisition. HBA, considered the country's leading benefits-management firm, provides health network management services, employee communications, and outsourced benefits administration for large companies. For many of its clients, HBA becomes the benefits department, providing all customer service.

ADP's philosophy is to combine software, outsourcing, and services into fully integrated end-to-end solutions. For companies with more than 1000 employees, ADP's CCS HRizon software is the basis for a family of products and HRMS solutions. CCS HRizon is a technologically advanced, easy-to-use, fully integrated client/server HRMS. For smaller companies, ADP has developed a series of new software products that run on client/servers and Microsoft Windows, while at the same time continuing to support its established products.

CCS HRizon can run on the client's machine or can be integrated with ADP payroll services. Databases such as Oracle, Informatix, and SQLBase are supported. Version 7.0 includes the industry's first embedded employee self-service function, plus workflow technology, position and compensation management, and training and development. The purpose of a system such as

TRACKER is to extend these services to medium-size companies with 75 to 999 employees. The use of user-friendly interfaces, such as voice-based Web access, can go a long way toward making such a product successful.

The existing self-service capability lets employees access information in two ways: either through a standalone kiosk in a nonoffice environment, or through a LAN-connected desktop via a Windows icon. The purpose of a system such as TRACKER is to extend access to the home or to dispersed (non-LAN-connected) home-office employees, using Internet and intranet technology in general, and Web-based voice in particular, to support lively interaction with the end user.

All of ADP's HRMS solutions are integrated with AutoPay payroll services, which allow clients to take advantage of ADP's outsourced payroll and other services, including payroll tax filing, direct deposit, unemployment cost management, and benefits administration.

ADP also offers an Alliance service, a new implementation option wherein ADP takes complete responsibility for providing, implementing, and supporting a client's HRMS, including the hardware, database (Oracle), and application software. This solution is designed for large companies that want the latest technology and HRMS functionality, but do not want to invest in client/server infrastructure. At its own facilities, ADP will install and retain responsibility for the operating system, database, and CCS HRizon application; the client's LAN or WAN is connected to ADP through a communications facility. ADP's Application Group provides all necessary implementation and maintenance services, including those typically handled by the client's in-house IT staff. Services include customization, performance tuning, database security, administration, and database and application software upgrades.

The goal of a system such as TRACKER is to utilize the same model in the self-service arena, but for down-market customers—namely, to shrink-wrap a system (with hardware, software, application, and access) for smaller companies that do not have the resources or the interest to make their own technology investments. Smaller companies have the same problems as large ones, but fewer resources to tackle them.

A new Microsoft Office–based product, HR/Perspective, offers smaller companies the same information management and analytical tools previously available only to large companies. It allows clients to arrange their HR information to replicate their actual organizational structure.

As noted, ADP may already have an outsourcing arrangement with a company, and thereby already have that company's data, communications connectivity, contracts, and SLAs. If ADP does not have a formal outsourcing arrangement with the company, but handles its payroll, it already has some of the company's data and has an existing business arrangement. If ADP has no relationship at all with the company in question, perhaps the basket of integrated payroll and benefit services might entice this corporation to become a new customer of ADP.

A payroll company has already made significant investments in data processing technologies, systems, and networking. The payroll company should clearly capitalize on this existing system and data infrastructure. Specifically, this infrastructure provides the payroll company a spring-board for the development of the necessary TRACKER informatics capabilities; it provides the outsourcer a set of core competencies and confidence to attack the project; and it provides a competitive advantage over the competition in terms of baseline capabilities, speed-to-market, experience, channels, technology supplier relationships, and overall industry know-how. Furthermore, the outsourcer may be able to cite and emphasize multidecade experience in selling, marketing, and advertising the service, to gain the mind-share of the prospective company.

7.4 System Synthesis

An integrated approach to delivering and marketing business is key to success. Companies are now focusing on global competitiveness and core competencies [4]. With the rapid pace at which new hardware, software, and networking technology is changing, corporations do not want to have to invest the technology and project-management resources required to deploy yet another broad-coverage system. A payroll processing company needs to suitcase the entire TRACKER deployment and the initial data acquisition, verification, and databasing.

Systems and technology for TRACKER have to be selected correctly by a payroll processing company in order to achieve both cost-effectiveness and speed to market. Generally, technology selection focuses on the following areas:

- Necessary technical features, including standards support
- Reliability and scalability
- Manageability
- Vendor strength (as related to technology providers)
- Pricing (initial and recurring) and terms and conditions

Analytical selection techniques based on list a of decision factors that are subareas within these key areas are indeed practical when looking at a single product category. TRACKER needs a whole range of products, therefore producing a Cartesian-product decision space and making the overall process more challenging; nonetheless, analytical methodologies will still have to be applied. A payroll processing company will need to select technology and systems in such areas as the following:

- Back-end and database, specifically hardware platforms, operating systems, DBMs, Internet or intranet server software, and Common Gateway Interface (CGI)–like access to legacy systems (company- or client-owned) must be selected. DBMs such as Oracle, Informatix, and SQLBase, should be considered.
- ICVR technology (voice over the Internet and/or intranet) should be secured. In addition, QoS-enabled Internet services (e.g., RSVP) should be explored.
- Front-end and interface, specifically user platforms, operating systems, Internet or intranet browser software (e.g., Windows, Windows 95, NT, Explorer, and Netscape) must be selected.
- Communications and networking infrastructure for both the intranet extension and the Internet access cases. This also includes the communication apparatus for both the payroll processing company end and the customer or employee end. The payroll processing company may want to consider broadband transparent LAN services (such as provided by TCG). This analysis may also include an assessment of Web-hosting services (such as those provided by TCG CERFnet). If voice over IP and voice over Internet are considered for call and

service centers, then the appropriate server-end and client-end (HR department and employee) software and hardware must be selected and suitcased.

An increasing variety of Internet access technologies have evolved in the recent past to support intranet extensions, including dial-up dedicated line, cable modems, ADSL, and frame and cell access. A payroll processing company needs to identify an access technology menu that is based on the target company's service profile, throughput requirements, size, Internet or intranet architecture, security requirements, and willingness to pay.

7.5 Marketing Issues

Although the challenges associated with the development of a feature-rich system such as TRACKER are significant due to the breadth of the system and communications issues of the undertaking, marketing and sales issues should not be underestimated. As noted, a payroll processing company starts out in a position of strength, given the existing customer base and long-standing reputation. However, outsourcing decisions are always difficult for the company affected, because of the ultimate staffing implications. Therefore, it is incumbent upon a payroll processing company to have a solid marketing and sales strategy.

In particular, a payroll processing company needs to define the market it wants to own; possibly a multitiered approach can be used, identifying first the most likely prospects, then the midprobability prospects, and finally the lower-probability prospects. Such tiering can be done geographically, be based on a vertical industry segment, or be based on the kinds of payroll processing services already utilized by the prospective company. In defining a downscale market, a payroll processing company needs to place both an upper bound and a lower bound on an appropriate company metric, whether this be number of employees, annual revenue, or technological savvyness. An initial target range may be 75 to 999 employees, but then the tiering overlay just described needs to be defined.

The market identification in specific terms gives rise to specific strategies, tactics, and execution plans. This should include a coordinated sales-visit and media blitz. Based on the tier, customer contact may be through an on-site visit by a traditional salesperson or by a telemarketing call. Trade shows can also be utilized. A service prospectus, along with a marketing guide, needs to be developed. Exact TRACKER service definitions; SLAs; pricing; company informatics, HR, and baseline data requirements; technology elements required for deployment; benefits versus trade-offs and short-term versus long-term impacts; and the competitive advantages of outsourcing all need to be documented in the marketing guide, so that the sales force can prepare itself and immediately be effective on customer calls. Scenarios and illustrative case studies should be included in the guide. Functions-based individuals to be sold the service need to be identified in the guide. The guide should also contain basic technology tutorials, glossaries, and sample methods, checklists, and talking points for HR individuals in target companies, such as IT managers, networking managers, and possibly even CTOs (these may be new people to be brought on board, in addition to the traditional finance people normally involved in a payroll-only decision). On-site sales training must be set up for rapid field familiarization with the new product and its features.

A payroll processing company should also consider technology to sell the new service. So, in addition to targeted print media, radio and TV, trade shows, and direct sales force calls, a company can use multimedia mailers, Web sites, and desktop sampler software. Of all these demonstration alternatives, a live Internet or intranet demo with ICBV and multimedia may be the most compelling for prospective HR customers.

7.6 Rollout Issues

While the technical side of the house may have its hands full with the traditional software development and system and network integration, it is important that services planners develop a rollout plan well in advance of the actual release of the product to either the general market or even to an alpha customer or partner. Naturally, this plan will have to be fine-tuned as experience with both the technical aspects of the product and the market or target reaction are empirically acquired.

It may be appropriate to set up separate subject matter expert (SME) teams to address the various aspects of the product launch. (Such a team may, in fact, be a virtual team, and may eventually also involve people from the friendly user.) This enables a payroll processing company to leverage niche expertise and use best-in-class methods, rather than have novices, who may perhaps be intimately familiar with a specific aspect of the technology, make policy decisions about other aspects where they may only have a superficial understanding. Teams should include people with expertise in the following areas:

- System and application development, including database technology
- Platform development
- Networking technologies development
- Call center development and management
- Service development, marketing strategies, launch, collateral development, media, and advertising
- Alpha customer program management

Telemarketers need to be given effective scripts and be given decision-making contacts to call. The goals and parameters of the campaign have to be defined in specific terms in the product launch plan.

These methods will also be applicable to many other Web-based services.

7.7 Conclusion

With the advances in PC and intranet technology, along with voice and video over data networks (including the Internet), and their widespread deployment, in conjunction with payroll processing companys' possible account ownership at the payroll processing level, such a company may find itself in an ideal position to capture the HR benefits-outsourcing and self-service market at this time. In addition, this allows a payroll processing company to retain its competitive hold on financial and related data of large and medium-sized firms, or may allow an an upstart payroll processing company to erode the market share of embedded providers, thereby *owning* that nascent market. A payroll processing company needs to understand the market, the services to be rendered, and the systems required to deliver those services in a cost-effective and quick-to-market manner. Each of the various corporate constituencies involved in the product must be individually addressed by the company's product introduction plan. The company also needs to develop strategies to leverage the existing relationships, the customer base, and the deployed infrastructure. Beyond technology, the company will have to focus on marketing strategies and processes to execute the introduction of TRACKER in a synergistic, effective, rapid, and seamless manner. In particular, an effective advertising campaign directed at HR print media, coupled with telemarketing focused on prospective corporate segments, will be required. An effective approach is to use the technology itself (specifically, a live multimedia ICVR Internet or intranet demo) to sell new systems-based business solutions.[3]

References

1. D. Minoli and E. Minoli. *Web Commerce Handbook.* New York: McGraw-Hill, 1998.
2. D. Minoli. *Internet and Intranet Engineering.* New York: McGraw-Hill, 1997.
3. D. Minoli. *QoS-Enabled Communications.* New York: McGraw-Hill, 1998.
4. D. Minoli. *Analyzing Outsourcing.* New York: McGraw-Hill, 1995.
5. *Business & Health* (February 1997): 64.
6. *Business & Health* (February 1997): 41–42.

Notes

[1]The authors wish to thank J. Dressendofer of IMEDIA, Morristown, NJ, for the assistance provided in this project.

[2]For example, refer to *Human Resource Executive* (November 15, 1996): 12–17.

[3]Other references utilized in preparing this chapter include: (1) *Business & Health* (1996 and 1997 issues), (2) *Workforce* (formerly *Personnel Journal*; 1996 and 1997 issues), (3) *Human Resource Executive* (1996 and 1997 issues), (4) *HR Magazine* (1996 and 1997 issues), (5) *ACA News* (1996 and 1997 issues), and (6) *Employee Benefits Journal* (1996 and 1997 issues).

Case Study: Lucent Technologies' Internet Telephony Server—SP (ITS-SP)

A.1 Introduction

This appendix provides some detailed information on a leading server-based VOIP product, for illustrative purposes. The Lucent Technologies' network-based Internet telephony solution includes a hop-on/hop-off functionality that merges the traditional public switched telephone network (PSTN), the Internet, and other data packet networks.* Figures A.1 through A.4 depict typical applications.

Lucent's Internet telephony solution is based on the Internet Telephony Server—SP (ITS-SP) hardware and software platform upon which several applications are being offered, including Internet voice telephony and Internet FAX. The ITS-SP optimizes the economics of the PSTN and other TCP/IP-based data networks (e.g., Frame Relay, ATM, intranets, etc.) to deliver voice message traffic conveniently, inexpensively, and reliably. This includes a traditional phone-to-phone conversation and fax-to-fax voice types of transmission. Future releases will provide Computer-phone interfaces.

*This material is included with permission from Lucent Technologies.

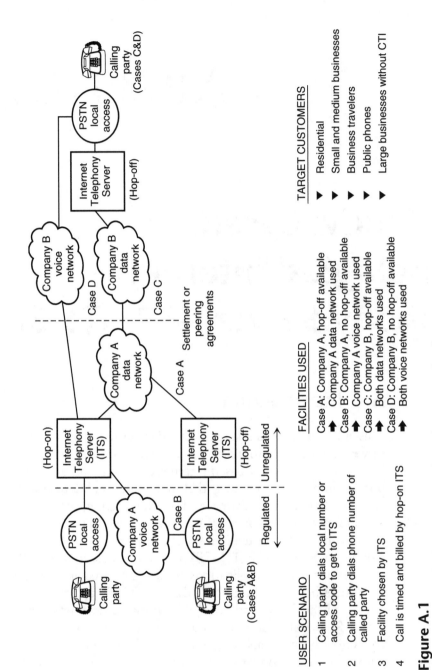

USER SCENARIO

1 Calling party dials local number or access code to get to ITS
2 Calling party dials phone number of called party
3 Facility chosen by ITS
4 Call is timed and billed by hop-on ITS

FACILITIES USED

Case A: Company A, hop-off available
        Company A data network used
Case B: Company A, no hop-off available
        Company A voice network used
Case C: Company B, hop-off available
        Both data networks used
Case D: Company B, no hop-off available
        Both voice networks used

TARGET CUSTOMERS

▶ Residential
▶ Small and medium businesses
▶ Business travelers
▶ Public phones
▶ Large businesses without CTI

Figure A.1
Second brand telephony service—long-distance or local.

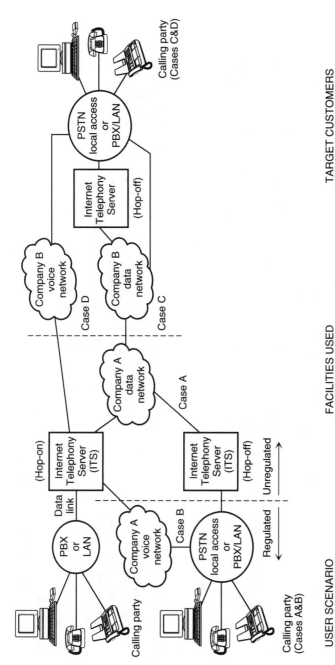

TARGET CUSTOMERS

► Large businesses without CTI

FACILITIES USED

Case A: Company A, hop-off available
    Company A data network used
Case B: Company A, no hop-off available
    Company A voice network used
Case C: Company B, hop-off available
    Both data networks used
Case D: Company B, no hop-off available
    Both voice networks used

USER SCENARIO

1 Calling party dials as they do today.
2 Corporation administrator sets call routing policy.
3 ITS screens all data packets.
4 Voice and fax packets stripped off and routed according to policy.
5 Calls are timed and billed by hop-on ITS.

Figure A.2

Flexible routing enterprise service for voice, data, fax, and voice messaging.

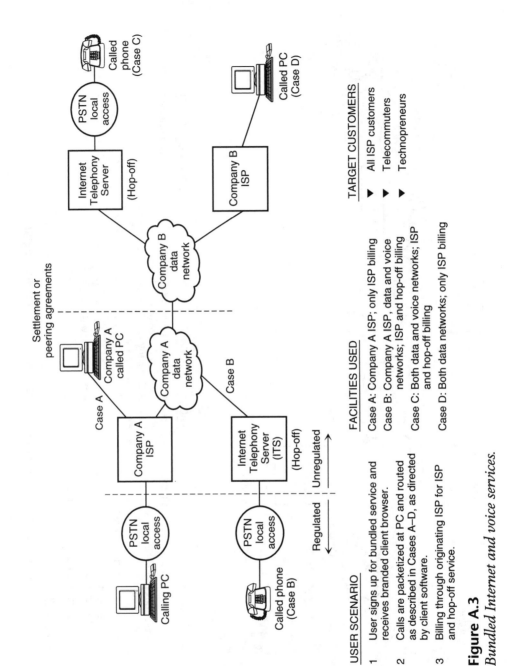

USER SCENARIO

1 User signs up for bundled service and receives branded client browser.

2 Calls are packetized at PC and routed as described in Cases A–D, as directed by client software.

3 Billing through originating ISP for ISP and hop-off service.

FACILITIES USED

Case A: Company A ISP; only ISP billing

Case B: Company A ISP, data and voice networks; ISP and hop-off billing

Case C: Both data and voice networks; ISP and hop-off billing

Case D: Both data networks; only ISP billing

TARGET CUSTOMERS

► All ISP customers
► Telecommuters
► Technopreneurs

Figure A.3
Bundled Internet and voice services.

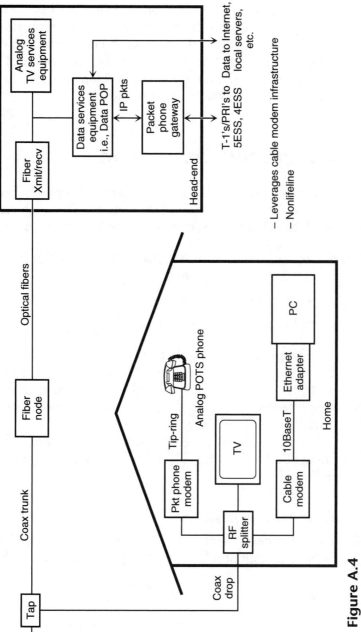

Figure A.4
Cable modems and packet telephony—alternate local access for voice.

259

The Internet telephony solution employs Lucent intellectual property to provide a higher-quality voice transmission, in addition to voice and fax transmission over the network of choice. By leveraging a scalable platform, and incorporating application programming interfaces (APIs), the Internet telephony solution provides an evolution path to value-added services.

A.2 Product Description

The basic configuration for the Internet Telephony Server is the single T1/E1 termination unit (see Figure A.5), which can be ordered as T1-based or E1-based, and has the following features:

- Supports 24 bearer DS0s if T1, or 30 DS0s if E1
- Requires a single T1 or E1 circuit
- Table top or rack-mounted (19″)
- 115/230 VAC power supplies

The product is scalable to 144 bearer channels by stacking multiple units within the same rack. Thus, six T1 or E1 termination units, providing 144 channels if T1 or 180 channels if E1, can be supported in a single rack. Each termination unit requires its own T1/E1 circuit (see Figure A.6).

The ITS-SP will receive incoming PSTN calls and generate outgoing PSTN calls using T1 or E1s. A typical configuration is shown in Figure A.7.

Channel Independence

Each channel is independent of others. Each channel may support both voice calls and fax calls. The port will dynamically determine

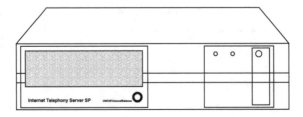

Figure A.5
Single T1/E1 termination unit.

Figure A.6
Six stacked T1/E1 termination units.

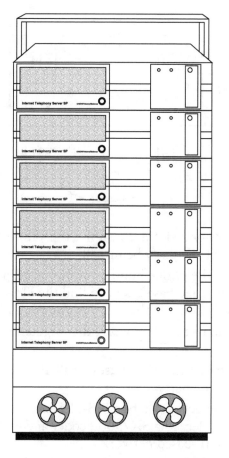

the type of call being placed. Thus, the ports do not have to be reserved or configured as voice-only or fax-only ports.

Operations Sequence

To introduce the features and configurations of the Internet Telephony Server, the steps required to establish a ITS-SP based call are summarized in the following.

Voice Calls

- The consumer uses PSTN to dial the local ITS-SP.
- The ITS-SP (i.e., the originating ITS-SP) answers the call on an incoming T1 and prompts the user for an authorization number.

Figure A.7
Typical ITS-SP configuration.

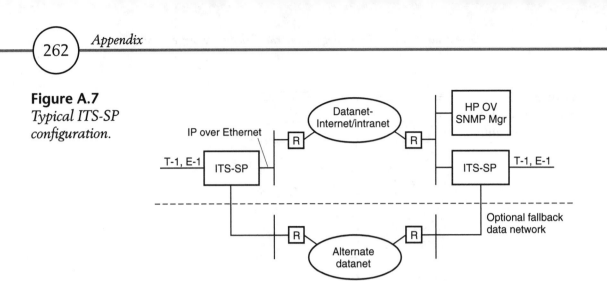

- Once authorized, the consumer is prompted for the phone number of the party being called.
- Based on the phone number of the called party, the ITS-SP performs a database query to find the ITS-SP that will most effectively connect the call (i.e., the terminating ITS-SP).
- Using the IP-based network, the originating ITS-SP contacts the terminating ITS-SP.
- The terminating ITS-SP uses its T1 to dial the phone number of the called party.
- Once connected, the two ITS-SPs encode/decode the voice using the elemedia SX7300P coder and exchange the packets using the IP-based network.
- Each ITS-SP keeps statistics on each call, collects billing information, and monitors call quality. If call quality falls below a given threshold, the call can be routed to a secondary data network, if available.

Fax Calls

The exact sequence will depend specifically on the fax machines used. In general, the sequence will be as follows:

- The consumer lifts the fax handset.
- The consumer uses PSTN to dial the local ITS-SP via the fax machine's keypad.
- The ITS-SP (i.e., the originating ITS-SP) answers the call on an incoming T1 and prompts the user for an authorization number.

- The consumer is prompted for an authorization code, and then the fax number of the party being called.
- Based on the phone number of the called party, the ITS-SP performs a database query to find the ITS-SP that will most effectively connect the call (i.e., the terminating ITS-SP).
- Using the IP-based network, the originating ITS-SP contacts the terminating ITS-SP.
- The terminating ITS-SP uses its T1 to dial the phone number of the called party.
- Meanwhile, the user presses the fax START button and replaces the handset.
- Upon reception of the fax tone initiated by the receiving fax machine, the originating fax machine begins fax transmission.
- The two ITS-SPs encode/decode the fax and exchange the packets using the IP-based network.
- Each ITS-SP keeps statistics on each call, collects billing information, and monitors call quality. If call quality falls below a given threshold, the call can be routed to a secondary data network, if available.

Incoming/Outgoing PSTN Trunk Specifications

The specification for each T1 interface is:

- T1 interface with D4 framing (1.544 Mbps)

The specification for each E1 interface is:

- E1 interface with ITU-T G.704 framing (2.048 Mbps)

The network interfaces should provide the following capabilities:

- North American Numbering Plan (NANP), International, and/or private network dialing schemes

ITS-SP User Authentication

A user authorization interface will be provided to prohibit unauthorized access to the ITS-SP. For connections originating from the PSTN (i.e., public connections), users should be required to enter an authorization number (up to 20 digits). This number will be used to identify the user for authorization and billing purposes. Private network numbering plans can also be supported.

Inter-ITS-SP Call Routing

The ITS-SP will provide the mechanisms that will enable an originating ITS-SP to locate a terminating ITS-SP that best meets the business needs of customers. The ITS-SP database will contain at least three fields for each terminating ITS-SP:

```
ipaddr/name; Number served; Comment
```

where:

- `ipaddr/name` is the IP address or machine name, as found in the DNS, of the terminating ITS-SP.
- `Number served` is most significant digits of the called number. In the NANP, `Number served` can be of two formats: NPA-NXX or NPA. For international dialing, `Number served` can be of two formats: Country Code–City Code or Country Code.
- `Comment` field.

Given the following entries:

ITS-SP1; 908-582; ILEC
ITS-SP2; 908; GTE
ITS-SP3; 201-386; ILEC
ITS-SP4; 201; MCI
ITS-SP5; 215; AT&T

calls destined for area code 908 will go to ITS-SP2, unless specifically destined for area code 908, exchange 582 in which case they will go to ITS-SP1. Similarly, calls to 201-386 will go to ITS-SP3 while the rest of the calls to area code 201 will go to ITS-SP4. Calls destined for area codes not provided for in the table will receive a verbal error message and be asked to reenter the destination number.

Applications may be altered using the API interface (see the "API Interface" subsection following) to make use of the comment field to customize the routing algorithm.

Inter-ITS-SP Connectivity

Each ITS-SP will be connected to the data network using 10BaseT Ethernet cards and RJ45 connectors. All traffic over this interface will use the TCP/IP or UDP/IP protocols.

Each ITS-SP will require the following IP-related items:

- IP address
- Machine name known to the domain name server (DNS)

SX7300P Speech Coder

The SX7300P coder is a member of the elemedia product family. Key characteristics of the SX7300P coder are shown in Table A.1. These characteristics enable the ITS-SP to deliver high-quality voice with low CPU overhead.

Call Detail Record Logging

To support the generation of billing records and other gateway statistics, information will be collected at both the originating and terminating gateways, as follows. Call 1 refers to the PSTN to the originating gateway connection. Call 2 refers to the communication between the two gateways. Call 3 refers to the terminating gateway to the PSTN connection. All times and dates are GMT.

This information is stored on the local hard disk drive of each ITS-SP. The data format will be provided. The extraction of this data and its subsequent integration into a customer billing system is outside the scope of this trial.

Collected at originating gateway
- Call 1 arrival time at originating gateway
- Call 1 truck group ID and circuit ID

Table A.1 SX7300P Coder Characteristics

Parameter	*Value*
Rate	7.3 kbps
Frame size	15 ms
Echo cancellation	Yes

- Call 1 answer time at originating gateway
- Calling party number (if available)
- Dialed number (if available)
- Authorization number entered
- User ID validated as XXX
- Destination number entered by user
- Type of coder used
- Selected egress gateway (IP address and interfacing carrier)
- Time Call 2 setup sent
- Time Call 2 connect received
- Time voice path was initiated
- Number of packets received
- Number of voice samples received
- Number of voice bytes received
- Call 1 disconnect time
- Call 1 disconnect reason
- Call 2 disconnect time
- Call 2 disconnect reason

Collected at terminating gateway

- Time Call 2 setup received
- Call 2 originating gateway and interfacing carrier
- Time Call 3 setup sent
- Time Call 3 connect received
- Time Call 2 connect sent
- Time voice path initiated
- Number of packets received
- Number of voice samples received
- Number of voice bytes received
- Call 3 disconnect time
- Call 3 disconnect reason
- Call 2 disconnect time
- Call 2 disconnect reason

Each record will contain a record ID that can be used to synchronize the two records.

Data Network Fallback

Each gateway will have two Ethernet ports to allow connection to two different data networks, for example, the Internet and a private frame relay network. Mechanisms will be provided that will enable the application to direct IP traffic toward one port or the other depending on various network performance measures, for example, latency, packet loss, and jitter.

Network Management

Local ITS-IP administration access is provided to perform the initial configuration. An ASCII terminal may connected via the serial port to allow an installer or administrator to configure the system. Typical information configured at this time is the server's host name, its IP address, and the name of its domain server. The rest of the information needed to run the Server is provided via the SNMP Manager.

The ITS-SP is managed via an SNMP Manager, consistent with HP OpenView. An ITS-SP specific MIB is provided. Via the SNMP, the following functions are provided:

- Routing table administration
- Authorization table administration
- Reporting of traps and alarms

API Interface

The ITS-SP is provided with voice to voice and fax to fax applications. These applications make use of a standard API interface provided by the ITS-SP platform. The user may change the applications provided and/or develop new applications using this API. In this way, users may define their own service definition, using the ITS-SP as a platform. The list of API functions will be available separately.

Index